Martin McGuinness
THE MAN I KNEW

JUDE COLLINS

MERCIER PRESS
IRISH PUBLISHER - IRISH STORY

To the memory of my much-loved sister,
Patricia Friel, and my brother, Fr Paddy.

MERCIER PRESS

Cork

www.mercierpress.ie

ISBN: 978 1 78117 601 6

10 9 8 7 6 5 4 3 2 1

A CIP record for this title is available from the British Library

Printed and bound in the EU.

Contents

List of Contributors

Gerry Adams was president of Sinn Féin from 1983 to 2018 and has been teachta dála (TD) for Louth since 2011. From 1983 to 1992 and from 1997 to 2011 he was member of parliament (MP) for West Belfast. During his time as president, Sinn Féin became the third-largest political party in the Republic of Ireland, the second-largest in Northern Ireland and the largest nationalist party in Ireland.

Dermot Ahern is a former Irish TD for the Louth constituency. He was chairman of the British–Irish Inter-Parliamentary Body from 1993 to 1997, minister for foreign affairs from 2004 to 2008 and minister for justice, equality and law reform from 2008 to 2011. Since his retirement from politics in 2011, he has become an accredited mediator and uses his experience and contacts to work in the area of alternative dispute resolution.

Martina Anderson is a former political prisoner and a Sinn Féin politician. She was a member of the legislative assembly (MLA) from 2007 to 2012, and served as a junior minister in the Office of the First Minister and Deputy First Minister from 2011 to 2012. She has been a member of the European Parliament (MEP) from 2012 to the present.

Denis Bradley was educated at St Columb's College, Derry and later studied in Rome. He served as a priest in the Bogside and was a twenty-six-year-old curate on Bloody Sunday. He left the priesthood later in the 1970s. He was a founding member of Northlands alcohol and drugs residential counselling centre in 1973 in Derry and remains involved with the work of the centre as a consultant. Denis is also a consultant to the North West Alcohol Forum in Co. Donegal. He was vice-chairman of the Northern Ireland Policing Board from its formation on 4 November 2001 to 2006. In 2007 he was appointed co-chairman, along with Rev. Robin Eames, of the Consultative Group on the Past in Northern Ireland. A well-known political commentator, Denis also writes a monthly column for the *Irish News* and received an honorary doctorate of law from the University of Ulster for his contributions to the community and the peace process.

Bill Clinton served as the forty-second president of the United States from 1993 to 2001. Prior to the presidency, he was governor of Arkansas from 1979 to 1981 and again from 1983 to 1992.

Thomas P. DiNapoli is the fifty-fourth comptroller of the state of New York. He has served in this position since 2007. One of his primary responsibilities is to oversee the New York state pension fund – the third largest public pension fund in the United States, which provides retirement security to over a million public workers and pensioners. Under his leadership, the fund has invested nearly $270 million in Irish companies and made $30 million in private equity commitments specifically targeted at Northern Ireland. His office also examines how American companies are implementing the MacBride Principles legislation and where these companies invest their capital in Northern Ireland.

Pat Doherty is director of corporate governance in the Office of the New York State Comptroller, where he helps develop and administer social and environmental responsibility initiatives for the $184 billion New York state investment fund. Before coming to the state comptroller's office in 2010, Pat was director of corporate social responsibility in the Office of the New York City Comptroller.

Peter King, a member of the Republican Party, is serving his thirteenth term in the US House of Representatives. He is a member of the Homeland Security Committee and also serves on the Financial Services Committee and Permanent Select Committee on Intelligence. He served as chairman of the Homeland Security Committee from 2005 to 2006 and again from 2011 to 2012. He has been a leader in homeland security and is a strong supporter of the war against international terrorism, both at home and abroad.

David Latimer grew up in Dromore, Co. Down. Before becoming a Presbyterian minister, he worked as a systems analyst with Northern Ireland Electricity. In 1988 he was appointed minister of First Derry and Monreagh Presbyterian churches. During 2008 he served as a hospital chaplain in Afghanistan. David is married to Margaret and has three daughters.

Aodhán Mac an tSaoir is from a strongly republican family. In 1971, as the conflict deepened, he joined the republican struggle and has been a full-time political activist for most of his life since then. From 1992 he worked as political adviser to Martin McGuinness and was a close friend.

Eamonn MacDermott worked in the film business and was involved in making a documentary about Johnny Walker of the Birmingham Six, among other projects. He was also a reporter with the *Derry Journal* for many years. He subsequently was editor of the *Sunday Journal* before leaving to go freelance in 2009. He is a former republican prisoner, having served almost sixteen years in the H Blocks.

Martin Mansergh is a former Fianna Fáil adviser and politician, and a historian. He was a member of the Irish Senate from 2002 to 2007 and TD for Tipperary South from 2007 to 2011. He played a leading role in formulating Fianna Fáil policy on Northern Ireland.

Pat McArt was editor of the *Derry Journal* from 1982 to 2006. During those years he had almost daily contact with local leaders such as John Hume, Martin McGuinness and Bishop Edward Daly. He began his career in his hometown of Letterkenny, Co. Donegal, before moving to RTÉ in Dublin in 1980. He has frequently broadcast on both national and local media.

John McCallister was born and grew up on a family farm in Glasker near Rathfriland, Co. Down. He was president of the Young Farmers' Clubs of Ulster from 2003 to 2005 and MLA for South Down from 2007 to 2016. He was the first MLA to pass a private members bill (PMB), the Caravans Act of 2011, and the only member to have a second PMB passed, the Assembly and Executive Reform (Assembly Opposition) Act 2016. An Ulster Unionist Party member from 2005 to 2013, he resigned over an electoral pact in a Mid-Ulster by-election. Co-founder of political party NI21 in June 2013, he resigned in July 2014. He is currently the Northern Ireland human rights commissioner.

Eamonn McCann is a long-time socialist and member of Derry Trades Union Council. He is involved in campaigns for workers' rights and women's liberation, and against state repression and defilement of the environment. 'If I can't dance, I don't want to be part of your revolution' is his favourite quotation, which was first uttered by political activist and writer Emma Goldman.

Mary Lou McDonald is a Dubliner, mother and unrepentant Fenian. In 2004 she became Sinn Féin's first MEP and is currently TD for Dublin Central. She was deputy leader of Sinn Féin from 2011 and became its president in 2018.

Michael McGimpsey is a former Ulster Unionist Belfast city councillor and MLA in the Stormont Assembly. He worked closely with David Trimble and was made minister for the Department of Culture, Arts and Leisure, and later minister for health in the Stormont Executive.

Mitchel McLaughlin was a lifelong friend and confidant of the late Martin McGuinness. Until he retired from day-to-day politics, he was a leading strategist and spokesperson for Sinn Féin over a forty-year period. In public life he served as Sinn Féin's national and regional chairperson, local councillor, MLA and speaker of the Assembly. Mitchel also played a key role in developing the peace process, engagement with the unionist community and in the development of Sinn Féin's economic policies.

Joe McVeigh was born in Ederney, Co. Fermanagh in 1945. He attended Moneyvriece Primary School, St Michael's Grammar School, Enniskillen and St Patrick's College, Maynooth. He was ordained for the diocese of Clogher in 1971 and has served in parishes in Monaghan and Fermanagh. He is assistant priest in St Michael's parish, Enniskillen. His hobbies are music and reading.

George Mitchell served for several years as chairman of the global law firm DLA Piper. Before that, he served as a federal judge; as majority leader of the United States Senate; as chairman of peace negotiations in Northern Ireland, which resulted in an agreement that ended an historic conflict; and most recently as US special envoy to the Middle East. In 2008 *Time* magazine described him as one of the 100 most influential people in the world. Senator Mitchell is the author of five books. His most recent are a memoir entitled *The Negotiator: Reflections on an American Life* (2015) and *A Path to Peace* (2016).

Danny Morrison is a writer and media commentator. He is the author of seven books, including novels, non-fiction, memoir and political commentary, as well as several plays and short stories. Formerly, he was the national spokesperson for Sinn Féin, editor of *An Phoblacht/Republican News* and MLA for Mid-Ulster. He was imprisoned several times between 1972 and 1995.

Niall O'Dowd went to America in 1979 from Drogheda, Co. Louth. He is the founder of IrishCentral.com, *Irish America* magazine and the *Irish Voice* newspaper. He was awarded an honorary degree from UCD and an Irish Presidential

Distinguished Service Award for his work on the Irish peace process.

Terry O'Sullivan, general president of the Laborers' International Union of North America (LIUNA), is a proud descendant of Irish immigrants, holds dual American and Irish citizenship, and works tirelessly to build bridges between the Irish and American labour movements. He is a vocal supporter of Sinn Féin and serves as president of New York Friends of Ireland and chairman of DC Friends of Ireland.

Eileen Paisley, Lady Bannside, Baroness Paisley of St George's, is the widow of Ian Paisley, former leader of the Democratic Unionist Party (DUP). She became a life peer in 2006.

Jonathan Powell is director of Inter Mediate, the charity he founded in 2011 to work on conflict resolution around the world. He was chief of staff to Tony Blair from 1995 to 2007, and from 1997 to 2007 was also chief British negotiator on Northern Ireland. He is author of *Great Hatred, Little Room: Making Peace in Northern Ireland; The New Machiavelli: How to Wield Power in the Modern World* and *Talking to Terrorists: How to End Armed Conflicts.*

Dawn Purvis was a former leader of the Progressive Unionist Party (PUP) and MLA for East Belfast. Dawn left politics in 2011 and worked with Marie Stopes International to open the first sexual and reproductive health centre offering abortion services on the island of Ireland. Dawn is currently CEO of a housing charity.

Peter Sheridan OBE is a former assistant chief constable of the Royal Ulster Constabulary (RUC) and of the Police Service of Northern Ireland (PSNI). He is currently chief executive of Co-operation Ireland.

James T. Walsh is a government affairs counsellor in the Washington DC office of K&L Gates LLP. He served in the US House of Representatives from 1989 to 2009 and during his tenure was a deputy Republican whip from 1994 to 2006. He was a member of the House Committee on Appropriations from 1993 to 2009 and became chairman of four House Appropriation subcommittees: District of Columbia; Legislative Branch; VA, HUD and Independent Agencies (NASA, EPA, FEMA, NSF, Selective Service); and Military Quality of Life (which included jurisdiction for Military Base Construction, the Defense Health Program and Housing Accounts) and Veterans Affairs.

Foreword

I first considered writing a book about Martin McGuinness some years ago. We'd met on a number of occasions, including the 2010 launch of my book *Tales Out of School: St Columb's College Derry in the 1950s,* where he was a guest of honour. But a series of obstacles and distractions intervened and as Martin himself said of his intention to retire from the position of deputy first minister in May 2017, 'The best-laid plans of mice and men often go awry.'

His sudden illness and death in March 2017 shocked everyone. Much was written at the time about this youth from the Bogside who became an Irish Republican Army (IRA) leader, a forceful politician and finally deputy first minister of Northern Ireland. What was lacking, in my view, was the direct testimony of people who had met and interacted with him at different points in his life.

In *Martin McGuinness: The Man I Knew,* I have tried to bring together as wide a range of voices as possible: from those who knew him as a neighbour and an IRA leader, to those who worked with him in the Stormont Executive; from Gerry Adams and Mary Lou McDonald to Eileen Paisley and former Ulster Unionist MLA Michael McGimpsey; from prominent Irish-American Niall O'Dowd to peace talks chairman Senator George Mitchell. If I have a regret, it is that I have not been able to include more voices from political unionism.

The focus of all the interviews is Martin McGuinness, but inevitably contributors range beyond the subject, commenting on the turbulent social and political circumstances in which he lived. What I first thought of as digression, in fact provides a background and context for the life of the late deputy first minister. And of course contributors, in telling us about Martin McGuinness, tell as much about themselves. I'd like to thank them all, on both sides of the Atlantic, for giving so generously of their time. I am also indebted to those who facilitated the interviews and to those who provided unforgettable photographs taken at different points in Martin McGuinness's life.

No book can tell the full story of a person's life. The modest ambition of this volume is to offer the reader a range of perspectives on a man who helped shape recent history and whose death has left Irish politics poorer.

I

Mitchel McLaughlin

Martin and I played on the same soccer team when we were young. At that time he was nine or ten. He was a passable goalkeeper – he wasn't quick on his feet, but he was a big cub for his age and there was never any doubt that he'd be the goalkeeper; it seemed to be his natural position. He also had very quick hands so he was a decent schoolboy keeper. That was soccer, although we played Gaelic football too. Mind you, back then you couldn't admit you played both. But he wasn't somebody I'd be meeting coming from school every day, although we'd parallel paths. If there was a football game you'd have known to look out for him.

In the early 1970s we became reacquainted. At that stage he was already a considerable figure in the republican movement. The thing to remember is that, although it didn't have the depth or breadth of counties like Tyrone, Armagh, Antrim and Down, where the republicans could trace their ancestors back to the United Irishmen and 1798, Derry did have a republican tradition. It was Catholic and nationalist. My father's family were serious supporters of the old Nationalist Party. On my mother's side, my maternal grandmother was a member of Cumann na mBan at the time of the 1916 Rising.

Growing up, we lived in a nationalist environment where the injustices of gerrymandering and unionist control of the council were being badly felt – so radical politics, such as those espoused by the Derry Housing Association, were of interest to us. In the early days Martin was already involved in the civil rights marches. He was energised by the whole campaign against gerrymandering and discrimination. If the state hadn't reacted the way it did, he'd probably have gone on being a van driver and working for Doherty's butchers. Instead, he got drawn into it with a whole lot of other people, a new fraternity who were developing their politics. They were not revolutionaries waiting to strike: they started from a very low base. But from all of that, he emerged as a significant player and came to the attention of the national leadership.

Martin and I became involved separately in supporting the protests against discrimination. That was 1967–68 – running up to the first civil rights march. I was on the march on 5 October 1968, opposing unionist gerrymandering and discrimination – I don't think Martin was there. But it was the beginning of a political journey that would bring us closer together. Neither he nor I was particularly vocal then – the radical and strident voices were the Eamonn McCanns of the day [a radical young socialist agitator in Derry]. If there was a platform, you would have had business people, clergy, Eddie McAteer [leader of the Nationalist Party], John Hume – the emerging professional people – taking to the stage. We were more the foot soldiers of the day for people who didn't see this as a militant process. But I think our instincts were that it could be.

I was listening to all the messages about Martin Luther King and so on – but their impact didn't last too long. People talk nostalgically of the changes that came about through non-violent agitation for civil rights in other countries, including the US. But what really made an impression on me was what happened on 5 October [when the RUC attacked civil rights marchers] and the reaction to it. I don't remember Martin's reaction to it and I never discussed it with him.

My first proper conversation with Martin coincided with the Free Derry period. There was the division between those just cutting their political teeth and the older, establishment people, who had a completely different view of what would happen. And it was a confused situation. Not only were there barricades round the area, but there were armed people driving around in cars they'd hijacked – they always seemed to be Ford Cortinas. So there was a meeting in Free Derry, which I think had mainly to do with antisocial issues and the tensions that had emerged between the Official IRA and the Provos. The meeting was held in a community hall, an old wooden structure. And there were maybe sixty, seventy people at it.

At the meeting you had all these young insurrectionists – a different generation – who were questioning how antisocial elements should be dealt with; in other words law and order in Free Derry. Martin was on the same side of the discussion as I was [arguing for sanctions other than kneecapping to be used in dealing with antisocial elements].

At this point the army was on the streets, the IRA was on the streets, Bloody Sunday had come and gone. And this was a time when people with authority emerged – Martin was one of those. He spoke with the authority of the republican movement – that was very clear.

The next time I remember Martin being part of a discussion I was involved in was about the monument that had become Free Derry Corner. Free Derry Corner at that point was a derelict terrace of houses where Caker Casey – a local character of fame and renown – had painted 'You are now entering Free Derry' on the gable wall. There were proposals in place to knock it down because a road, a fly-over, was going to be built – something that I suspect the security forces would have had a big say in.

Martin could turn the heat up in meetings such as this. His normal tone was the flat, unemotional line in response to arguments that people were putting forward. But whenever there was a persistence not to his liking, say with the Free Derry Corner, Martin just cut to the chase and said, 'Look, everything's up for discussion except the removal of that wall.' Calmly put, but the end of the debate.

A British sapper, who is said to have hijacked his vehicle, drove into the Bogside and crashed into the wall of Free Derry Corner, destroying part of it. The reaction was to build it again, stronger, with buttresses – the road was eventually built round it. It was originally a handy gable wall for putting up the message; it later became a symbol of what could be. When the wall was rebuilt, it was repainted and the lettering of 'You are now entering Free Derry' was reinstated as well, only this time it was done neatly. Eamonn McCann had a strange reaction to all this. He lamented that we had institutionalised Free Derry Corner.

Following on from this, Martin in particular became very conscious of the fact that the barricades in the area were not only symbolic. They were in fact a barrier to those going out and coming in, and sometimes you were putting limitations on people who were maybe involved in IRA activity – there were only a limited number of ways you could get back into the area. So at one meeting Martin argued that the barricades should be taken away – and that was against popular opinion in the Bogside then. He said, 'Do you really think those barricades would stop the British Army from coming in here?' So they took the barricades away and they painted a white line round Free Derry – and the British Army agreed not to cross over this white line! Martin felt the barricades were a complete waste of time and energy, and gave a false sense of security. And that was where I began to see his leadership capacity.

Martin stood out in any grouping. You saw the press conferences and the delegations sent over to London to negotiate with the British government and he was part of the IRA leadership. In Derry he was already recognised as the go-to person. And he was on the run – the British knew about him, the same as everybody else. But the Free Derry area was one where the British Army couldn't come in and be undetected for very long. So he wasn't skulking about – he didn't have to – nor did any of the IRA volunteers when within Free Derry, the Bogside or the Creggan. He couldn't have gone into the centre of town though.

The British knew he was there. There were many instances of them coming in, usually in the dead of night. There was a community alarm system – bin-lids – and that meant that people were mobilised very quickly, though a number of people were killed. The British had that ability, always had.

Martin stayed in different houses. He wasn't going to his own house and he wasn't going to the same billet every night. He just had to assume there was surveillance of some kind – as well as informers.

***

Derry at the time was re-establishing a republicanism that had been very reduced. The growth of republicanism there was far greater in proportion to anywhere else because of the standing start. In Belfast they had the expectation – we didn't have that in Derry, there was only a handful of people. But not only was it reassembled, it became a formidable operation in the city. The bombing campaign which characterised the IRA campaign during the 1970s was particularly prominent there. Yet Martin McGuinness was one of the first I heard saying, 'This bombing campaign has its limitations. Do we really think that's going to force the British to negotiate or to withdraw from Ireland?' He had a very tight grip on the types of bombing operations that were permitted.

I'm quite sure there were tensions among republicans. Some were of my father's generation, and some beyond that. So they weren't all about to pick up the gun and go out, although some did. But they weren't resentful of a younger generation coming along, with new leadership emerging. This was a new type of struggle. Martin and his cohorts from that generation were largely unknown at the start, but they gradually became known.

There is a lot of fairly crass speculation as to what Martin's military capability was. I've read that he was a crack marksman. Well, I know that he had weak eyesight. It was his leadership, his judgement, his authority that got people locally to accept his leadership and to do it with great loyalty and commitment to him. You saw the turnout there was for his funeral – how that loyalty to him had permeated public opinion on the island. Nobody was basing his authority on the grounds that he was a crack marksman.

He had an ability to carry his own natural personality with him. Mostly he was the warm Martin McGuinness. But an issue emerged if you tried to pressurise him, if you tried to bully him or threaten him; then the other side – a fearless, indomitable aspect of him – emerged.

I've seen that come out. Here's an example. There was a raid on a house not far from here. Both he and I turned up at it. It was the RUC. This would have been the mid-1980s, when we both had a public profile. So we got the call that somebody was being raided and we went round to a situation that quickly became quite nasty. There was a very well-known Special Branch officer and it was his brother who was leading this raid. I think they were from Omagh. What emerged was, basically, some sort of sectarian remark that both Martin and I reacted to. After that things got quickly out of hand. Martin ended up grabbing this sergeant by his tie through the railings in the staircase in this house. There were about four or five RUC men trying to pull him off. The harder they pulled the tighter he held onto the tie – it was strangling the cop. It was hilarious in retrospect, but at the time it was hairy – I thought he was going to kill the sergeant, just by holding onto his tie.

A side issue of this: after the incident my wife, Mary Lou, used to see that cop down the town, and she would be making strangling motions at him every time. He eventually disappeared – he was involved in some civil prosecution. So Mary Lou broke him!

But that was the side of Martin McGuinness you rarely saw. I don't think it was reckless. It was the way he responded to a set of circumstances that could have gotten out of hand anyway. Three or four of these guys would maybe have given him a beating. He grabbed the sergeant maybe as a way of asserting a different dynamic.

Another example. We all went to the Sinn Féin Ard-Fheis in Dublin one year, in the early 1980s. Myself and a man called Gerry Doherty were travelling together, and we hit this tailback of cars before we got to the bridge. And Gerry said to me, 'That's Martin McGuinness.' This was before we got to the bridge. We knew that he was going to the Ard-Fheis and he was ahead of us. The tailback went on so long we left somebody else to drive the car and we went on foot to the bridge and then on up. Martin McGuinness had this car across the bridge and was refusing to move it. They wanted him to drive to a search bay and he was refusing to do it. 'You can search here or you can stay here all night.' In the end they gave up – they sent for an inspector and he said, 'Take a look at the car and then let him go on.' The Brits couldn't resist trying to subjugate him, but they were learning that there was no point in taking this guy on.

Sometimes he created a situation just for devilment. We travelled together everywhere and it'd depend what mood we were in. The first time he ever cursed at me it was because he felt it was all right if he started a row with the police, but if I started it, it wasn't! 'I never fucking know what you're going to do!' But you got fed up being stopped all the time. In this instance I had started it – picked up on something they said, or refused to do something they said to do – though usually I was the peacemaker. Normally it would be him who would start the aggro – and he wouldn't need a carful of people to back him up either, he'd do it on his own.

***

Martin was quite a devout Catholic – which I am not. And we used to have some arguments about it. But he genuinely did have his faith. Bishop Eddie Daly had a sort of love-hate relationship with Martin. Daly condemned the actions of the IRA many, many times, and Martin would challenge him publicly. The weakness of the Catholic Church in that kind of argument was that they didn't balance it with the injustice of the state or the British, and they certainly didn't offer an alternative. That debate around an alternative was maybe the seeds of the peace process. You want the IRA to stop? OK – give us an alternative. Bishop Daly would have been condemning and issuing edicts about IRA funerals in churches.

At other times the bishop would engage with the IRA. There might be a family in trouble and he thought he could find help. There were issues relating to conscience or social justice which you could put forward and discuss. It wasn't exactly a back channel, but there was always a dialogue.

Years later, Daly, when he was the bishop and Martin was in the IRA leadership, said he had come to recognise that McGuinness was at peace with his conscience. In other words he believed in what he was doing. The bishop was pressed on this and said he didn't think that this could be interpreted as meaning that Martin McGuinness made choices he had to live with but wished he had done something different. He said it was quite possible if those circumstances were repeated that Martin McGuinness would have made exactly the same decisions. That was an insight that could only have come from private conversations – certainly I wasn't party to it. But when I heard Eddie Daly saying that, I said to myself, 'You've taken the time to explore this with Martin.' So Martin was at peace with his conscience, and that's not to be interpreted as him wishing he had made different decisions.

Martin was also quite a progressive thinker. I attribute to him two things: one was ending the policy of 'disappearing' the bodies. There was an informer shot in Derry, a man called Duffy, who had been buried secretly. Martin was opposed to the practice of 'disappearing' bodies and made a direct intervention; there are famous photographs of the body being located and the hearse waiting at the border for the family. Then, in subsequent years, there was the ending of the policy of kneecapping. He was the person who challenged the thinking behind this policy, querying whether it was an appropriate response. Was it a solution to the problem? It wasn't.

He was a strategic thinker even when he was a young man in his late teens and early twenties. He had developed a strategic capacity over all those years. So when it came time for the peace process, there was nobody with a clearer understanding of what that meant. His role – public now but secret then – was of being the contact point with the British government – the back channel. His appointment as the sole point of contact and his ability to deliver messages on behalf of the republican movement – and to deliver them in a coherent and sufficiently succinct manner – meant that Martin was completely on top of that brief.

In the early days such contact with the British was very dangerous. There were people who were involved in the 1970s in ceasefires and there were people who were involved in negotiations during the hunger strikes – particularly the first hunger strike – where the commitments that were given were reneged on. All of that left a view among some – which was a disaster if it had prevailed – that you couldn't trust the Brits in any circumstances. In effect that was saying, 'There's nothing else for it but to shoot people and blow the place up.' Martin's argument was that everybody has interests, everybody has outcomes in mind, nobody is operating on an agenda that's fixed. We are going to sort this out. Now Maggie Thatcher may have been fixed. Martin

McGuinness, on certain issues, might have been fixed. But on the overall situation, nobody believed that sustained warfare for generations was possible. There had to be a purpose and a direction, and there had to be momentum.

Whenever we produced the discussion documents – internal but subsequently published as *A Scenario for Peace* – it laid a claim for a very under-developed peace, though it was fairly revolutionary for its time and context. *A Scenario for Peace* was an attempt at laying a foundation and putting down a marker on record that republicans were interested in peace.

This was the late 1980s. *A Scenario for Peace* was, I think, written up around 1987. Then you'd the talks with the Social Democratic and Labour Party [SDLP], which followed that year. Then you had things like the Downing Street Declaration, the contact between Gerry Adams and John Hume, the publication of *Towards a Lasting Peace in Ireland*. All those things really required people with prescience and vision, such as that ascribed to Gerry Adams – though others also had to have the same skill-sets. Martin had those skill-sets. It wouldn't have got off the ground without Gerry's vision and Martin's leadership. It was just a priceless combination.

As well as that, Martin was consistent. The evidence for that is his attitude to rolling devolution in the James Prior years. [In 1982 British Secretary of State James Prior set up a Stormont Assembly with limited powers, which were to be increased as it learned to operate constructively.] Martin was elected to that and I was his director of elections. Once elected, he was immediately aware that it was going nowhere. Martin knew instantly that this Assembly and rolling devolution were a dead duck. We forced the SDLP to pull out of it.

Never at any time was Martin an isolated figure in the republican movement – although it was dangerous at certain times when some very senior people in the IRA were saying that there never again would be a ceasefire, because the decision to call a ceasefire in 1975 was abused by the British to introduce Ulsterisation. [An initiative by British Secretary of State Merlyn Rees to replace units of the British Army with the local RUC and Ulster Defence Regiment (UDR).] Despite this, Martin never let go of the possibility of a negotiated outcome and was pursuing it through contact with British military intelligence.

***

Martin clearly loved Donegal. He went there every chance he had down the years – to walk along the beach at Lisfannon, to go to his mother's home in the Illies, just outside Buncrana. He was a fly fisherman, but he very rarely would have been fishing on his own. There's a great fisherman in Derry, who doesn't live that far from here, Jamesy Quinn. He taught him all he knew. He'd have been a constant companion. There was also former republican prisoner Gerry Crossan, who was a formidable fisherman. So it wouldn't have been solitary. The walks along the banks of the River Fahan [a few miles from Derry] would have been with his family – the children and his wife, Bernie.

He also wrote poetry, though where he got the time to I don't know. I remember us driving up and down from Derry to Belfast in the days before the by-pass at Toome, when you had to drive through Toome. And there was this local character; you would have seen him in the mornings, standing outside the shops as you're driving through. We'd have been coming home again in the evening and the poor craytur would have been slumped on the ground with drink. So Martin had figured out by observing him that there was someone who looked after him and loved him: out each morning clean, dressed, fed, upright; by the evening, collapsed at the side of the street with a feed of drink. Martin wrote a beautiful poem about it. He read it to me as I was driving. I said, 'I want you to give me that poem', and he said he would – and he fucking never gave it to me! And when I went looking for it, I challenged him about it, and he couldn't find it then. But that's the kind of person he was. We were driving and thinking about all the high politics we thought were extremely important to the whole world, and in the middle of it he had taken time to observe this man whose name he didn't know. I find that revealing about the kind of person he was.

***

I found out about his illness at pretty much the same time as everybody else. Bernie and I had a conversation – an unconcerned conversation – about this kind of ticklish cough, and she made a remark that came back to me like a hammer-blow subsequently when more detail emerged. This was late 2016 and before anything else emerged – it was just this ticklish and persistent cough. She told him to go and get it checked and said to him, 'I think that's your heart.' Now why she said that she doesn't know – I asked her – but it turned out she was right.

He went and got tests. Initially there was no alarm, but there was a question about the quality of the blood. It turned out that this was the source of the problem – his body was producing too much protein. And it was far too late at this stage to fix – major damage had been done to a valve on the left side of his heart. They developed a regime of treatment that was to run from the turn of the year to August of this year [2017] – that's how serious it was. At this stage it was fairly obvious to me it was a life or death struggle. The prognosis from the doctors was that they had a treatment devised that was going to succeed, going to save him, but it was going to take time and it was going to be a long and difficult process. It was in that context Martin made the decision not to stand for the 2017 election. He knew he was going to be incapacitated.

Right up to the weekend before he died, the doctors were still confident. His family obviously were blinded to what the situation was, because he was in intensive care for about three weeks before he died. I hadn't seen him during that period because I respected the family and I knew the kind of man Martin was, that he wouldn't want people interfering. I know one or two people went over, but I quite consciously and deliberately stayed away. It was an awful shock when he died.

The last time I saw him was just before Christmas. We live just round the corner from each other. He was in the house after he'd been diagnosed and I left him up a collection of Seamus Heaney poems that I had. I'd always meant to give it to him. It was a very good quality book that was presented to me, but he had a far greater interest in Heaney than I did. Seamus Heaney and I had a wee bit of history. We fell out over whether he ever addressed the core of the situation here.

At Martin's funeral I was devastated. I knew he had arrangements made to retire in May of this year. One of the things that impressed him and reinforced his decision was the fact that I'd retired and was obviously so happy. He'd see Mary Lou and me about the town, just wandering about and having time to ourselves.

He and Bernie contributed so much of their own time to everybody else. His house never emptied. I had a far greater discipline. We run offices and I used make myself available to people, but I never encouraged the idea of people suiting themselves and coming to the door, except in emergencies. But Martin had an open door. I don't know how he did it.

He was first and foremost a friend. Probably my closest friend. I'm not claiming I was closer than anybody else – he was hugely admired within republican circles, as reaction to his death would testify. But we could speak at a personal level and took an interest in each other's family. So I lost a friend first and foremost, and I think we've all lost, and the unionists in particular have lost, the best friend they could have had.

Stormont opened a book of condolence for the family and it's a very interesting read. Every single party, including the DUP, signed it, made comments. My own contribution – and I thought about it – was a play on the Seamus Heaney line from 'The Cure at Troy': 'Martin was a man who made hope and history rhyme'. That's how I saw him. He was a friend for fifty-odd years, but he was a man – a leader – who made hope and history rhyme.

2

Peter Sheridan

When I first went to the police in Derry in 1978 as a young Catholic RUC officer, Martin McGuinness would have been well known to officers of the city – or at least spoken about. The picture I got was of somebody who saw me as an enemy, somebody who was prepared to use extreme violence against me and police officers and the army in the city.

There was an element at that time that figured the way to prevent Catholics joining the police was to concentrate on attacking such Catholics. I was forced to move out of my house twice when people thought I should visit the next world before I wanted to. Obviously, when I was out on duty they couldn't particularly pick me out from others. But the fact that I became over time a senior officer in the police in Derry meant I'd have been reasonably well known. As a result I became a focus of attention.

I have often thought about not just Martin McGuinness but the other people who were intent on killing me then. Personally, I never went to bed any night wondering whom I could shoot, kill or maim. Nor did I get up any morning thinking the same. And that included Martin McGuinness and others in the IRA. It's not how I was brought up to think about people, as my enemy.

Martin was seen as somebody who was on the other side – the leader – and was involved, therefore, in what was happening, not just in Derry but further afield. But it certainly wasn't a case of hatred. I've never hated anybody in life. I pride myself at working hard not to let others fall out with me. I remember stopping people in the street who would have been known IRA people. On those occasions I would have been at pains not to be antagonistic towards them, even if they were trying to antagonise me. There are very few people in life who I haven't got on with, and that includes people in paramilitary organisations.

At that time, when we were searching people's houses, I used to try to put myself in those people's shoes. How would I have felt if the police were coming in, people I didn't know, who I saw as the opposition, coming in and searching my house? How would I have felt about the way they left the house? I was always conscious of those things, particularly when I became more senior in the organisation – how we left people feeling.

I'd have stopped Martin at checkpoints several times in the city. There was no let's-get-to-know-each-other conversation, but I didn't find him objectionable to me. I didn't find him rude or anything. I didn't find him nasty in any way. I wouldn't use the words unpleasant or objectionable. When I became more senior he'd have recognised me, but not in those early days.

I first met him formally in 1997, when I was in Downing Street with Hugh Orde. Tony Blair called a meeting where Sinn Féin were going to meet the police. It was part of the build-up to Sinn Féin supporting policing. So we met them in Downing Street that day.

We were in the Cabinet Office with Prime Minister Tony Blair, Jonathan Powell and one or two Northern Ireland Office [NIO] people. Then there was myself, Hugh Orde and Sinead McSweeney, who was our director of communications in the PSNI at the time. So we were all in the room first, and then in came Gerry Adams, Gerry Kelly and Martin McGuinness. I don't remember any shaking of hands at the beginning of the meeting. Gerry Adams said something along the lines of 'You're welcome' to me, and I quipped back, 'You'd think it was your house – it belongs to him!' – pointing at Tony Blair. There was no need for introductions – everybody knew everybody else in the room.

We sat at the cabinet table. They were on one side; we were on the other. Hugh Orde sat beside the prime minister and I sat beside Hugh Orde. Jonathan Powell sat on the other side of the prime minister and the NIO civil servants further on up. The discussion was about policing – very high level. I said, 'My view from an operational perspective is, unless people down and around Shantallow [a nationalist working-class area in Derry] see a substantial change in policing within a year, this initiative for acceptance of the PSNI could be lost.' I was asked some questions about policing. At that point we were reintroducing officers on bicycles back into the Creggan and we'd done it successfully. But I made the point that I was worried it wouldn't last.

It was a professional, business-like meeting – there wasn't any sense of personalities coming through. I think Sinn Féin at that stage were on a mission about what they wanted before they would join up with policing. I'd have seen Martin McGuinness quite a bit on television in the run-up to this. He and Gerry Kelly were probably more on the warm side. There was almost more distance at the table with Gerry Adams.

Tony Blair left the meeting slightly early to go to something else and Jonathan Powell continued in his place. At the end there was a shaking of hands. When that began to happen, I remember thinking how one of my father's friends was murdered by the

Irish National Liberation Army [INLA]. He was a Protestant man engaged in nothing – a businessman in Derry – who was mistaken for a police officer. His daughter was a friend of mine. She wouldn't have got beyond the fact that these sorts of people had murdered him.

This was the image that came into my head as I was going to shake hands: knowing that, and having walked behind the coffins of other murdered colleagues and so on, and conscious of how this meeting would be read by the police organisation, the handshakes felt awkward – something not quite right about them. It took literally a couple of seconds. I'd never met Martin to shake hands with him before. So I shook hands with Gerry Kelly and Gerry Adams. And as I shook hands with Martin I said, 'Your mother makes good soup.' He looked at me and said, 'How'd you know my mother makes good soup?' And I said, 'I'd a bowl of it on Saturday.' And he looked at me and said, 'Where'd you get a bowl of my mother's soup?' So I said, 'You come back to the next meeting and I'll tell you then.'

What had happened was that the previous Saturday I'd bought a book in Dublin called *Nell* by Nell McCafferty. So I rang her and said, 'I refuse to read your oul' book unless you sign it for me.' She said, 'I'm going to the Bogside at the weekend to see my mother.' So I thought I'd nip over on the Saturday morning and get the book signed.

I drove over and Nell met me at the door, the hair standing on her head, in the dressing gown, fag in her hand, and insisted that I come in to see her mother. It was a small terraced house; her mother had had several strokes and she was in the living room in the bed – they'd made the room a bedroom. It had a window out onto the street almost. So Nell brought me in and said, 'I want you to meet my mother', and sat me on a commode at the side of the bed. I said to her, 'It's probably a good place for me to sit, Nell, because I need to be out of here soon.'

She was having a conversation with her mother, who was having difficulty speaking at that time, and I discovered that her mother's grandfather was known as 'the good Sergeant Duffy' – he had been a Royal Irish Constabulary officer. So we were talking and the mother produced this bell-push that they'd had an electrician rig up for her, so she could call for assistance during the night. But when Nell was making the bed that morning, she'd pulled the covers and pulled the wire out of the thing. So Nell hands me this bell-push and a huge screwdriver and says to me, 'Can you fix that f–ing thing?' I started putting the wires back into it and she's shouting in her mother's ear, 'He's a top cop, Ma!' Meanwhile I was aware there were people passing outside and my car was parked out there.

So anyway I fixed the bell push and then Nell brought me in for a bowl of soup in the kitchen. I was having the soup – I didn't want to show I was afraid and didn't want to hang about – and she had this wee tray with a doily on it, pieces of French roll and a bowl of soup. Nell is not the most domesticated.

So anyway, she gave me this soup and she said, 'Do you know who made that soup?' And I said, 'I know you didn't make it anyway.' And she says, 'Peggy.' And I says, 'Peggy who?' And she says, 'Martin McGuinness's mother.' So I said, 'Are you trying to poison me?' Eventually I took a police business card out of my pocket and wrote on it 'Peggy – wonderful soup'. And I gave it to Nell and told her, 'You give that to Peggy the next time you see her.' And Nell said, 'Oh, she was in the other night to see my mother', and she set the card up on the mantelpiece.

What I didn't know was that on the way back home from Downing Street, Martin must have rung his mother and his mother said, 'Martin, there was a cop in Nell's house on Saturday.' And in Nell's book [Nell rewrote her book with a new chapter about the first cop that'd come to her house since 1969] it says that he told her, 'Me and Gerry Adams negotiate with the peelers, not you and Nell McCafferty's mother.'

***

That following summer of 1998 there was an Apprentice Boys parade banned from the walls of Derry, and all sorts of prophecies of Armageddon were made. I had responsibility for all events on Apprentice Boys' day. So I was based in Derry and there were about 1,200 police and soldiers on the streets, but in the end it passed off generally peacefully.

But in Dunloy [a small nationalist village in County Antrim] the commission had given the Apprentice Boys permission to walk out of the Orange Hall, go 200 yards down the street, turn back again, get on the bus and go. But the street had been blocked by people – probably at that time Sinn Féin people – in the middle of Dunloy. There was a kind of stand-off and the Apprentice Boys hadn't left the hall. You could sense that it was building up throughout the day. And the rallying cry had gone out for the Apprentice Boys in Derry, when they were finished the parade, to travel home by way of Dunloy. That was the intelligence we were getting.

So I could feel another Drumcree building up. [In 1995 there had been a massive stand-off between thousands of Orange Order marchers, the police and local residents at Drumcree.] We even had a water cannon on the way from Belfast. But I took one last throw of the dice and rang somebody I knew in the Bogside and asked if there was anyone who could do anything about this. So he said, 'Hold on.' He hands his phone over and then a voice says, 'Who's this?', and I said, 'And who's this?', and the voice says, 'Martin McGuinness.'

I told him about the situation and I'd no sense he was going to do anything about it. It was a fairly cold, not all that engaged conversation. But about twenty minutes later I had a call from the guy I'd rung and he said, 'What happens if I get caught for speeding through Greysteel?' He was obviously saying they were on their way. I told him not to kill anybody or knock anybody down – if it's only speeding we'll hopefully resolve that.

So they got to Dunloy and between us we were able to resolve the situation. In policing terms we were within our rights to move the people off the streets because the commission had said the march was allowed to go down. But big burly cops in riot gear hoofing people off the streets is a no-win for policing, even though you're legally in the right. They still wanted some things like the police taking off their riot gear. But we resolved it between us, and I often say it had to do with the bowl of soup I had in Nell McCafferty's house. Or the handshake in Downing Street, treating him like a human being. I don't know, but I think out of that experience both of us knew we were trying to achieve the same thing. We were going to come at it from different directions – there were different audiences, after all – but we both wanted effectively the same thing, which is a more peaceful place here.

Further to the soup story – in 2012 my brother was in Eason's bookshop in Derry, buying his wife a cookery book for Christmas. He spotted Martin McGuinness, who was doing the same thing, and my brother wondered, 'What do I do here?' Martin was deputy first minister at the time. So he lifted this book – probably the cheapest book he could get in the shop – *Two Hundred Soup Recipes* – and he goes over to Martin McGuinness and says, 'Would you mind signing this?' And Martin said, 'Would you mind buying it first?' So he says, 'Oh yes, I'll buy it, I'll buy it.' He bought it and asked him to write, 'If you liked my ma's soup you'll like these.' So McGuinness says, 'You want me to write that on it?' And my brother says, 'Yes.' So he's halfway through writing it and Martin looks up and says, 'Are you a cop?' My brother said, 'No, no.' So Martin writes on it and signs it, and on Christmas morning I get it as a gift. I still have that book.

***

Given what I knew about Martin's background, I was puzzling over how to make sense of his life. I put it in three phases. I didn't know him in the first twenty years of his life, when he grew up in poverty with an outside toilet, discrimination, gerrymandering, housing – all the things that happened in the Bogside. I wasn't exposed to that. I knew of him in the next twenty years, which was when he responded to that discrimination, etc., through violence. But I would see that Downing Street meeting as a marker after which I got to know him.

We met umpteen times after that and it was always an easy conversation. It was never one of those, 'Will you and me and Bernie and Michelle go on holidays together?' things, or 'Let's go out for a meal together.' But it was always a pleasant conversation with him. I met him in Derry one Sunday – we happened to be in the same restaurant and we had a conversation there. So I got to know him; and I think I also got to know him by watching what he was doing in politics.

There are people who'll look at the middle twenty years of Martin McGuinness's life and that'll be the only bit they'll comment on and look at. There are others, however, who'll only look at the last twenty years – Bill Clinton did that at his funeral, looked at his last twenty years. If I only focused on the twenty years that I knew of him, I'd come up with a certain viewpoint, whereas I can look across when I knew him and also have some recognition of where he came from. I was head of murder, organised crime, intelligence and all, so I'm not naïve about the middle twenty years. But I do have some difficulty with people now who couldn't convict him in this life but are trying to convict him in the next, when he's not here to defend himself.

People consistently ask me about his involvement, and I say, 'We didn't convict him in this life – it's not my job to try and convict somebody when they're dead.' And I think it's unfair to people. If you believe in justice and law, then you can't just fire stuff around – that he was involved in this, that and the other. It just strikes me as morally wrong, ethically unfair to do that.

I came to like Martin. It wasn't that close a relationship. But this guy was very personable. I didn't get any impression that this guy hates you or hates what you stand for. When we talked, it was a warm conversation.

I don't think his was a set-up charm. I think this is who he was – he was a people's person. He liked people, had an understanding of people. Maybe one of the reasons, in the second twenty years of his life, why he got caught up in violence was because he was so passionate about people and he thought that that was the only way to help them. I doubt very much if there were many people, once they engaged with him, who wouldn't have said there was warmth in him. I'm not naïve – I didn't come up the Foyle in a bubble. Like any of us in life – and I'm sure he was the same with me – he was trying to work out where this guy really was coming from. And I think we ultimately came to a conclusion about each other. Certainly in later years, he had the same desire to help people, to change things.

We engaged in conversations about violence. He did umpteen events for us in Co-operation Ireland [an all-island peace-building charity]. Trying to deal with the past was always a big issue. I had the view that we are never going to do justice to the scale of injustice on any side.

I remember when Harry Holland [a well-respected West Belfast greengrocer] was murdered [by a local youth in 2007]. Gerry Adams came out and made a statement that the police weren't up to it or the investigation wasn't, or some such. You just had to swallow hard because you knew they were talking to their own community. There was this whole 'holding the police to account' – wagging the finger. It was a particularly difficult one because, when you're trying to do a murder investigation and the MP in the area is telling the people that the police aren't up to it, it really doesn't help in terms of getting evidence and witnesses. So I went down to Hugh Orde and said to him, 'You're going to have to say something publicly about this.'

Of course Hugh, in his inimitable style, didn't miss. A clash set in and it necessitated a meeting in Hillsborough with the secretary of state at the time, Shaun Woodward, to try to thrash things out. I remember saying to Gerry Adams – and I think Martin was there, 'Look, I'll make a deal with you. I'm willing to accept that you have an understanding of the last thirty-five years. I'm not going to say it's right or that I agree with it, but I will accept it's yours. Because I wasn't at every house search, at every checkpoint. I don't know how soldiers and police officers behaved every time to you. But there's one condition: that you accept that I have an understanding of the last thirty-five years. I'm not asking you to say it's right – just accept it. Then we can get on to the future.'

And he said – I remember it because I wrote it down – he said, 'It's much more complicated than that.' I told him, 'Yes it can be. But that'll mean we'll need to look at everything and see who is to blame in every case, and we'll be at it for forty years and still not get it right. We've already spent twenty-five years trying to do that.'

I remember suggesting to Martin, 'What if we decide at the Maze/Long Kesh site to build a women and children's hospital? Let the British and Irish government build a women and children's hospital – it's about saving lives, it's a memorial to everybody caught in the conflict. Without saying it's a memorial to victims. It's a memorial to everybody, because everybody who grew up in this place is some sort of victim of the conflict, because they couldn't walk down the street and go into a shop without being searched. So let's build a memorial. The British and Irish governments were in charge at the time, let's hold them responsible.'

I said to him, 'We're all in this together. I didn't get up or go to bed wondering who to shoot or bomb. I didn't think about you as my enemy.'

He replied, 'Well, if you grew up in the Bogside …'

And I said, 'I understand that – you got involved in this because there was no other way of changing it.'

At one point in 1994 they were planning to shoot at me after chapel in Greysteel, but the guards intercepted the guy in Donegal. So I asked Martin, 'Is justice for me the guy who's going to do the shooting, or is it the guy who hijacked the car, or the guy who provided the safe house? Or is it the guy who gave the order? Or is it the bollocks who's sitting in Mass on Sunday and, instead of saying his prayers, is taking notes that I was there? Which of those is justice?'

I don't remember what he said to all that – I suppose I wasn't looking for a response. I wasn't talking about it just for me – I was talking about dealing with the past.

I believe Martin was a thinker around those things. He didn't always respond by saying, 'You're right' or 'Here's my alternative argument.' Part of it was me giving him a view of something. I think he was open to that. I think he genuinely was. I believe that because of what he has done in politics.

People now dismiss his meeting with the queen, but I think that was a huge event. I dealt with him in the run-up to the event, and afterwards. He was across the hall on 8 November when the queen unveiled a portrait. The next day I met him in Belfast and he was giving off to me about how that was to be a private event and yet here's a front-page photograph in *The Irish Times* that featured him and the queen. But it had every other political party leader in Ireland as well, and yet he was giving off to me about it!

'Martin, if you weren't there, Sinn Féin would have been the only party not there. Fianna Fáil, Fine Gael, the tánaiste – everybody's in that photograph. We're trying to normalise relationships.' The event was on 8 November 2016 so I spoke to him on the ninth. Two months later he resigned and the Executive collapsed.

What I think now is – and at the time I didn't cop on – he was getting it in the neck from his own people. 'You're doing all this reaching out, there's nothing coming back the other way.' We had the queen, Prince Philip, the tánaiste, Mike Nesbitt, Colum Eastwood – we'd all the politicians and a range of business people from across the island here [at Co-operation Ireland]. We had dinner afterwards. All the party leaders made statements and talked glowingly about the Executive; then two months later it was gone.

But his point to me was that he'd met the queen several times and in his own organisation there was a bit of a kickback. He wasn't getting anything out of the Executive. I didn't realise that at the time. But the relationship he had with me was strong enough that he could say those things to me and I didn't take offence at them; likewise I could come back at him. So that's what I mean when I say he got it. I think there was a willingness to reach out – to stretch himself – but at the same time not go too far.

That was the last time I saw him. He wasn't showing any signs of ill health at the time. He was kind of cross, but I put that down to the fact that he'd just come from America the day before, was feeling some jet-lag and was a bit grumpy.

***

The night before his funeral someone contacted me and said, 'You know you'd be welcome down at the house.' So I met a guy I know on the edge of the Bogside and we drove in. It was like the parting of the waves at the Bogside Inn. We drove up close to the house and there was an hour, an hour and a half of a queue snaked round the house. I thought 'God!' – it was an uncomfortable place to be. Quite a lot of the people would have known me.

Somebody shouted from the crowd to the guy who was with me, 'You're a turn-coat!' He stopped and I thought, 'Bloody hell!' He walks over to the guy. The impression I got was there was some sort of apology. The next I saw, two guys with green jackets went over to the guy and told him, 'Look, if you can't behave about this house, you're not welcome.' He was a pretty well-known guy in the area, you know. But he said, 'I was only joking.'

There were a couple of guys who'd have been former IRA men who came out of the queue and shook hands with me. Then they took me in a side door, where I met Willie McGuinness, Martin's brother. He took me in to where the coffin and Bernie and the girls were. I met them, paid my respects and said a prayer. As I was going out again I met Martina Anderson. She said, 'There's a seat reserved for you tomorrow in the church.'

Saying a prayer for him – it was like you would do for any human being. All of us are going to be there one day. There was a finality to it all. I was just watching his family around him, the few brief moments I was there, and I was thinking that now there was an hour and a half of a queue, but in a few weeks' time there'd be just the family.

It was that human instinct at the loss of a father. He clearly was loved by his children, his grandchildren. They didn't see him the way some other people saw him: they saw him as a father, a good father, a loving father. I had sympathy with them for the loss of somebody who'd exited this life the way he did.

As I understand it, there was a bit of a stand-off the night before the funeral because the church didn't want the tricolour on the coffin. But in the end I think they knew that these people were going to force the issue at the front door. He probably would have wanted the tricolour. I think the family were adamant that there'd be no other trappings.

Thirty thousand people, or near enough that number, attended the funeral – you couldn't but be in awe of how he was thought of. And I believe he was thought of better in later life. I think the reason there were 30,000 people there was not because of his IRA past; it was that people genuinely thought he had helped bring peace to this place. The people who turned up included Arlene Foster. It wasn't a private funeral and I'm sure the family got some comfort that the funeral was the size it was. But on the other hand there was a lack of privacy around all that.

I didn't understand many of the hymns because it was Seán Ó Riada. No offence to Seán Ó Riada, but if you'd asked me to pick hymns for a funeral service, I think it'd have been very different, and I think Martin himself might have picked more everyday hymns.

That night I did a TV interview with Denis Bradley and Gregory Campbell on the walls of Derry. I thought Gregory behaved a little better than Jim Allister. At least Gregory didn't say anything negative about McGuinness until after the funeral. He might have waited another few days, but he did it that night after the funeral; whereas Jim came out against Martin from the moment he was dead.

I think of the comment Bobby Kennedy made at JFK's funeral: there's a tendency in death to elevate people more than they were in life. It's apt for all of us. You go to funerals of people that you know, and you know there was a bit of a rogue and a scoundrel about them. Yet the oration will only be about the good side of them.

I understand that, for the sake of the family and so on. But how do I look at Martin's life? He grew up in poverty and discrimination and he used violence to try to resolve those issues because he thought that was the only way. And there was some horrendous violence. I remember saying to him one night, 'Even in a war situation, you will never convince me it's right to go out in the middle of the night, put a bomb under another human being's car, and go back to bed and hope it blows up the right person, that there's nobody walking past. You have to have some sort of depraved heart to have that indifference to human life.'

So there had to be a period in Martin's life when he had that indifference to human life – there had to be. But then you move it on to the later part, where I believe he was genuinely focused on saving lives and protecting lives. So it's all of those things. I'm reluctant to pigeonhole him or anybody else in one aspect of their life, as if that defines their whole life. What defines their life is the beginning to the end.

I think he had it all rationalised in his own mind. Who knows with any of us coming close to death – you would make your peace with God. I think Martin McGuinness probably in his own mind – now this is only supposition – believed that all the things in this last twenty years would compensate for that middle twenty years. Like most of us in life – how do we compensate for the bad things? We hope that when we get up there and the scales are weighed, we'll come out on balance. That's the best we can hope for.

He was complex. I don't mean complicated. He was complex in that he may well never have envisaged, when he first got involved, how far this would go and how much he would be involved. When you throw the first stone, and then go on to become the leader of an organisation, you get almost caught up in it. And then how do you change it, as the leader of that organisation, which is what I think he did? I think that's where he was trying to take it to, and with his personality he built sufficient support for that in the organisation. I do think he was hugely influential.

A comment Ian Paisley once made struck me: it's how we end our lives, not how we begin our lives. If that's right, then history will be kind to Martin.

When I was thinking of joining the police originally, one of my teachers was Fr Peadar Livingstone, who was an Irish historian. He probably hadn't the greatest of love for anything British, but he persuaded me into the RUC. I remember the discussions at home – would it not be better going to join the Scottish police, or the guards? That was 1975, one of the biggest years for murder. So my grandmother, who lived with us at the time, said, 'Well if he's born to be shot, he'll never be drowned.' I told Martin McGuinness that one day, and said, 'She turned out to be right!' He laughed.

3

Denis Bradley

The thing with Martin McGuinness and me is that our association predated our actual meeting. His aunt and my sister were best friends. He would have known that and so would I. I met his mother through her sister, and she would have known me and I would have known her and all her people. Although I didn't know Martin's father in the early days, I would have known his brother reasonably well because his brother palled around with a lot of the boys who would have been in the club where I worked. But it goes even further than that. His aunt married my first cousin. So our lives were intertwined before we ever met.

The McGuinnesses lived on the border between the Long Tower parish and the Cathedral parish. I think they lived on the Cathedral parish side, but his mother always went to the Long Tower church. Anyway, around this time, in the early 1970s, I was twenty-four years of age and back in Ireland after six years in Rome. I was in the Cathedral parish as a priest for three months before they sent me to Long Tower parish. Because I had been a boarder at St Columb's College, the Bogside and that whole Long Tower area was known to me, but I didn't know it close up.

Now there I was, living in the midst of a turbulent situation and, as it happens, I was very happy to be in the midst of it. I couldn't get back from Rome quick enough to a place I had some interest in. My mother used to send me two copies of the *Derry*

Journal every week when I was still in Italy, and I read it from cover to cover, front page to back page.

So with regard to Martin McGuinness, it wasn't 'Here's this person whom I don't know.' We met in my car, when I was giving him and three or four other boys a lift. Most of the boys would have been in my youth club, although Martin wasn't. I was fairly heavily involved in the youth club but was more interested in the political world and what was happening on the streets. And my introduction to Martin was on those streets. I knew that all these boys had joined the IRA – you knew it instinctively – but I didn't feel particularly uneasy being in the car with them. That was the world I had walked into – one of political upheaval and violence.

Martin wouldn't have been my first introduction to that world either. My first introduction to that world was the Brandywell, which was part of the Bogside. There were a lot of families in the Brandywell that I'd have known and been visiting, and I got to know that area very well. I also got to know the boys in the IRA very well. I think that most of the young boys I knew were either in the IRA or expecting to join the IRA, because the flood into the IRA at that time was enormous. Absolutely enormous.

I remember a British Catholic chaplain once asking me why I didn't report these boys to the authorities. I think that's a pathetic question – 'Why did you not report them to the police?' – it shows a real British mentality. My answer was to throw him out of the house.

The night after Bloody Sunday I remember having a conversation with Tom O'Geara, who was my best friend. Both of us agreed that we'd lost. Civil rights was finished; it was dead. This was now a full-out conflict/Troubles/war, whatever you wanted to call it. There was no sense in being moralistic about it. The morals were out the window. Gone. The politics in this had been lost.

***

I find myself resisting this notion that Martin stood out as a leader from the first time he walked into a room. That's not how I saw him, not how I remember him. I do remember him as being reasonably tall and good-looking, with an innocent-type face. But then again, the place was full of young fellas like that. He wasn't the only one.

There was a reticence in Martin at that age. He was quiet; he was shy. And it was only later on as I got to know him better that I saw the steel in him. If he fell out with you, he could be rough. He used to have this saying, 'You're a disgrace!' And he would say it with a passion and venom that was almost scary. That same steel was in his mother. His aunt, whom I knew very well, was a good-looking woman, gentle, beautiful in every respect – physically and personality-wise. His mother was a nice woman and a fine-looking woman, but there was a toughness in her. I think Martin was a mixture of both of those aspects.

By the way, some people say the same of me that they do of Martin: that I'm very nice, but that I'm a ruthless bastard, that I've done things that have shocked them. Personally I would have thought I was much less ruthless than him.

There was a gap between the old IRA and the new breed of youngsters who were coming in at that time. They weren't joining up for the same reasons that the old IRA came into being, which was some ideological conviction. This new breed were coming from the circumstances in the north and as a reaction to the development of things post-civil rights, with the gradual escalation of violence. In Derry at that point the best-known names associated with the IRA were the likes of Seán Keenan. He and others like him were still around, but they were getting old and there was a gap between the two generations. Seán Keenan wasn't speaking on behalf of the new generation, who were drawn in for a completely different reason to him.

I often tell a story that somebody told me, which I think is probably true. The IRA didn't have very many spokesmen then. And they weren't prepared to put anybody out as a spokesperson, because if they did they were identified. The person who was the obvious spokesperson was Dáithí Ó Conaill, but Ó Conaill was in Dublin or Ballyshannon or wherever – he wasn't living in the north. The other known spokesperson was Ruairí Ó Brádaigh, but Ó Brádaigh was in Roscommon or wherever, and he didn't appear that often in the north.

Anyway, a group of the younger guys were in a place called the Lourdes Hall in Derry when somebody came in to say there was a TV crew outside and they were looking to speak to somebody who knew something of what was going on in the IRA and republicanism. So everybody went, 'I'm not going out there!' Then somebody said, 'McGuinness, you're going out', and they pushed him out the door. He went out onto the platform and never came off it. In other words, what they were saying was he took to it. I think that's a true story.

That's the way things happen. It probably happened to me to some degree too. If you'd come to the Long Tower parochial house looking for an interview, all the other priests would have run a mile. I probably was pushed out – 'You're young, you're used to this type of thing.' Then afterwards you think, 'Well, I didn't do great, but I didn't do too badly.' So that's the first time, and then you get a bit better at it.

At Cheyne Walk [where talks between the British government and the IRA were held in 1972] the republican movement wanted to introduce this new young breed, this new generation, and they had to have somebody from Derry. But the boy who was in charge of the IRA in Derry at the time was not a publicist and to this day he's hardly known. So that's one reason for Martin having a slightly more public persona than perhaps others had at that time and in that situation.

But there is another reason: he presented a good figure. He didn't smoke, he didn't drink and he didn't womanise. He had all the virtues of Catholicism and came from a good, well-known and well-respected family. He himself looked good and he had all the attributes that were acceptable within that community. As for paramilitary activity, while I don't know if this is true or not, some people claim Martin was as blind as a bat. The point being that militarily that hardly puts him in the front rank.

Martin very quickly presented himself as being trustworthy. That is, trustworthy to the organisation that he was involved in, trustworthy in his relation to the community in which that organisation existed, and trustworthy in his words. The IRA needed that at that particular time. He was very much a product of his time – I think he'd have said that himself. If the Troubles hadn't happened, what would he have done? Probably a whole lot of things, but he certainly wouldn't have ended up in jail. Remember, republicans were struggling at that time with a reputation – within unionism and to some degree within the media – that they were bad people, they were criminals, they were thugs.

This stereotype was applied to a lot of us and not just to people who were in the IRA. I was involved with John Hume in that famous sit-down at the time of Operation Motorman [when the British Army overran the 'no-go' areas in Derry]. In fact, I probably led that sit-down more than Hume – Hume fell in on that accidentally. But all these photographs appeared of us sitting down – I think it was in the *Daily Mail*. The following morning the photographer came to me to apologise because right across the photograph that he had submitted was printed 'Rioters and Thugs'. He had put in the word 'protesters' and the sub-editor had scrubbed those words. He came to me the following morning and said, 'Fr Bradley, I apologise very deeply – I had nothing to do with that, I just did the photograph.' That was happening constantly.

Martin had an image that was contrary to that. His image said this is not about thuggery, this is not about criminality; instead, it suggested that this is about good youngsters and a political eruption. And it wasn't just him – there were other normal fathers and mothers whose sons were involved.

In those early days you were coming out of a past where the IRA wasn't heavily respected in Derry. The city had kind of drifted into support for the old Nationalist Party, with Eddie McAteer, James Doherty, Eugene O'Hare – all that group of people – and there were a small number of Labour Party supporters. There were only about five known republican families in Derry pre-1967–68. And they were kind of … they weren't sneered at but … there was a guy, Larry Boyle, who was supposed to have said he wouldn't cut his hair until Ireland was free – you had that kind of situation.

And there were divisions among the Catholic clergy over the IRA. Most of the clergy of that time who were working in

Derry city were on the streets. I'm talking about Eddie Daly, I'm talking about Anthony Mulvey, about Joe Carlin in Creggan, George McLaughlin – all of them weren't out condemning the IRA every day of the week because they were aware of both sides of the situation. The British Army had shot people on Bloody Sunday – it had happened. The killing wasn't all on one side. They were aware that the situation was out of control, that there was wrong on both sides. And it was hard to put all this back in the box again. It couldn't really be put back. At the same time the clergy out in the country were looking at the clergy in the city and asking, 'What are those guys up to?'

The situation with middle-class Catholics was interesting. It was hard to know what the middle class thought because the violence was all happening within working-class areas. The middle-class people were looking at it and wondering where it was all going. They were probably more republican than they wanted to admit, mainly on the grounds that at the time unionism was represented by the face of Ian Paisley.

Because this wasn't all happening with unionists standing back being neutral and quizzically analysing it. This was Paisley doing Paisley 'Protestants are in terrible peril' stuff. And not just Paisley but that entire movement.

***

None of Martin's family were involved in republicanism right through the Troubles. Tom was a bit older than him, Paul a bit younger – Martin was the right age. Geraldine was the only daughter. Martin drifted into it by the accident of timing. But I think both the military and the political aspects were within his nature and his personality. When he got into it, he was very involved, very committed. He had a streak of ruthlessness in him and he had that other side of him, which was far gentler. No, gentle's not the right word. Just more aware of humanity, I suppose. The reason I stayed in close touch with Martin, and he did the same with me to some extent, was because I always believed that if he could make a situation better, he would.

'It'll be the cutting edge of the IRA that'll make the difference' – Martin said that, but those are the words of a young, enthusiastic fighter. The world is full of young, enthusiastic fighters. It happens every-bloody-where. England has always been full of these young, enthusiastic fighters, who go out to fight the Germans and ISIS and everybody else.

There is a split in the world between those who believe in pacifism, which is very few, and those who don't. And one of the great problems was that Catholicism never really confronted the whole question of violence in the world. One of my big difficulties during those years was that I couldn't find a pacifist. Not even in myself. Which was kind of disappointing. Because there weren't any on the ground – even those who were on the ground and were advocating anti-violence weren't necessarily pacifists.

I knew that the political situation was changeable. You must remember I was around Martin for years and years; I was involved in a back channel [secret communication between republicans and the British government] for a long time with him as the main contact. Then I drifted away because I left the priesthood and went off to get married and those were difficult years for me. I only came back when Martin said to me, 'I think that we have to become peacemakers.' And the minute he said that, I said, 'I'm in. This is going to work.'

His was the first voice that I knew which made any difference. A thousand other people could have said the same thing but, when he said it, I knew we were in. The republican movement was prepared to move because Martin McGuinness was prepared to see things in a completely different context.

Decommissioning was a difficult one for them, but it wasn't an extremity, in that you cannot be in government with guns. The only people who can have guns in government are the state's armed forces under the government's control. That's the logic of politics. So in some ways they had to come to terms with that and that was a difficult one for them.

I went on the radio one morning and said the IRA had to decommission. It was the logic of the situation. Unionism had a point – you cannot do this without decommissioning. And that night I had to go to the wake of Martin's brother's wife, and I walked into the middle of all these hard republicans from Derry and from Belfast. I knew they'd all heard me because one thing that Shinners were always good at was listening to the radio – they didn't miss much. The only thing was, you can't tackle anybody at a wake house. So I knew I was on safe ground.

But the only time Martin really fell out with me was around the acceptance of the police as a legitimate authority. He came on radio and tackled me on it. I was on the Policing Board at the time, so I had already decided that the republicans had to accept the police. There's a logic in politics, and part of that logic is that you can't be in government and say you don't support the police. His line was that there hadn't been enough reform of the police yet and all that kind of stuff.

***

In 2005 the dissidents physically attacked me in a pub just down the road in the Bogside, not far from where Martin lived. I was there and a few dissidents came in and they sent out for some young fella to hit me with a baseball bat. I was lucky that I have a hard head. Everybody was supportive of me over that, but Martin in particular. He was the first person up at the hospital to see me. I landed in hospital about 11 p.m. and Martin was over there at midnight. He was great at that.

If you're lying there sick and somebody walks in the door to see you, it doesn't matter what the disagreements are, it kind of takes away the sting of the nettle. I know he did that for a lot of people. There might have been an element of calculation, but there was also a natural, genuine warmth. He was incredibly charming – always. That was something he got from his own people. His granny was the most charming woman you would ever meet.

He asked my advice often; although he wasn't particularly good at following it. Republicans aren't very good at asking for advice. While Hume had a self-protectiveness and self-interest, and an ego that was quite big, the Shinners were even more protective about their organisation. And I used to shout and roar, 'Is this about a united Ireland or about Sinn Féin's united Ireland?'

I had a major, hour-long battle with Gerry Adams one day in that back-channel situation about 'Who are you to tell the Irish people that they will have a socialist republic? That's up to the people.' I used to argue with Martin that they needed a kitchen cabinet made up of people who didn't like the Shinners. They needed to hear the reality; they needed to hear the opposite, to hear the complexities of argument.

Then they went into government with the Democratic Unionist Party. The DUP culture had fifty to a hundred years' experience of government, even if it was only at the local level of administration. The Shinners had none. They had nobody on board who knew anything. And very interesting – if you look at the history of Sinn Féin and McGuinness's office: he had about seven different advisers within a very short period of time. They ended up with a situation where supposedly the Executive fell because the DUP were running rings round them. They were never particularly good at government. And how could they have been? It's not possible to walk into that world and know everything.

Some say the unionists lost the best friend they ever had when Martin McGuinness died. That's not about competence in government. Martin's project started when he said, 'Let's make peace. Let's become the peacemakers rather than the war fighters.' And he did shift that ground and did it incredibly well. His project was: we'll move this situation to that one; we're going to be talking to the Brits.

I was against Martin talking to the Brits during the time when John Major had a majority of only fourteen or fifteen people, most of whom were anti-European and particularly anti-republican, and I told him so. I remember warning him, 'Let Hume, let the Irish do the talking; stay outside, because they're not going to make a deal, they can't make a deal. So let that happen. You stay outside. Because the minute you go in that door, they can read your body language, they can tell you what's happening.' He didn't agree with that. He said, 'You don't know the republican movement, we need to be in there.'

I do think he had difficulty bridging the realities between

how far you can bring the organisation and still trying to achieve good politics. He said to me, 'You don't understand', and he was right. I thought in the end, however, that they did an incredible job around policing and securing acceptance of the new-look police by republicans. I was saying, 'You're too late to policing, you should have made the leap earlier. You're going to have to make it sometime, so make it on your terms.'

The republicans did make a great effort to prepare their people. The number of local meetings, some of which I went to, they handled that incredibly well. They handled decommissioning very well. All of those were historical, major efforts through which you had to bring an organisation. Martin would have been travelling around, meeting the important people before the local meetings. In whatever conversations I would have been having with him, I pushed him into realising that he actually had the control and the authority that people would follow him. And I think his view always was, 'You're overestimating my authority.' I don't know if I was or not – you'd have to have been there to really know. That's only conjecture rather than actual fact.

Despite my sense of his authority, I don't think Martin had the experience of the outside world to the degree he thought he had. I believe his warmth and charm, which was natural, got him through an incredible amount of stuff. And lured a lot of people into his den. And I don't mean that in a bad way; I mean it in a good, human way, where people felt comfortable with him. But that doesn't mean a wild lot was achieved.

I also think he became charmed in turn by the big world. He loved the 'we made peace in Northern Ireland; we're going to make peace in the world' type of thing. I used to go, 'Oh God – come home, Martin. Come home out of Colombia. What the fuck do you know about it? What do I know about it? What does anyone know about it?' The lesson of Ireland is: you have to make peace in your own country. Let other people make peace in their own country.

I also think that he was charmed by big personalities and lacked a little bit of cynicism, although I wouldn't include the queen in that. The queen's not the most charming personality in the world. I remember being at a function one time in Washington and Gerry Adams arrived: he was treated like a superstar. And I thought, 'Jesus, this is dangerous stuff.' It's very hard to live in that world. I mean, I couldn't do it. You get your head very easily turned. I think every human being I've ever met is at least partially that way. There are only a few people I ever met who stayed away from it, like maybe Jean Vanier [Canadian Catholic philosopher, theologian and humanitarian]. I can think of about three people and that's it.

As for Martin's meetings with the queen and attending that banquet, I think he believed that was good – not so much for republicanism as for unionism. He realised that he had to reach out, and that was natural for him anyway – he wanted to reach out. The difficulty was that he ended up feeling they didn't always reach back to him. I met him a few weeks before he died and he seemed to be of the opinion that he didn't get back what he gave – at that level, the symbolic level. The arguments that are now going on about this were well developed even before he died: that the unionists are too afraid, they're too defensive, they see everything as a threat.

My take on the meetings with the queen is that people can and do make those 'he's rolling over' remarks – and he was aware of those remarks. But if the politics had gone well, and if everything was up and running, people could make those remarks and they wouldn't have much impact. They'd be just that: remarks. It wouldn't have made any real difference to the people on the ground, to the republican movement itself. Republicans are always going to be critical of that type of situation, but it doesn't mean they're going to turn on anybody or that they're going to have a revolution. Laughing with Paisley – yes, there were people who were uncomfortable with that, but in general it was all right. Martin was controlling all of that and he was very good at that.

I put a lot of store by him in the sense that once he said we were going to make peace we made peace. I thought he had the authority or even genius to do that. It takes a lot – it takes stamina, it takes insight, it takes determination, it takes a bit of ruthlessness. And I thought he had it. What surprised me was how good he was at the political symbolism. And what really delighted me about him – and I took a little bit of pleasure in this throughout all the years that we would have been chatting, sitting here and sitting in his house, arguing, having debates about politics and so forth – was his ability to read the situation and take it on and go out and grasp it. Not too many people have that ability, but he had it.

Hume had it as well, but Hume did it in a different fashion. Hume had the reputation that when he was in doubt and when there were big things going to happen he would visit the pubs and talk to the dockers. Now I don't know if that's true or not, but that is the reputation he had. He would go round and he'd ponder for a day or two. And then he'd come out with something big and grand.

McGuinness had the ability to sit back and then, at the big

moment, come out and slam it – kill it if it needed to be killed or grow it if it needed to be grown. Like the type of situation whereby he walks out the door at Stormont with Hugh Orde [then PSNI chief constable] and Peter Robinson and says of the dissidents, 'You're traitors to Ireland!' That changes the whole dynamics of a situation.

That is the manifestation of something that he said to me the day I got hit by the dissidents: 'It's not you they're after, Bradley, it's me.' That is 110 per cent right. I was only a man who symbolised notions of reconciliation that were really embodied in him. And the dissidents could never win while McGuinness lived unless they took him out. Because his first statement was that they were pathetic, militarily speaking. He said that in public again and again – long before he said the thing with Orde. But the Orde thing was the big moment of bringing all that together and slamming it and saying, 'This is where we stand.'

I think he thought meeting the queen and visiting Messines and so on – he thought that was necessary and that was right. He also thought it was progress. He thought that despite the fact that the politicians were very difficult to deal with, he thought the unionist community was far more on his side. He did get a very warm reception from the Protestant churches, although they didn't necessarily represent the Protestant people. But Martin mightn't have understood that distinction.

His relationship with Catholicism and with the Catholic Church was a whole lot like other people's – he was very *à la carte*. He wouldn't be the only one around the place. He had little to no relationship with Edward Daly, the bishop of Derry, who once said to me, 'Denis, you're far better at the politics than I am.' And I said, 'Yes, you're bloody right, Eddie.'

If it were simply a matter of Christianity denouncing violence and meaning it, the morality of violence would be easy. But that's not true. Christianity does violence every day of the week. My memory goes back a bit on these things. Who was it – Cardinal Spellman – sprinkling holy water on the American air-bombers during the Vietnam War? I think Martin was aware of things like that. And most Catholics are. The Catholic Church doesn't ever address it, so it's not a major problem. It will come up, but it hasn't come up yet.

***

A whole lot of images come to mind when I think of Martin now, but one that comes often is the day he 'dumped' me. He walked in the front door of my house with a bottle of wine and he was dumping me in the sense that he was saying bye-bye to me and the others who'd been involved in the back channel. He was dumping us and he was creating another back channel – or thought he was. There was a directness in the way he did it, a decency, although he didn't drink and it was a pretty bad bottle of wine! It was a mixture of ruthlessness and decency. And it was inevitable. We had predicted two years before that we were coming to an end, that we'd be dumped some day because we'd used our brief in a proactive way, which you have to do if you're going to achieve anything. But that's another story.

So I have mixed memories of Martin. That's the case with anybody I know – there's that mixture. I don't do heroes very well. But I liked him. Yes, I liked him. But I think I lost him. I lost him to the new world of politics. It was inevitable. I would have felt kind of lonely about the fact that I lost him. Men do not make friendships that much. Women do better in that regard.

I've had a thousand acquaintances, but I've only had about three or four people that I'd call friends. I know I'm lucky – I've seen men who have plenty of 'friends' but not intimate friends. And I don't think Martin and I quite reached that stage because we lived in two different worlds and there was too much separating us. But we came close to it at times.

I didn't lose him when he first went into politics. It was when he became deputy first minister and was travelling the world, wining and dining with everybody. Let's remember this: it's not as if I was some wee young fella sitting at home. I was out doing the Policing Board and other things. It was the same tree in some ways, but the branches were going in different directions. He was busy over there and I was busy over here. And there was a crossover the odd time. But I felt I wouldn't have been able to talk to him with the same intimacy and the same honesty and openness in the years after he became the big, public Martin McGuinness. When I knew him and we were close, he wasn't the public Martin McGuinness.

On his death I felt the loss at a one-remove level. Sometimes when I walk through Derry I think, 'Jesus, McGuinness is dead!' It all happened so fast. I went to see him a couple of weeks before he died. He didn't think he was dying – he was at home at that point, though he was in and out of hospital. But, as I say, I still walk through Derry and suddenly think, 'McGuinness is dead!' It kind of hits you in a very personal way. So I'd feel the loss of him.

But I had already lost him. The conversations we used to have stopped happening quite a while ago, along with his need for me and my need for him. I mean, I used him and he used me during the hard times. Numerous times he'd have come to me about a problem, asking, 'Can you sort this out?' or whatever. And the reason I trusted him was that if he could do that kind of thing for me in return, he would. I used him in the sense that I'd go to him and tell him, 'You know, this isn't going to happen. I know this person and it's never going to happen', or whatever, and he'd listen. Those intimate exchanges went on for years and in very private situations, involving a fair amount of trust. You don't get that in life all the time.

His ego was his greatest weakness and his ego was his greatest strength. But I think that's true of most men. It was his greatest weakness, in the sense that it's very hard to keep a balance and clarity when you're surrounded by people telling you that you're the greatest thing since the sliced pan. And it was also his greatest strength, in that he had the requisite confidence and conviction – it takes an ego to say, 'I'm going to take this situation and drive it through.' So I think the same thing was his strength and his weakness. I don't know if that's true of everybody or not, but I believe it was true of him.

4

Dermot Ahern

The first time I met Martin McGuinness would have been in the early 1990s, when he and Gerry Adams came into the meeting room that Bertie Ahern had on Floor 5 in Leinster House. I had met Adams a couple of times before that, but this was the first time I met McGuinness, and it would also have been the first time Bertie met him.

He said very little during the meeting – Adams did all the talking. I remember Bertie saying later that McGuinness just stared at a picture Bertie had on the wall of Patrick Pearse. At some stage he said to Bertie something like, 'How do you stick it?' The interminable meetings are what I think he was referring to in his Derry accent.

This was the first occasion he had, you might say, popped up his head. In the past he had always stayed in the background. To us his appearance was confirmation there was some merit to these meetings. We would have regarded McGuinness as being the main IRA aspect at the meeting. Adams was doing a lot of discussing and talking about historical perspectives – fairly academic stuff about the whole process of republicanism from Wolfe Tone on up, whereas McGuinness was the more practical side of things. At this time we in Fianna Fáil still regarded McGuinness with great suspicion. He didn't make any bones about it: he had been in the IRA and probably still was.

Over the intervening years I met him again at various north–south ministerial meetings. He was at the very first of these, held in Armagh on 13 December 1999, and I've a framed menu card from that occasion. It was a very uneasy meeting but not because of McGuinness. It was uneasy because of David Trimble. Quite apart from the fact that Trimble didn't want to meet nationalists, here he was sitting round a table with the Irish government. He was throwing tantrums and all sorts of things. Quite a lot of my colleagues who didn't have any real interest in the north were saying to themselves, 'What the hell are we doing here? We could be back in Dublin or Cork or Kerry doing other things.'

At the end of our meeting, which was a kind of lunch, someone suggested that since it was such a historic occasion, we'd send round the menu card and we'd all sign it. As usual in those circumstances, when one person takes out a pen they hand the pen around to use for signing. And on that occasion the pen went missing and there were jokes about 'Who took the pen?' But when I got my menu card back, it had gone round the table a second time and the only person who had signed it twice was Martin McGuinness. So the joke was that Martin McGuinness was so delighted to now be inside the tent, he signed it not once but twice. We had a good laugh about it.

***

Martin was a much easier person to deal with than Gerry Adams. When I saw him at meetings, we had a definite sense of movement. Although I'm not saying that I didn't believe Adams. I first met Adams in 1988 when Martin Mansergh, Senator Richie Healy and myself met with him, Mitchel McLaughlin and Pat Doherty in a Redemptorist monastery in Dundalk.

In a second meeting between us, it was a Monday morning – the Saturday before, eight British soldiers were blown up in a bus in Ballygawley [on 20 August 1988] and the following Monday morning we were due to meet Adams and co. at the Redemptorists' place. I remember I rang Richie Healy and I said, 'Richie, about this incident on Saturday night. I've no stomach to meet these fuckers, excuse the language.' And he said, 'Neither have I.'

I was a young TD – had been a TD for only a year, in fact – although I was cute enough and the meeting was in my home town. Anyway, I said to Richie, 'Look, we're going to have to meet them but we'll lay down a marker at the start of the meeting.' It was agreed that I'd say something to Adams, though we didn't tell Mansergh that we were going to raise this.

When the meeting started I said, 'Before we go any further' – and I spoke directly to Adams – 'How can you expect us to continue to meet with you when an incident such as happened in the last forty-eight hours happens?' I didn't really know what sort of answer I was going to get, but the answer I got was: 'Isn't that the very reason why we're meeting? In order to convince those people that did that to stop doing that? That's what we're trying to do.' Which to a certain extent cut the feet from under me. That was the first time I heard that mantra, which we heard many times subsequently – the reason why all these meetings were taking place was in order to achieve peace.

Mitchel McLaughlin and Pat Doherty were two fine people; I had great regard for them subsequently. But to me Adams was the devil incarnate. He was trying to make out by saying that he was having an internal battle within the IRA and Sinn Féin to bring people onto the political route. McGuinness coming in, whom we knew to be in the IRA, was a clear indication that there was a move afoot. Up until he became involved, we were never really sure. However, the minute McGuinness appeared on the scene, southern politicians who'd met Sinn Féin on a regular basis would have regarded that as a clear indication that there was movement.

Early on, our meetings with Adams and others would have been hugely criticised if they had been public knowledge. My political career wouldn't have lasted five minutes if it had got out in 1988 that I had met Gerry Adams. In fact, it was only after the 1998 Good Friday Agreement that it came out that we'd met then.

***

I think Martin McGuinness got fair press in the south – mainly because of his personality. But at the end of the day, during the presidential election he was never going to get away from his past. That's what did for his candidacy in the end. He was a good choice from a personality point of view for president, but it was his past that did for him. And I think the questions asked of him and the accusations made against him were fair enough. While I had a regard for him, what he and Adams would have done over the years – it wouldn't make me vote for them.

Neither did I talk with them much, not that there was much opportunity for small talk. Most of the time we'd have met in fairly formal circumstances – maybe a little bit of chit-chat over a cup of coffee after the meeting, but we certainly wouldn't go off to the pub for a pint.

One of the most difficult meetings we had was directly after the Northern Bank raid [the largest bank robbery in Irish history, which occurred in Belfast on 20 December 2004]. That's when I was minister for foreign affairs and Michael McDowell was the minister for justice and Bertie Ahern was the taoiseach. We had been briefed by our security people – the top gardaí – that Adams and Sinn Féin had prior knowledge of what went on, that they knew more than they were saying.

We met Adams and McGuinness out in St Luke's – Bertie's constituency centre – rather than in government buildings. Of course the two of them denied everything. McGuinness was extremely angry and agitated that we had some knowledge as to what had gone on. They kept challenging us, 'Show us the proof.' Naturally we weren't going to say, 'This is the proof.' But it was the very strong advice of our own gardaí, whom we would trust, and also intelligence from the British side. We were adamant in telling them that it wasn't just the British response; it was our own guards.

McDowell and myself, we would have been very tough about things at that meeting. We felt it was bigger than the £26 million or whatever it was. It was really a shot across the bows of the political discussions that were coming to a close at that stage. We were on the final lap and next thing fecking this happens. We felt completely duped. So we stopped negotiations with them at that point. There was a cooling-off period.

***

I don't think McGuinness particularly liked me because I was forthright. He always knew McDowell was anti-him, but I was a wee bit more forthright in some of my comments. I came from a constituency [Louth] where I knew what the IRA was up to over the years, so I was inclined to take a tougher line.

Apart from the meeting to discuss the Northern Bank raid, the only other time I saw McGuinness agitated – although it was more Adams, really – was at the end of the St Andrews Agreement. [This was an agreement between the British and Irish governments and Northern Ireland's main parties pertaining to the devolution of power in the region.] It was just before the press conference on the final day at about four o'clock. Adams and McGuinness – although it was admittedly more Adams than McGuinness – intervened. We were in a room with Tony Blair before we all went over to the press conference in the room opposite. Basically Adams and to a lesser extent McGuinness had a shouting match with Blair over the final communiqué that the governments were intending to give at the press conference.

Despite this both Bertie and Blair got up at the press conference and announced the St Andrews Agreement. Adams and McGuinness weren't happy with the results – neither was the DUP. When Bertie and Blair announced the agreement, immediately after the press conference the media rushed off to Paisley on one side of the room and Sinn Féin on the other side of the room for their comments. Adams and McGuinness were upset about some of the finer details in the agreement – I can't remember exactly what. But a couple of weeks later, Sinn Féin first and then the DUP said they'd work with it.

***

Looking back, I think McGuinness was a natural politician. He had the personality for it. He was a good negotiator. He was able to make people like him. He showed that to a lesser extent with David Trimble but to a greater extent with Ian Paisley. It was a very good choice that Sinn Féin picked him rather than Adams to be the leader in the north and to be the deputy first minister. His personality was such that he was able to show the nicer side of republicanism, as it were. Other people wouldn't have been able to carry it off.

Over the years, I found he was very easy to work with and I came to regard him very highly. We met on a number of occasions off-camera. He had a great love for soccer in the form of Derry City, as did I for Dundalk. Shortly before he died I was up at a game against Derry – which we won handsomely. Before the game I met him. We had a chat about football and, though it was not long before he died, he didn't look that bad. I met him again at the funeral of Dermot Gallagher, the former secretary-general of foreign affairs, who died on 14 January 2017. I had a chat with him at the funeral and wished him well.

Given his affable personality, I think he would have succeeded in reconciliation, given time. He was able to sit down with people like Paisley and Peter Robinson and others. We used to find it very difficult to meet with some of these people, so I often wondered how he did it.

We went into the meetings in 1998 in an effort to convince Sinn Féin that there was a better way and a less counter-productive way of achieving a united Ireland – by negotiation and politics, rather than trying to shoot and bomb people into a united Ireland. The fact is the IRA was a patent failure in getting the Brits out. But ultimately, despite all the talk of getting a united Ireland, Sinn Féin is no closer to achieving this than they were at the start of the campaign. So McGuinness and Adams did fail in the main objective of their careers.

However, in fairness to them, they got people sitting round the table talking and they brought about an absence of violence.

And McGuinness – with his journey from IRA gunman and leader to a consummate politician, which is what he turned out to be – certainly played a central role in that.

5

Dawn Purvis

I can remember Martin McGuinness appearing on TV as part of a Sinn Féin delegation; this was back in the 1980s when their voices were dubbed. He was a scary figure, very much viewed as someone who was instrumental in the IRA's war and someone who had taken a leading role in that war, thereby viewing all things British – including myself – as dispensable. He was indeed a frightening figure. And the fear was strong. People like my granny would have taken a knife to the TV screen. Working-class unionists would have feared the IRA. If they said something, people in my community would have said, 'Oh, if they said it, they mean it.' What I'm getting at is that they were regarded as people who, whatever they said, they followed up on it. So, if there was sabre-rattling, that was believed.

But there came a point where their word was no longer their bond. That was around the time of Castlereagh [in 2002, the heavily fortified Castlereagh police barracks was raided and sensitive intelligence documents were stolen] and Stormontgate [also in 2002, when police raided Stormont amid allegations of an IRA spy ring operating there], and everything that flowed from those events. Things like the claim that Adams was never in the IRA, or that the IRA was never involved in the Northern Bank robbery – all these things were hard to swallow. I think up to that point people would have believed what they said because they followed up on it.

Until the time when Martin McGuinness became deputy first minister, Martin and Gerry Adams were viewed as two sides of the same coin, although Adams was more the bogeyman than McGuinness. I think McGuinness's admission that he was a member of the IRA gave him some integrity within the unionist community.

In 1992 my home was extensively damaged by an IRA bomb and I remember the anger in the local community. I recall Ian Paisley coming down to the street and getting chased by the local people. I remember Peter Hadden, the Labour representative, coming in and getting chased. I remember the Ulster Unionist Party [UUP] representative, Martin Smyth, coming in and getting chased. They all wanted their photograph taken with this devastation – but where had they been before that?

I wasn't angry – I was bemused. Why would anybody want to plant a bomb that would have no impact on a police station at all? It wrecked the benefits office and it wrecked our homes. I walked into our house and I could see the sky. I remember thinking, 'This is a product of the society that we have created.' I had no hatred for the person who did it. He was as much a product of this society as I was. From that point, I realised that people were products of the circumstances in which they grew up.

Working-class unionist outrage at that time was channelled more towards Gerry Adams than McGuinness. Within loyalist working-class areas, there was a sneaking regard for the IRA and Sinn Féin, a sneaking regard for their inextricable links. It was like the Prods were looking at the Catholics and asking, 'Why can we not be more like them?' They seemed a homogenous unit: they had the GAA, they had the Catholic Church – so there was something of a green-eyed monster within unionist working-class areas towards the IRA and Sinn Féin. Even my granny, if she was watching the news and a bomb went off and it was attributed to the IRA, would say, 'Ah, sure they always get it right.' But if she heard it was loyalists who were involved, 'Ah, sure they'd muck it up, they'd muck it up.' There was a regard for the solidity of the relationship between the IRA and Sinn Féin. And people used to measure that against unionist politicians and loyalists and say, 'Naw. That doesn't exist.' I'm talking here about the 1980s.

In later years, when I was in the Progressive Unionist Party [PUP], there was a much finer analysis of the Provos and their leadership, and what they were trying to do. I sat at many meetings where we unpicked their language and actions to try to work out what they were saying and what they meant. In the early days, there was no analysis of what the republican movement was up to.

***

I remember the first time Sinn Féin came into talks. It was June 1996 and I was in my late twenties. I was petrified. The PUP saw republicans coming into the talks as a good thing. I remember Gusty Spence [a veteran loyalist paramilitary leader] saying, 'Ah, we need them in, we need them in!' I was saying to him, 'Are you mad?' But Gusty kept saying, 'We need Sinn Féin in the democratic process. We need them in to see the whites of their eyes and to start working with them.'

I'd seen cardboard cutouts, media caricatures on TV. It was only when they came into the talks – at which point the DUP and Bob McCartney [the then leader of the UK Unionist Party] walked out – that I began seeing members of Sinn Féin as real human beings.

What was perhaps most difficult for me, at first, was that Martin was a purveyor of a mantra that was repeated over and over: about them being the most oppressed people, how this was a war against British colonialism, how we needed the Brits out of Ireland – with no real consideration of *this* Brit. No real consideration of the unionist community. No real consideration of the impact of IRA violence on the unionist community. That didn't happen until much later. In fact, there are still those in the republican community who don't recognise the impact that killing RUC and UDR men had on the psyche of the unionist community.

I met Martin during the peace talks. I was a member of the PUP delegation, and while we didn't have bilateral meetings with Sinn Féin, you'd see them in the corridor or the dining room, and I have to say, they were very personable, very friendly and genuine. My first face-to-face came as I was walking down the corridor in Stormont – and I was petrified, absolutely petrified. I was on my own and here was this 'government' of forty people moving towards me. The Sinn Féin delegation always walked in clumps around the place. I suppose I'd got comfortable because I'd worked in the place and I knew my way about. But now I was going, 'Oooh ...', shaking. Do you stop; turn in the other direction; run?

Gerry Adams stopped and said, 'Hello. How are you doing?' I was like a rabbit caught in the headlights. I went back to the office: 'They know me! They know my name! How did they get my name?' They didn't offer to shake hands, which in hindsight I thought was actually very big of them. They didn't want to put me in an uncomfortable position. I remember reflecting on that. I'm a very huggy sort of person and that's the usual thing I would bounce to do. I remember reflecting on their approach and thinking, 'Fair play.'

But we were hearing the same rhetoric from Sinn Féin over and over again. The fact is that Sinn Féin never negotiated [in the peace talks leading to the Good Friday Agreement]. In each of the three strands they set down their *Éire Nua* document and said, 'This is it. This is our negotiating position.' And I think it wasn't until the last forty-eight hours that the serious negotiations got under way. So every time we went into a plenary session, we heard about the discrimination, we heard about the hard time the Catholic community had suffered.

I remember an occasion where Martin himself laughed. The talks had moved to Dublin Castle and he was giving his single transferable speech about being a young man growing up in Derry and not getting a job and so on. And we were all sitting there going, 'We've heard this, we've heard this.' The first time you hear it, OK, but you don't need to hear it repeated over and over and over again. Hugh Smyth [a senior PUP figure] would sit near the microphone and tear up paper or rattle the coins in his pocket. On this occasion, he interrupted Martin McGuinness's story. The very patient Senator Mitchell said, 'Yes, Mr Smyth?' And Hughie said, 'I just wish somebody had given him a job all them years ago because then we wouldn't be listening to this over and over again!' Martin McGuinness smiled and Adams had to put his head down, and other delegates were going, 'OK, Hughie, we feel your pain. We know where you're coming from.'

There was sometimes a sense they were trying to wear us down, a sense of cynicism. Gusty Spence used to say of loyalist communities, 'Ye'd neither in ye nor on ye, but we were in power.' He meant you were left in poverty but didn't dare speak out because unionist leaders would say, 'You think you're doing bad? Look at them ones over there!' It was this notion of 'Just shut up – youse are doing all right!'

Certainly from people within the PUP, there was a clear recognition of the discrimination that existed towards Catholic communities, but also that it was replicated in some ways in Protestant working-class communities. We always felt that wasn't recognised within republicanism because it didn't fit with the narrative they were trying to put forward.

**

I'd say I really only started to get to know Martin McGuinness after the Assembly got up and running in 1998. That year David Ervine and Billy Hutchinson of the PUP were elected to the Assembly and I was the party's spokesperson on women's affairs at the time. It was during that time and then after 2007, when David Ervine died and I got elected to the Assembly, that I got to know Martin much better.

I was in the Assembly when Martin was announced as the minister for education, but I was not part of the collective gasp that went up when his name was announced. I was delighted because Sinn Féin was opposed to academic selection and so was I.

From 1998 to 2004, when I worked in the Assembly for the PUP, my boys came in during the school holidays and met whoever was about. They didn't distinguish between anybody. The year before my youngest son was about to sit the Eleven Plus [an examination taken at age eleven, which decided if a child would attend a grammar or a secondary school], as I was taking the two boys down for their lunch, we met Martin coming slowly up the corridor – he'd broken his leg playing football.

The two boys said, 'There's Martin McGuinness!'

So I said to the younger one, Lee, 'That's the man who's in charge of the Eleven Plus.'

Lee said, 'Can he not do away with it?'

And I said, 'Why don't you ask him?'

As Martin came up I said, 'Good morning, minister. This young son of mine has something to ask you.'

'Does he? What's your name?'

'I'm Lee. I'm supposed to be doing the Eleven Plus.' Then he said, 'Would you not do away with the Eleven Plus before I have to do it in November?'

And Martin said, 'If I can do that, son, I will definitely do it.'

'Well, do your best,' Lee told him.

'Yes, son, I'll do my very best.'

And he shook hands with both of them.

My two sons were very astute with regard to politics. They watched events on TV and I had them out tramping the streets canvassing from when they were no age. They were watching the talks process and I asked, 'Who do you think is the best in terms of negotiation?'

The big one said immediately, 'Seamus Mallon. He's the best.'

'What about David Trimble?'

'Don't like him.'

Seamus Mallon was a schoolteacher [and deputy leader of the SDLP], whereas David Trimble didn't have the same nature or personality – he could be quite short, aloof.

After Sinn Féin and the DUP made their big announcement about agreeing to share power in 2007, both parties set up meetings with the rest of the parties in the Assembly to talk about 'Devolution Day', which was going to be 8 or 9 May. Sinn Féin still hadn't worked out that Martin McGuinness was going to be deputy first minister. But we got an official request for a meeting and I said, 'Yes, absolutely.' I made the comment David Ervine used to make when Sinn Féin asked for a meeting, 'Can you send me somebody that hasn't been in Castlereagh Interrogation Centre and knows how to impart information?'

I met Michelle Gildernew and Martin. It was the first time I'd had a meeting with Sinn Féin and it just felt very informal and comfortable. It was clear talking: 'Here's what we're going to do and this is how we're going to go forward.' It was great. We had a series of meetings with Sinn Féin before the PUP got its first meeting *ever* with the DUP. Up to that the DUP had refused to meet our party. I felt much more comfortable in meetings with Sinn Féin.

During the talks, I don't think Sinn Féin regarded us as an enemy or a political threat, or in any way chipping away at their electoral base. However, we were treated with absolute contempt by the DUP and by Bob McCartney. I had to complain to the chair of the talks about McCartney and his attitude towards me. And I remember during the referendum campaign on the Good Friday Agreement, Paisley and the DUP were canvassing in Sandy Row and we were called traitors and all sorts of names. We were despised because we were pro-peace and pro-Agreement.

Martin McGuinness and Sinn Féin were aware of that and it was reflected in meetings. They talked about our socialism and about how our policies were not too far from their own, in terms of wanting to help communities. The whole idea of scrapping the Eleven Plus, for example. They didn't see the DUP as representing the interests of working-class loyalism – they saw the PUP as doing that.

I don't think Martin visited any state/Protestant secondary schools while minister for education. It was such a toxic time. I think the fact that he didn't reflects badly on our community. I saw that throughout that period. While Martin wasn't able to go and visit a Protestant/state secondary school, I saw Gregory Campbell as minister for regional development in the [Catholic] Lower Ormeau area when the place was flooded, talking to residents with no worries about his safety or security. I thought, 'Why can't we reciprocate that? Why can't my community do that?' It was the same when former President of Ireland Mary McAleese was visiting the Women's Centre in the Village [a working-class, unionist area of Belfast] and people were up in arms about it. Why?

Was Martin a good minister for education? It's hard to tell, because devolution was stop-started so many times then that my memory is a bit blurred about what was actually done. I don't think his abolition of the Eleven Plus worked out successfully. I do think it was the right thing to do and the moral thing to do, in terms of our children and our education system, but I think he could have handled it better. He left us with the hodgepodge system we now have of private tests and that's not a good thing – although I do think his heart was in the right place. Had we had a stable time, I think he would have been a very good minister.

When I first arrived at the talks in 1996, I was a very naïve and timid young woman. Seeing people like Paisley and John

Hume up close, I was very intimidated. Gusty Spence said to me, 'You've as much right to be here as any of them. Do you think you're any less qualified than any of them?'

And I was going, 'I'm sure I'm less qualified.'

He said, 'No, you're not. No you're not. You've every right to be here.'

I felt the same about politicians in the Assembly being nominated as ministers. In the first Assembly, when devolution was restored, what our politicians lacked was experience of governing. They'd lots of experience of opposition and political activism and that sort of stuff. But confidence only comes with being in office. I mean, what is a professional politician? What experience do you need? What education? Peter Robinson was an estate agent with, I think he said, five O Levels. But he was a very good minister.

I watched Martin mature over a period of time and I thought he was a great deputy first minister. He sometimes talked a bit too long, but he was statesmanlike. He went out of his way to get people onside and he had a natural way of doing that. He had the likeability factor: when you met him you were left with an impression. And there are not many politicians who have that. But also he was genuine. He listened to you. He was sincere in what he said.

I saw his outreach for reconciliation as a massive gesture of leadership – bravery, stepping out from your own tribe to reach the hand of the other. We haven't had enough of those types of gestures in Northern Ireland. I know there are people who see those gestures as cynical and say, 'Oh they're only doing this because they want something else, there's a *quid pro quo*.' I didn't see any *quid pro quo*. I didn't see any equalising of that or follow-up from that, any magnanimous gesture coming from unionism. I thought they were serious gestures and at the right time.

I particularly remember the big one. I was watching TV at the time and I remember going 'Wow!' when he stood at the steps of Stormont Castle in 2001 with Hugh Orde and Peter Robinson, after the killing of PSNI officer Stephen Carroll, and called the dissidents 'traitors to Ireland'. I thought, 'My goodness, my goodness! This is the type of leadership that we need to see here – from both sides – in order to take this place forward.' And I was really hopeful that Peter Robinson would reciprocate and show the same level of courage and bravery in relation to his own tribe. I thought we started to see elements of it, for example when he talked at his party conference about one system of education, rather than the present system of separate Protestant/state schools and Catholic schools. I also remember how the flags in the audience stayed down when he gave that speech, and I thought, 'Oh-oh. I think Robinson knows where he wants to go, but he hasn't his ducks lined up yet.' But sometimes political bravery and courage is about not waiting to have your ducks lined up. It's about taking that step.

I think Martin McGuinness was outstanding, unparalleled in that. If you look at other peace processes, like with Nelson Mandela and F. W. de Klerk and other such processes, you had those big gestures, but they were reciprocated and that's what made them work. Martin's great gestures included meeting the queen at the Lyric and going to Irish President Michael D. Higgins's first state visit to Britain and putting on all that regalia for the formal dinner. Yes, there were rumblings of dissent from his own people, but that's what great leadership is about.

It was shameful that there was no reciprocation. 'Will you go to a Republic of Ireland football match?' [McGuinness offered to attend both a Republic of Ireland and a Northern Ireland football match with Arlene Foster.] 'No, I'm not going,' she said. Get a life! All that humming and hawing – what's it going to do? Just go. Just *go*. What is attending a football match going to do?

Working-class unionists don't vote in large numbers. They will tell you they are fed up with their politicians and that they do nothing for them. Then they meet them face to face and tell them they are great and doing a good job. But when they are out of earshot they spit on the ground and curse them. So the people are partly to blame for the politicians they get. The politicians have no real sense of the people. They need to get out more and not surround themselves with back-slappers. They need to get out of their own comfort zones and really engage with people. We live in a false world where people can't be honest with one another.

I think Peter Robinson and Arlene Foster missed the boat in terms of reciprocal gestures to McGuinness. Here was a leader who was prepared to make these big statements, take these big steps, in order to accommodate unionists and unionist feelings, and say, 'We've got to work on this, we've got to move forward.' And I think in return McGuinness's hand was slapped out of the road. Big opportunities were missed, are being missed, and will continue to be missed.

I think the more working-class unionists Martin met, the more they warmed to him. He got himself out in the community, meeting with people – and you can see throughout his term in office that he got to meet more and more people.

The relationship McGuinness fostered with the Presbyterian minister in Derry and others also started to soften unionist attitudes. When you have a Presbyterian minister saying, 'I regard Martin McGuinness as my friend', that's a big thing. That Presbyterian minister would have got it in the neck if his congregation thought he'd been doing something wrong. He would have been checking the pulse of his parishioners.

I remember talking to groups who had been up at the Assembly, whether it was women's groups, youth groups or whatever, and they all would go, 'We met Martin McGuinness and he was lovely!' It was like complete disbelief that this man was so warm and so generous and so personable, and they didn't think he'd be like that. Or they'd hear him speaking at some event and it would be, 'Oh – he was very good! He was great!'

It reminds me of the time during the talks process, if I'd gone into my own local at the weekend, when you'd get the lads coming up to you:

'What're they like?'

'What's who like?'

'The Shinners – what're they like?'

'Well, they're all right. They have two arms, two legs, a head–'

'Ah, I don't mean that! What're they like?'

'What do you expect them to be like? They're human beings.'

'But what are they like – are they tough or what?'

'They're representing their people, they're negotiating.'

'Right. As long as you're doing it and I don't have to do it.'
There was that sort of attitude – 'I don't want to go near them.'

Then, twenty years later, you have people from a loyalist, working-class background coming up to the Assembly, meeting Martin, his staff and special advisers and everybody else, and going, 'He's all right! He's all right, you know!'

So there's this persona built up in the community and then that's smashed. That's what I mean by the likeability factor – he had a gift of putting people at ease and coming across as genuine and sincere – and he listened.

***

I have no doubt there were still lingering doubts about Martin's past, especially around the Saville Inquiry [the public inquiry into Bloody Sunday events, which said he was the IRA's second-in-command in Derry at the time]. There were also the constant images being shown of a young Martin in his polo neck on top of a wall with his hands up as the Derry IRA commander. I've no doubt that in Claudy [where three car bombs killed nine people in 1972] and places like that, there's a completely different view of the man – what he was involved in, what he represented.

For me, I saw him for what he was when I knew him, and not for his past. Similarly with people in the PUP – I saw them for what they were now, for what they were doing now. And they were working damned hard for peace. More than others, such as the DUP. These were people who were absolutely committed to a better future. They were putting their lives on the line for it, and Martin was putting his life on the line as well, by showing leadership, by driving change within the movement. And making those big gestures. And I really think he could have been killed for that. It wasn't just political courage – it was literal physical courage.

That being said, he was seen by loyalists as a less important figure than Gerry Adams. What brought that home to me was during a meeting of the party leaders in Stormont, convened by the first and deputy first ministers. We were trying to get over some hurdles and Martin was talking about the way forward from Sinn Féin's perspective. Peter Robinson turned round and said, 'Well, we need to hear that from Gerry. No harm to you, Martin, but the unionist community needs to hear that from Gerry.' I thought that was an indication of the status that Adams has in the unionist community, as opposed to Martin.

From my point of view, knowing members of Sinn Féin and Martin McGuinness, but also knowing members of the PUP and David Ervine, having had them as close friends: they wouldn't have been the people they were before they died had they not been through what they'd been through earlier in their lives. So whilst I regret and am very much saddened by the sort of life they had and what they were involved in – as well as feeling sorry for the victims and survivors that have come out of that violence – I'm also very thankful that they were here and were in a place to bring about the relative peace that we now have. I think the dynamic to bring about peace in Northern Ireland is not just down to the environment, it's down to the actors and the agents that are involved. And it takes a special set of circumstances for that to happen. I think David Ervine was one of those special people and he brought loyalism as far as he could. And I think Martin McGuinness did similar work with republicans.

Martin's greatest strength was, I think, his ability to put people completely at ease. You felt that he was genuinely interested in you and genuinely listening to what you were saying. And that matters. When I was involved in politics, 90 per cent of what I did was listening. Making sure that people got the feeling that, when they left the meeting with you, they had off-loaded onto you. I certainly felt that and saw it in action when Martin interacted with people.

I think he's a massive loss to the republican movement, but he's also a great loss to the process. In the years that he shared an office with a DUP first minister, he began to understand the psyche and the mentality of some of those within unionism who would be most fearful of change and making progress. And because he had that insight, he was able to use his influence within Sinn Féin to go further than they'd ever been before. I'm afraid that just wasn't recognised within the DUP: they were always pushing for more, more, more. The DUP never had a period of Provo-watching, they never had a period where they said, 'Let's do some serious detailed analysis on the republican movement. Let's listen to what they're saying, watch what they're doing, see what the next action is going to be.' They don't do that. It's constantly *us, us, us, give, give, give.* There needs to be more.

Was there a good and a bad Martin McGuinness? I wouldn't know. I only met the good one. I think, like others who've been through this transformation, he realised that the best way forward was through political dialogue and not through violence. He and others like him saw violence as being destructive to their own community and realised it was not what people wanted. I think he saw that the democratic process and political dialogue was an alternative way to achieve what they wanted to achieve.

I'm sure there are people who will remember Martin Mc-Guinness for all the horrible reasons: for his leadership within the IRA and the period that entailed, which involved some of the bloodiest acts we witnessed within this country. Others, who don't have that memory of the awfulness of what went on here during that time, will look at him as someone who was involved in the peace process and who tried his best to bring about change within our political institutions but sadly failed. Not through anything he did but because of the broken state of our political institutions and because of his partner in government.

I think he will be remembered for all of those things. And that's good because it means people can pick and choose how they want to remember him. There are those who'll venerate him and those who'll condemn him. But he will have historical permanence.

6

George Mitchell

I was aware of the long-standing nature of the conflict in Northern Ireland. The actual peace negotiations began in June 1996 and I had been in the country off and on since January 1995, so I served in other capacities before chairing the talks. I initially served as President Clinton's special representative on economic matters in Northern Ireland and then the British and Irish governments requested that I review the difficult issue of decommissioning. That occurred in December 1995 and January 1996. So by the time the negotiations began I had been exposed to and was familiar with the difficult issues. And I saw how hard it was even to begin to address these, so I was under no illusions about how difficult it might be to bring this process to a successful conclusion.

I can't remember when exactly I met Martin, but it would have been some time in the year of 1995 and I think, without a doubt, early in that year, because the assignment President Clinton asked me to organise on economic issues in Northern Ireland was an effort to underpin the then just-beginning peace process. The IRA had declared a ceasefire in the summer of 1994 and the loyalist militias had declared a ceasefire in October of that year. The effort was to encourage that process and increase trade and investment with Northern Ireland, and the conference itself was held at the White House in May 1995. I'm reasonably certain it was sometime in the period between January and

May of 1995, during which time I was travelling throughout Northern Ireland meeting with business leaders and other leaders in connection with this conference, that I met Martin.

Shortly after agreeing to accept President Clinton's request that I go to Northern Ireland, I undertook as much study of the issue as I could. I had compiled a fairly lengthy bibliography of books and magazine articles, and read quite a lot about the history of the conflict and of relations between Britain and Ireland, and Ireland and Northern Ireland. So over that period of time and over the period of time that I was there, I read thirty or forty books on the subject. Not only books but also newspaper and magazine articles. I'd had some assistance, of course – people finding things for me to read. So I was aware of who Martin was and what his background was but also what his role was at the time that I met him.

Martin was an outgoing person, very friendly, at least on meeting me, and I believe he had an outgoing personality with others as well, not just with me. He was also easy to talk to in the discussions, well focused on what his and his party's objectives were. I had read about his past – although I knew nothing more about it than what I'd read – but my relationship with him was a cordial one throughout, as was the case with most of the participants in the talks. At the outset, Dr Paisley and his party were opposed to my participation [traditionally unionist politicians argued that Northern Ireland was an internal UK matter], so it was a little difficult, although on personal grounds I ended up getting along well with everyone, including Martin, and later spent a great deal of time with him.

I'd been in politics long enough to know that what appears in the newspapers doesn't always correspond with the reality, and that continues to this day, particularly with the television news – controversy makes news; inflammatory statements make news; colourful statements make news; sensational statements make news. So I have learned that it's important to inform myself as much as possible about people but make my own judgements based upon my own discussions with them. And I can't say that I was surprised that I ended up getting on well with Martin.

I think you could say of everybody I met from Northern Ireland that there was a tough streak in them. They all were tough negotiators. On the first formal day of the negotiations, in front of a large crowd of the negotiators, David Ervine said to me, 'Senator, there's one thing you must know about us in order to be any use in this process.'

I said, 'What is it?'

'We in Northern Ireland would drive one hundred miles out of our way to receive an insult.'

So I was on pretty good notice that they were all tough guys.

I don't think the ability to be a tough negotiator and knowing how to break tension with a joke are mutually exclusive qualities. Martin was a tough and effective negotiator. He was always focused on his objective. But we got along well. We had disagreements, but they never had any effect on our personal relationship. That was true of many of them. At one point or another I disagreed with almost everybody – not surprising, with so many issues and so much history of and room for disagreements in Northern Ireland. I'll give you one example.

On 27 December, two days after Christmas, in 1997, Billy Wright, who was a prominent loyalist paramilitary, was killed in prison by a group of Catholic prisoners. That touched off a round of back and forth violent acts, mostly assassinations. The British and Irish governments had long planned to try to change the location of the talks, as a way of getting maybe a change of mind or a change of heart. So when we returned to the talks in January 1998, after the break for Christmas, we went to London, where we met at Lancaster House. These were very difficult meetings, mostly concerned with who should be expelled from the talks as opposed to the subjects we were discussing.

The following month, February, we moved to Dublin. We had temporarily suspended one of the loyalist parties in London. The loyalists wanted to expel Sinn Féin at the talks in Dublin. And Sinn Féin was in the process of trying to stall or delay the talks. And Martin was the spokesman for that and I was the chairman. Martin repeatedly objected to the talks continuing and sought an adjournment, and I repeatedly denied his request. And we went through this several times. If you could read a transcript (I don't know if there is a transcript) it would sound very harsh. But in fact he was engaged in an initiative that he and his party thought useful. I disagreed with it, as did both governments, and so after several repetitions of the same thing, Martin again sought an adjournment. And I said – I don't remember my exact words – I said, 'Request is denied. And I'm not going to consider any further requests. We're going to proceed with the business of the meeting.' And Martin looked across the table at me and gave me a nice smile. A twinkling of his eyes, a nod of his head, OK. I think it was Mo Mowlam who then took up the next item of business.

If you could read it, it would look like a harsh exchange, and it was a pointed exchange, but it was all in good spirit. After the meeting we talked as though we'd just had a cup of tea together.

Much of the discussion was in bilateral or three-party

meetings, much less of it in plenary session where all parties attended. I think you have to distinguish between their relationships internally and their relationships with others. I said to both sides many times, 'If you treated each other the way you treat me, you'd get along much better.'

Look at the way Martin eventually got along with Ian Paisley. They didn't talk directly, certainly in the early stages of the discussions. Keep in mind that the talks began in June 1996, and it was not until August 1997 that Sinn Féin entered the talks. They were not in the talks for the first fourteen or fifteen months. When they came in, Paisley and the DUP, and Bob McCartney and his smaller party, which was affiliated with the DUP, walked out. So Paisley never participated after that. Which meant there was no discussion between the DUP and the nationalist parties.

At first, the Ulster Unionists wouldn't talk with them. There was a famous incident when Gerry Adams and Ken Magennis [UUP] passed by each other at a urinal and Magennis allegedly swore at Adams. On a few occasions early in that time, we went through what many people would regard as bizarre procedures. For example, I can recall sitting at the head of the table with unionists on the right side of the table and nationalists on the other side of the table, and rather than speaking to each other, they would address me. With the others sitting right there. So someone would say, 'Well, tell him I said that' – and the fella to tell it to is sitting right there!

There was a long history of conflict and violence and hostility, so it was not surprising – difficult obviously but not surprising – that they didn't get along, didn't want to engage in dialogue. Remember, many of these people had been engaged in violence, some of them had been in prison for violent acts, some of them had been the target of violent acts. A famous American political pundit of the nineteenth century once said, 'Politics ain't beanbag.' He wasn't speaking of Northern Ireland but that phrase applies. It was very tough and yes, it took a while. They were hostile. But eventually they came around to talking – to their eternal credit – all of them.

There were problems with both sides, but they ended up with an agreement. Trying to measure who was most truculent and difficult is a waste of effort and time, I believe. There was a lot of hostility on all sides. It is to their great credit, and I've said this hundreds of times, in Ireland and in the UK and the US – the real heroes of the peace process were the political leaders. Think about the historical hostility, the violence, the grievances that had built up, think of the intensity of emotion on both sides. And yet they rose to the occasion. And despite great risks to themselves personally. Look what's happened. David Trimble's career came to an end almost immediately after the talks. The SDLP suffered enormous political losses and those two parties did a lot of the heavy lifting in the talks. So I don't think enough credit goes to all of the political leaders of Northern Ireland, Martin being one of the most involved and responsible leaders in the process.

I adopted a policy very early on of not getting socially engaged with any of the parties. I received many invitations: would I go to dinner with this group, would I attend this event with that group, and I scrupulously and politely declined. I felt that I had to be independent not only in fact but also in appearance.

However, I was there over a span of five years, and much of my time was taken up in discussions in my office or in small groups. I never drank tea before I went to Northern Ireland; the first few months I was there I had ten or twelve meetings a day and every group that came in, they'd bring a new pot of tea and McVitie's biscuits, and so as part of socialising I started drinking tea. And to this day I drink tea and have McVitie's a couple of times a day, because of my experiences in Northern Ireland. I saw Martin often in such discussions, just as I saw David Trimble and John Hume and Seamus Mallon and Ian Paisley and Peter Robinson and all the others. So I spent a great deal of time with those guys.

There was one occasion that has been somewhat publicised. You'll recall that agreement was reached in April 1998 and approved in May 1998. I left and returned home and the Assembly began to function. On 15 July 1999 – I remember the date so clearly – my two colleagues, Prime Minister Harri Holkeri and General John de Chastelain, and I were invited to Buckingham Palace in London, where the queen honoured us for our work in Northern Ireland. It was a very nice ceremony.

When we left the ceremony, we went to – I can't remember which embassy – and there were reporters there. And a reporter said to me, 'Senator, you have just been honoured by the queen for this peace process. Are you embarrassed by the fact that today, while you were in Buckingham Palace, the Northern Ireland Assembly collapsed and the peace process is over?' I had not known about it until the reporter asked me and I said, 'You're telling me something I'm not aware of.' And he explained to me what he had read in a wire service. I said, 'In that case I am embarrassed.' [The attempt to nominate ministers at the Assembly had collapsed when the UUP boycotted the meeting over the matter of the IRA decommissioning its arms.]

A celebratory dinner scheduled for that night was postponed. Taoiseach Bertie Ahern called me. Prime Minister Tony Blair called me the next day and asked me would I go back and try to put it back together. By coincidence David Trimble was in London so I stayed a few extra days in London. My wife went back to the United States. And then I met with Trimble and a few others and I did go back to Northern Ireland. By then, it was primarily a negotiation between the Ulster Unionists and Sinn Féin. The others were involved, primarily the SDLP, but the primary discussions were with Sinn Féin and the Ulster Unionists.

All the talks were held in Stormont in what had been a government office building that had been renovated to be a venue for the talks. And there was a gate and just outside the gate the press were encamped. At one point they had trailers and other stuff brought up. Print, television, everything. So that every day when the delegates came out of the talks, through the whole process, the reporters were there. Trimble and Adams came to me and said, 'It's impossible with all this back and forth.' They asked would I find a neutral location we could all go to privately and secretly, outside the context of the press. Adams and McGuinness would have come on behalf of Sinn Féin; Trimble would have had Reg Empey and others with him.

So I searched around and discovered that the United States ambassador's residence in London had just completed a two-year renovation. I contacted the then ambassador – it was a big, beautiful home – and asked if we could use that. He agreed, and in November 1999 we went to London for a couple of weeks. I think it took the press about a week to find us.

On the first day I made up a set of rules. I said, 'First off, we'll have meals together. Lunch and dinner.' I gave them each separate rooms for conferences and discussions. And when we got to the first dinner, I said, 'I have been around you guys long enough to know that one side sits all together on one side, the other on the other. I want you to mix it up. There'll be no discussion about business.'

'Well what are we going to talk about?' they said.

I said, 'Talk about your families. Your dog. Your vacations. Hobbies. Family history. Talk about the things that human beings talk about in ordinary life.'

It was a little bit tense at first. But the ice was broken when one of the fellows across the table said to David Trimble, 'David, we know you love opera. Have you been to the opera lately?' And Trimble said, 'No, but I listened to one last night at home', and he described it.

And one of them said to me, 'Senator Mitchell, do you go to the opera?' And I said, 'Yes, in fact, I do. I went to the opera the night before I came here. And,' I said, 'that has been my practice for several years. To prepare myself for dealing with you guys I go to the opera the last night.' And they said, 'Well, why is that?' And I said, 'Because when I go to the opera, I know in advance every word that's going to be spoken or sung.' I said, 'I've seen *La Bohème* twelve times now. And every time the lead singer, Rodolfo, sings exactly the same song, says exactly the same words, and that gets me in the right frame of mind to deal with you guys, because I know one thing with you guys: you say the same thing all the time and you never vary.' Well, they got a big laugh out of that, and they all joked, and they did start talking about personal things.

***

Martin had a sharp sense of humour, a keen wit and he had the kind of personality that meant even people bitterly opposed to his position and particularly him, in view of his background and experiences, warmed to him. That's what happened later with Paisley when he became the first minister and Martin became the deputy first minister.

I think what was true of Martin was that he was very focused on the objectives that they were seeking. One of the difficulties I think the unionist side encountered was their internal disagreements. I wrote in my book documenting my experience that sometimes the subplot of internal unionist dissension outweighed the main plot, that is, unionists versus nationalists. Paisley and his related parties spent a great deal of their time attacking David Trimble and the Ulster Unionists, seeking to embarrass Ulster Unionists in terms of an internal plot. Nationalists, thanks primarily to John Hume, had earlier reached what you might call a tentative agreement on nationalist unity. The Irish government – Albert Reynolds was involved – and John Hume, they brought Adams in and then McGuinness and the rest of Sinn Féin. And so they had less overt disputes among themselves – although I'm sure they had plenty internally. Martin was very focused on what their objectives were, and didn't get distracted, didn't go down side roads as the unionists often did.

Much of my discussion was with Adams and McGuinness together – though not all of it. They at least presented in a public sense a unified position. They never criticised the other privately or engaged in disagreement, although I'm sure there were internal disagreements that went on that I was not privy to.

It's hard to say if the Good Friday Agreement could have happened without Martin McGuinness, and you could say the same about a lot of people. All were great contributors. It's pretty clear that John Hume was the visionary, the architect of the overall structure of the talks. But in the negotiations Seamus Mallon, who was his second-in-command in the SDLP, was a hugely important figure. A very smart, detailed guy. It's very clear that Trimble was a decisive factor in bringing the Ulster Unionists along, despite much internal dissent. It's also true that Adams and McGuinness were central figures on the nationalist side, and Martin was, I think, a critical factor in presenting the views of Sinn Féin. I think it's probably the case that most of the unionists disliked Adams more because he didn't have the same level of charm as McGuinness. At the same time, the same has to be said of Dr Paisley at the end of the talks, when they got to St Andrews. So you could say of several people in the process that it probably wouldn't have happened without them on both sides. I think it's fair to say that about Martin, but it's also fair to say it about others.

I think Martin ranked higher than 'middle-ranking officer material', as someone in the British Army is reputed to have said. After all, he was the deputy first minister of Northern Ireland, which I wouldn't call middle ranking. I myself was a politician – I spent much of my life in politics – and there are many qualities that go into success in politics. When I spoke at Martin's memorial service at St Patrick's church after his death, I remarked on the three phases of his career: the earlier phase, in which he was part of a protest; his negotiating phase, the only time I really knew him and participated with him; and then there was the governing phase of his life. And when you look at it, he was a leader in each of those efforts, different as they were and although they required different skills and different talents. He certainly was a leader in the protest, as far as I can tell, although I was not there and knew nothing personally about it. He was certainly a leader in the negotiations, and he was certainly a leader in government as the deputy first minister. So, to me, I think it's fair to say that he – though not exclusively, for there were others – was a central figure.

Will Martin have a place in the history of Northern Ireland? Without a doubt. Particularly if you think of it in the manner that I've described. This was a process that extended, some people would say eight hundred years, some one hundred years, but for our purposes you could take it back to 1970 when the latest round of violence erupted, and carry it forward for about thirty or forty years. In that period, Martin certainly was a dominant figure in each phase: the phase of protest, the phase of negotiation and the phase of governance. I think history will make that judgement.

7

Eamonn McCann

I grew up in the same area as Martin, but I was eight years older than him. Fourteen-year-olds don't play with six-year-olds, so while I was aware of who he was, that was about it. I became more aware of him when he emerged in the civil rights movement, at a time I'd mainly have known him as Tom McGuinness's brother. Tom played at midfield for the intercounty Derry team – he was one of the very few people from the city who played Gaelic football at county level – and also played soccer for Finn Harps FC.

October 1968 was when the civil rights movement really erupted, with the RUC attack on the marchers in Duke Street during their demonstration in Derry. I can't remember Martin having been involved before that. But I can vividly remember November 1968. Just a few weeks after the RUC attack on the civil rights marchers in Duke Street, on 16 November 1968 a huge civil rights demonstration was held. If my memory is right it was a Saturday. Because of the earlier attack, many, many more people turned out in November than had turned out in October. The march came across Craigavon Bridge; there are photographs taken from the front showing 8,000 maybe 10,000 people marching. Craigavon Bridge is quite wide so there were fourteen, fifteen people in each rank. And right in the middle of the front row you'll see this blond-haired guy with a sort of diffident look on his face. That's Martin McGuinness.

I was heavily involved in the civil rights movement then

and I was always scurrying around from one meeting to another. But in the autumn of 1969, when British troops came onto the streets, things began to change and it became a struggle against the state.

They were tumultuous times and played a part in Martin's political formation. After half a century in which nothing had moved politically in Northern Ireland, suddenly there were troops on the street and Londonderry Corporation, widely known for its gerrymandering and discrimination against the large Catholic majority in the city, was abolished. There were meetings and ructions and occupying council offices, and more meetings to decide who to kick at next.

Martin would have spoken up at those meetings. He would have been among the younger element there – the young guard. I didn't see him as hotheaded. You didn't have to be hotheaded to be a very militant person. He was very self-confident, very self-possessed. He wasn't speaking rhetoric – he was serious. There were lots of young people who wanted to hurtle down Rossville Street and take on the British Army. Martin might have been involved in that to some extent, but from the beginning you were struck by the impression that here was a serious-minded person.

He tried to join the Stickies initially – the Official IRA, who split from the Provisional IRA [the Provos] in December 1969. Some people at that time had a problem finding the Stickies in order to join. That's absolutely true. Eddie Gallagher [an IRA volunteer involved in the 1975 kidnapping of the Dutch industrialist Dr Tiede Herrema], who I got to know well, told me that. Eddie went round Letterkenny, Buncrana, Ballybofey, asking if anybody knew where the Stickies were. Nobody knew – nobody could find them. So he went and joined the Provos.

Martin McGuinness: The Man I Knew

The journey from participating in civil rights marches to stone throwing and petrol bombs, and from that to armed insurrection in the IRA was common at the time, so Martin's trajectory through that wasn't unusual. Whether or not you agree with Martin's politics – and I very sharply did not – nevertheless there was about him an authenticity that a lot of others didn't possess. Many of the people who emerged as leaders in the new republican manifestation in the Provos tended to come from established republican families in West Belfast. Albert Price – the father of Marian Price, whom I got to know – the Adamses and the MacArts, they were republicans and would have experienced internment in the 1940s. They were the small group of families that kept the flame burning over the years. The Derry republicans then would have been well known because there were so few of them – Seán Keenan, Gerry 'The Bird' Doherty and so on. However, the McGuinnesses were not part of that.

I'm not aware of any particular event that catapulted Martin into the line he took. There were many shootings at the end of many streets and there were huge numbers of young people teeming around at the time. Most people didn't join the IRA, but Martin did and quickly became prominent in it. He took to it like a duck to water.

At the time I'd been saying and writing things that wouldn't have pleased republicans at all. [McCann took a consistently socialist rather than republican line and would, on occasion, have criticised IRA actions.] I used to have quite a tense relationship with some of them. Some would meet me in the street with a mild snarl. But not Martin – it may have been his personality. Martin would always say, 'How are you doing?' and chat away and wouldn't refer to what I'd been writing or saying. He was unusual in this in Sinn Féin at the time. Usually if I'd denounced something that had been done by Sinn Féin or the IRA, members of Sinn Féin would let me know they objected to it. But at no point did Martin ever come up to me and say, 'That was abominable', or that kind of thing. I found that quite striking.

Occasionally at community meetings I'd be attending, republicans would also be present, Martin among them. For example, I remember a meeting in Central Drive on the night of Bloody Sunday 1972. There was a lot of discussion about what to do. Johnny White, an old and dear friend of mine, now dead, was the Officer Commanding [O/C] of the Official IRA at the time and Martin was O/C of the Provos. There were normally bitter relations between the Official IRA and the Provos, but I remember Johnny and Martin coming together to call for a general strike throughout Ireland. The call went out from that meeting, as did an announcement that the barricades were going to stay up.

There were a couple of hundred people jammed into the hall and the atmosphere was very emotional. It would have been standard practice at a meeting like that for people to up the ante and say, 'We're going to drive out the Brits, it's the only language they understand.' That would have been expected. But this was a wider and more reasoned call going out to the people of Ireland to bring the country to a standstill. Everybody was angry, but Martin wasn't flustered or taken over by emotion. Both he and Johnny White were very cool, calm people – they didn't raise their voices when they wanted to make a point. Martin never shouted.

It's difficult to see clearly events that happened over forty years ago and perhaps there's a tendency to see those events through the prism of what has happened since. I'm often struck by how people can have remarkably different memories to mine of the same event; some of these remembrances can even be totally contradictory to my account. But they are simply telling the truth as they recall it.

The high-ranking members of the IRA at that time – Dáithí Ó Conaill, Seán MacStíofáin, Seamus Costello – were from a different era and place. What they didn't have were any significant leaders from the section of the population that was driving the resurgence of republicanism – brothers off the block. It must have struck MacStíofáin and the others that, in Martin, they had found one who spoke for the thousands of those who were active on the streets at the time.

One of the longest conversations I ever had with Martin was in White's shop, which is just round the corner from us here – he's Westland Street, I'm Westland Avenue. We talked about whether or not it was blasphemous to put raisins in soda bread. Whether it was necessary to put buttermilk in it. He was something of a fundamentalist on the buttermilk question. So, as you can see, there was a geniality about him. I was able to have that kind of conversation – although I shouldn't exaggerate it. While we might have occasionally met in the street and said hello and had a chat, I wasn't hanging out with him or having any kind of political conversations.

I do remember one time Martin arrived at my door. It was a Sunday morning in the early or mid-1990s and I had been writing a number of articles for *The Observer* about the clerical sex abuse scandals happening in Derry. He said he'd read the articles and asked if I knew much about the subject. I said I'd read a couple of books about it.

'Can I come in?' he asked.

I nodded.

In he came and we discussed this issue for two hours. We discussed whether it was about Catholic clergy specifically, if it was about the priesthood more generally or whether this form of abuse was simply more widespread in our society than had been commonly realised.

Obviously Martin was involved in other matters at that time – but he'd still arrived at my front door and asked if he could discuss the issue. The relationship between people with my views [as an atheist] and people with his [McGuinness was a practising Catholic], it wasn't such that they'd often arrive at my front door and ask if they could come in and talk to me. I cannot in a million years see Gerry Adams coming and asking the same question. Of course this occurred in part because Martin and I were neighbours. But I'd also attribute his more genial attitude to the manner in which he came to republicanism – off the street rather than through an inherited ideology.

After one IRA operation or another, the clergy on a regular basis would denounce them as 'agents of the devil', a phrase that was popular at the time. There wouldn't have been much debate in Derry about that anyway, in public or anywhere else. The church saw it as something they had to do: denounce violence, call for peace, blah blah blah, constantly characterising violence as un-Christian and so forth. I wouldn't know if Martin ever butted heads with the bishop over that.

And I don't remember him giving his reaction to the Church condemnations. But I do remember a meeting in the Creggan estate where Martin declared the morality of the armed struggle. And it struck me as I listened to him talking – without citing the source – that what he was giving was Thomas Aquinas's moral justification for war. There were a number of things you had to have, according to Aquinas, to justify war. It had to be a last resort, it had to have some prospect of victory, it had to be proportionate to the social evil opposed and every care had to be taken not to harm people not involved in the fight.

While Martin could produce pretty ferocious rhetoric for republicanism, he also gave an impression of reasonableness. It was the way he spoke. The traditional Irish thing – 'The fools, the fools, they have left us our Fenian dead!', fighting to the last drop of blood – he really didn't go in for much of that, as far as I recall. Many republicans did, of course. I didn't agree with the politics behind it, but it was a calm sort of militancy that Martin seemed to prefer, rather than a raging militancy.

Despite this, I was surprised that he moved so smoothly into politics. Once he embraced it, he was into it, even as the armed struggle continued.

There were two ways of looking at McGuinness after that transition. Some argued that he was responsible for the awful things that happened on his watch, both before and during that period of transition. On the other hand – and this is a strong argument too – others would claim that the armed struggle needed to be maintained at that time, if eventually ending it was to be effective. Without keeping the armed struggle going, in a sense, Martin wouldn't have been able to call it off at a later time. Now it seems to me there's a dubious morality behind that viewpoint and, inescapably, Martin would have been part of it. I suppose he proved you can be moderate and talk about the need for peace, and at the same time be pretty ferocious in your military life.

Regarding his relationship with Ian Paisley, the surprise for me was not Martin joining Paisley but Paisley joining Martin. There was a sign on a wall here – in fact, it's still there – saying 'West Bank loyalists under siege'. Unionism in Northern Ireland has seen itself like that for a long, long time. If you're under siege, you can't afford to be friendly with the people outside who are shouting, 'C'mon, let us in – we mean you no harm!' It was hard to see how Paisley thought he'd get away with this. But the desire for peace was very strong. It didn't really surprise me that Martin would go for it. There was always that capacity in him, even when Paisley was at his roaring, Bible-thumping peak.

***

Amid all the madness Martin's family were kept out of the limelight. Bernie, his wife, was a republican herself and interned – she is from the Canning family, who are an old republican family – but she didn't play any public role. I'd meet her around the area and she's a very friendly woman in my experience. People who'd share my views would get quite annoyed with my attitude to Martin and Bernie; perhaps they saw it as me weakening the rigour of the anti-republican argument. But these were personal matters, as well as everything else.

Martin was something of a home bird, though I've no recollection of seeing him with his children. He would have had a wariness, and necessarily so, about public life. Taking your kids by the hand to the park on a Sunday afternoon? Maybe there were people who advised Martin not to do that.

He was very fond of fishing on the River Faughan and throughout the Troubles he would have gone fly-fishing there. He fished for salmon as well – this while he was in the IRA.

Maybe he found it a relaxing pursuit, I don't know. It's supposed to take your mind off your work or so I'm told; I imagine there's something very calming about sitting by a river, dangling your rod.

Personally I didn't notice much change in him as he grew older. He always lived in the area he was from; and while he didn't advertise his Bogside credentials, it was very obvious in his manner and speech that he was from the Bogside. He didn't change in that sense.

After he died I was phoned up by several radio stations. I talked to one of them, but then I decided I wasn't doing it any more. I found it very difficult to separate the fact that he lived round the corner and that I knew Bernadette and how distressed she was, and that to some extent we had had a friendly relationship. Again, I wouldn't exaggerate that for a moment, but it certainly wasn't a hostile relationship. At the same time I was sharply different from him in politics and I'd have felt the need to explain that on public radio, so I just felt uneasy at the thought that one of Martin's neighbours was being harsh about an aspect of him with the man's body lying within a hundred yards and scarcely cold.

His funeral was a state funeral in all but name. In fact, the bishop of Derry used that phrase. There had been a ban for thirty years on political trappings at all republican funerals and that was lifted. The Church hadn't intended to lift it. But when the coffin arrived at the church door it quickly was made clear that it wasn't going into the church without the Irish flag. This was Martin McGuinness and it was a perfectly reasonable sort of argument.

Bishop McKeown, a nice man, said afterwards in a very

stumbling sort of way, 'It was decided that this had the character of a state occasion' – something like that. That is a really interesting phrase – it had been 'decided'. Decided by whom, I wonder.

It was also interesting that, after the ceremonial funeral with the dignitaries, there was the ceremony in the City Cemetery, a few hundred yards away, at which Gerry Adams spoke. The tone of that – inevitably, I suppose – was much more republican. Defending McGuinness's role in the IRA and comparing the situation to 1916 and all that. There was none of that in front of the dignitaries, including the chief constable of the PSNI. So there was a very different atmosphere at both events – on and off the main stage, so to speak. Yet they were just a couple of hundred yards apart. I thought all that was very much symbolic of where things are now.

The most interesting, and possibly symbolic, thing about Martin was the way his development, his growth and the changes in his perspective, which were clearly evident, followed almost exactly the trajectory of the community from which he came: march for civil rights, followed by the decision to fight back if attacked; then you fight against the state, bringing you into the republican army. At every stage Martin was in lockstep with the people in the streets of the Bogside. That was how he was perceived and how he perceived himself.

I don't think it's parochial to say that the whole struggle started in Derry. There were other demonstrations before it – in Dungannon and so forth – but the RUC attack on the civil rights marchers on 5 October 1968 was the key moment. Things developed more quickly in Derry because the movement for change started at an earlier stage. Things also ended in Derry at an earlier stage, as the IRA campaign in Derry was effectively over long before the ceasefire. The last policeman killed in Derry was shot outside the Richmond Shopping Centre in Shipquay Street in January 1993. A guy ran past two cops, shot one of them in the head and jogged away. It was a terrible, terrible thing, and a lot of people in Derry didn't like that, I can assure you. But as I say, the IRA campaign ended earlier in Derry than in other parts of Northern Ireland.

You see, Derry's different from the rest of the north. First of all, on the west bank you have the biggest single concentration of Catholics in the country. The Catholics here were more self-confident. They had the border at their back. I'm sitting in the Bogside now, and if you go three miles south, or three miles west or three miles north, you're in Donegal. That helped infuse confidence.

Moreover, the political arrangements in Derry before and during the Troubles were the most egregiously sectarian of any-where in the north. Two-thirds of the population was nationalist, yet the one-third that was unionist elected a majority to the cor-poration. This was absolutely glaring sectarianism, and no one in the world could say anything else. In Derry, people shrugged their shoulders and cracked jokes about it. You couldn't do that if you were in the New Lodge Road in Belfast. I remember Bernadette Devlin [civil rights leader and former MP] once saying – using slightly more flowery language than is included here – that Derry was 'the capital city in Ireland of injustice'.

But the discriminated section in Derry was not ground down. They felt confident enough to come out and march in the centre of town. That would not have been contemplated in those days in the New Lodge Road or Ardoyne, not at all. So that was the kind of city Martin came from, that's what shaped him.

I would say there was a sort of dialectical relation between the person and the place. It would be difficult to understand Martin McGuinness without factoring in that this was a Derry man. Not a Belfast man, not a Tyrone man, not a South Armagh man – a Derry man. It was inevitable that this would be reflected in his personality and his politics.

8

Danny Morrison

I'd heard of Martin McGuinness before I met him. There was a famous press conference in Derry in 1972 when I was nineteen. He appeared with Dáithí Ó Conaill, Seán MacStíofáin and Seán Keenan, and that was probably the first time that most people outside of the Bogside became aware of him. Seán Keenan, a veteran republican, recognised Martin's potential from the outset, and that's why he was at that press conference. What age was he then – twenty-one or twenty-two? But even then it was clear that he was one of those people who could naturally lead.

After 1972 his reputation was not simply restricted to Derry. The British and the media also identified him as a competent IRA leader. In Long Kesh in 1973, you'd be walking round the yard and different names would be mentioned as being great people, formidable people, though they were sometimes people you didn't know or hadn't met. I suppose Derry people who'd never seen Gerry Adams would have heard him spoken of in that same respectful way. I would have known which people were very influential in Tyrone and south Armagh. Even then Martin McGuinness's name and reputation would have preceded him.

Once Martin rose through the ranks, his activities wouldn't have been restricted to Derry city. He was very close to Francis Hughes [the second hunger-striker to die, after Bobby Sands], he knew those south Derry men very well, and he also travelled quite a bit throughout Ireland as his senior role grew.

Was he on the run during this period in the early 1970s? There are many situations that can put one on the run. For example, throughout the years of internment, hundreds of activists never slept at home and used false papers. When I was the editor of *An Phoblacht/Republican News*, the Brits came looking for me after I published a secret British Intelligence assessment of the IRA. During the supergrass period [the early to mid-1980s when often unreliable information from informers, known colloquially as supergrasses or touts, was used to jail hundreds of suspected terrorists], many republicans had to go on the run until the outcome of a court case or trial, which might have taken several years. After the Narrow Water attack of 1979, when eighteen soldiers were killed and the re-introduction of internment was mooted, the wise thing to do was to go on the run until things settled down. This was similarly the case after the attempt by the IRA to kill Thatcher and members of her cabinet in 1984 and after the Enniskillen bombing of 1987, when eleven civilians were killed.

Rather than stay in strange houses, it was always better to stay with a cousin, a school friend – people you knew. The problem for the state was that 100 per cent of the Bogside was supportive of republicans, due to the effect Bloody Sunday had on the Derry psyche. And that's what made it impossible for them to crush us.

The first time I actually sat down and met Martin was in 1976, in a house on the Falls Road in Belfast. He was twenty-five and I was twenty-three at the time. We were talking about the political situation, what had happened. The general feeling on the ground among young people at the time was that the 1975 ceasefire was a disaster and the republican movement had lost its way and descended into infighting.

There had been tensions between the Officials and the Provisionals since the split in 1969/1970, and in March 1971, during the first feud, the Officials killed a leading local republican from the Falls Road, Charlie Hughes. The Provisionals also suspected that the Officials were passing on information about their movements in places like Ballymurphy to the British Army. In early 1975 the Officials attempted to wipe out the Irish Republican Socialist Party [IRSP], which had been formed by former Officials in December 1974. The October/November 1975 feud between the Officials and Provisionals was preceded by a number of fights between members of both organisations. In total, eleven people lost their lives during the feud and sixty, maybe seventy, republicans went to jail. The nationalist community was fairly demoralised at the time as a result. That was the grim situation Martin and I sat and talked about.

Martin never intimidated me when we spoke – but he was strong-willed. He spoke with conviction. Could his mind be changed? Yes. You put forward a better proposition, another argument and his hand could be stayed. I worked with him during my European election campaign – I was the Sinn Féin candidate in 1984 and 1989. He handled a lot of my travel throughout the north as, through contacts he had known in a past life, he was able to facilitate me going everywhere – every hamlet, every town, every townland. I warmed to him during this period, yes, absolutely, though that didn't mean I didn't have arguments with him. I did.

***

Martin was a kind person. I remember when a Sinn Féin councillor in Castlederg, a friend of mine, took his own life.

Martin's mother had just died. I had just come out of hospital – I'd had a knee replacement and was on crutches. I arrived at the funeral and, to my surprise, Martin was also present. He had left his mother's wake to go to the funeral.

I remember doing an interview in 2016 and, when we finished the interview, the journalist and I continued chatting. It wasn't known that Martin was sick at this stage. The journalist asked me if I missed being in the thick of politics – which I don't, although I still put my spoke in. The interviewer then said, 'Martin McGuinness is a remarkable man – more remarkable than Gerry. My father died a few months ago and I come from [he named a very unionist town]. On a Sunday morning, Martin McGuinness arrived at the funeral and the congregation did not hesitate to line up and shake his hand. He had driven all the way from Derry, on a Sunday.'

It was yet another example of how considerate he was.

My wife Leslie's father is a Second World War veteran. One day the three of us went up to Stormont and Martin invited us all out to lunch. Leslie's father was wearing a badge – a poppy, maybe, or a Union flag – and Martin was laughing because members of the DUP were at the next table and could see this man with us wearing a Union Jack badge.

Even when he was minister for education I could bring up students to see him at the drop of a hat and there was none of this 'See my secretary' nonsense. Land in, would he see you? Yes, he would.

There was an air of authority about him. Conviction, too – massive conviction. And it was that leadership quality that allowed people to believe he had changed. When he changed and decided to buy into the peace, you knew it was 100 per cent.

Was he media savvy? Yes and no. I remember he spoke at Easter one year, at Milltown Cemetery, and he announced an end to IRA punishment shootings. I was a bit surprised at that – it wasn't something that had been decided.

***

Looking back, I think it was the hunger strikes that changed everything. The republican strategy became two-fold. You had the electoral strategy, which was causing the British difficulty, but we also began opening up community services for the people around this time. This is the God's honest truth – we always assumed the SDLP was doing constituency work. It wasn't until we stood for election that we realised that for ten years the SDLP hadn't done a tap! Some of the party did a little work, but the majority cruised through life unchallenged as they felt they had a monopoly on safe seats.

So we opened up constituency advice centres, we trained people, that was one aspect of it. The republican struggle had always been taking from people: 'Lend us your house', 'Lend us your car', 'Come out and march for the prisoners', 'Buy the paper'. Now here was an opportunity to give something back. The same thing began happening in Derry, Dungannon, Newry, Armagh, Strabane.

During this period, I'd have met with Martin probably weekly. I was editor of *Republican News*. [*Republican News* and *An Phoblacht* merged in 1979.] We also met regularly with others to discuss the growing crisis in the prisons over the withdrawal of political status. The blanket protest and that by the women in Armagh Prison – long before the hunger strike in 1981 – took up hundreds if not thousands of hours of attention by different sections of the movement. It got to the stage where a huge amount of resources was being devoted to the prison protest movement. They were our comrades, our relatives, our friends.

By this stage, Martin would have been a public spokesman. I'd have been pushing our people – Martin included – to do radio and television to build up everyone's profile. I'd fight with the media for us to be represented on programmes, only to find that half of them didn't want to go on. 'Oh, can you not go on yourself?' I ended up doing most of the election broadcasts and interviews for the October 1982 Assembly elections.

Martin's arm had to be twisted to stand in these elections. He realised, I think, that there would be considerable concentration on him. And on his family. At the time his wife, Bernie, worked in a café or in a shopping centre, I think, and he didn't want that level of prominence for his family – for understandable reasons of security. He also probably thought at the time that his role lay in areas other than politics.

But Gerry Adams persuaded him, because Martin personified Derry republicanism. Rural areas might resent this, but Derry and Belfast were central in terms of the history of the struggle: Duke Street 1968, the death of Sammy Devenney [in 1969 after being severely beaten in his own home by members of the RUC], the Battle of the Bogside, pogroms in Belfast, curfew, internment meeting huge resistance in both cities, then Bloody Sunday. So, Martin was forced into this public role in the electoral region of Foyle [the district of Derry] in 1982.

Martin's political public profile rose quite dramatically during this time. His name started appearing in *Republican News* with more regularity, some of the stories dealing with constituency issues, while more of them – his statements, my statements and Gerry's statements – had to do with national issues. His rising profile resulted in some strange offers. For example, Martin came to me at one point and told me that he'd been approached by the BBC for the TV programme *Real Lives: At the Edge of the Union*, which wanted to present Martin in a family context. That was a very important decision for us to make, whether or not we'd allow Martin to be shown with his wife and children. I said, go for it. I just knew that it was quite obvious who a British audience was going to like if they saw Martin McGuinness and Gregory Campbell [another Derry man and member of the DUP] on the show. It was a no-brainer. And if it was banned or censored, we could make hay with that as well.

In 1986, during the abstentionist debate, Martin would have travelled around the country extensively, saying, 'This is what we want to do.' The crisis at the time revolved round Sinn Féin's decision to contest local council elections across the north. In an attempt to force Sinn Féin to abstain from taking its seats, the British introduced a compulsory oath that each councillor must take, forswearing the use of political violence. With revolutionary pragmatism and with the councils in its sights, Sinn Féin refused to let that obstacle block its way, took the oath and began to take its seats in councils across the north.

After that, the abstentionist debate turned its attention to the south. For Provisional republicans, boycotting Stormont was a no-brainer. At Stormont you wouldn't have any power – nationalists had already tried it for fifty years. In the south it was different. The bulk of the people in the south – unlike in the north – identified the institutions of the state as being legitimate. We in the Provisional republican movement were outside that frame: we weren't going to get people voting for us on the basis that we were abstaining.

Martin was crucial during this debate. Republicans on the ground in the south – including ex-prisoners from Portlaoise – were telling us that our base of support, our electoral support, would never grow in the south while we continued the policy of abstentionism. Yet some of the old guard were against changing our stance. Dáithí Ó Conaill, for example, was one of those resisting the proposed new policy of recognising southern courts. He was told: 'Dáithí, if you're charged with membership you're going to have to recognise the court. Otherwise you're setting a bad example to young people who are then not going to recognise the court and as a result will be sent to jail for three years and deprive the struggle of personnel.' In all this – recognising the court, taking the oath – Martin was instrumental in persuading those who thought only in terms of militarism of the importance of political involvement.

You could see from this – and other instances – that he was a good organiser, he could delegate and he was a forward thinker. He was a good reader of people, identifying people's strengths and weaknesses – things I wouldn't have spotted. He was a real psychologist.

***

Martin introduced me to John Hume way back. Hume was quite a ruthless politician – something people don't always appreciate. He was also a gentleman as well as a tough person, which is why he got to where he was in the SDLP, how he had friends in America like Edward Kennedy and how he could get on with Garret Fitzgerald and different leaders in the south. But Martin and Hume – there was a friendship there, certainly no enmity, although neither would be soft on the other, nor bow to the other. It was a sort of mutual respect, intensified by both being Derry men.

Martin was also extremely close to Gerry Adams. I would say Martin respected and often deferred to Gerry's judgement. Which probably explains why Gerry was president of Sinn Féin and not Martin. From an early stage Gerry realised the importance of having a public face. Martin probably came to that position later and, for him, it was arrived at with reluctance. Having said that, many remark that Martin came across as a warmer person than Gerry. I don't subscribe to that; I actually think there's a certain shyness to Gerry. When we'd go into a house, Gerry would be laughing and playing with the kids, whereas Martin would be over asking the woman of the house what she was cooking and engaging with her. When we left, the people in the house might have had different views on their personalities. Maybe Gerry has always been conscious that he's walking on eggshells, while Martin might have been less circumspect.

Take the Paisley stuff, for example. I remember being at the removal of the remains of Leo Wilson in January 2014. [Wilson stood in the 1964 general election as a republican candidate, was a founding member of the Association for Legal Justice, a human rights group, and was the father of prominent republican and former IRA prisoner Pádraic Wilson.] Martin and I were both at the removal. Afterwards, we were having a chat and I asked Martin where he had been before the funeral.

'I've been visiting Ian Paisley,' he said.

I was quite astonished.

Martin elaborated, 'I've kept in contact and I'd phone now and again, or go up into the house.'

Now everyone approaches forgiveness differently; I find it very hard to forgive Ian Paisley. As I was growing up there was the Maura Lyons affair [when a sixteen-year-old Catholic girl went missing after getting mixed up with fundamentalist Protestants, including Ian Paisley], then the Divis Street riots, with sixty kids going to jail all because of Paisley. I suppose in a way I was a bit cynical about the whole thing. But it turned out to my surprise that this was quite a genuine meeting of minds between Martin and him.

In my book *Then The Walls Came Down: A Prison Journal* I note that Martin came out with a statement in 1990 that everybody in the jail where I was on remand at the time was speculating on what it meant. Did it mean peace? In my prison diary I noted:

19 February 1990

Lunchtime. Roy is under his blankets for his afternoon siesta. There is little activity out in the landings as everyone is locked up until two and I think most of the screws are away to lunch. A couple of orderlies can be heard kicking ball in the yard but apart from that I am on my own and it is relatively quiet. There was a lot of excitement in the yard this morning when someone who had caught the ten o'clock news on Downtown Radio reported that Martin McGuinness had issued a statement asking the Brits what was on the negotiating table if there was peace. I never heard so much speculation! It was perfectly understandable, especially among those facing life. But by the time we came back to the wing the item had dropped right down the news, which

seems to indicate that some journalist had been engaging in hype.
I think the jail is all under blankets this lunch-time!

The leadership had been dead set against ceasefires for a long,
long time because of our experience of the demoralising effect
of the 1975 ceasefire. I was in the prison canteen when I heard
the news that there was a Christmas ceasefire and I knew they
were talking. I didn't say it to any other prisoner, but I knew that
wouldn't have happened if there hadn't been some sort of contact.
I noted it in my prison diary on Christmas Eve, Crumlin Road
Jail, 1990:

> *We have moved cell yet again – this time at our request. We are*
> *in cell 30 whose previous occupant, Davy Clinton, got bail over*
> *a week ago.*
>
> *The cards are coming in thick and fast now. From aunts and*
> *uncles, cousins and nieces and nephews and complete strangers.*
> *I've a total of 150 spread across the cell. How is your Christmas*
> *in Toronto? I'm sure you've heard the news by now about the IRA*
> *calling a three-day ceasefire, the first in sixteen years! Of course,*
> *it's led to all kinds of false hopes. But, however! What else has*
> *happened? Frankie Quinn was sentenced to sixteen years. And*
> *that young lad from Strabane, Adrian Mole, got bail.*

When Martin decided to engage, he engaged totally and in a way
that some republicans weren't totally comfortable with. This has
been especially true the last couple of years, where, for the sake of
reconciliation, he appeared to turn the cheek too many times. He
had obviously made a decision at some stage that the peace was to
be defended, which is what probably took him into that territory

where he came out and publicly denounced the killing of a PSNI officer by dissident republicans, calling them 'traitors to Ireland'. I would have found it difficult to say that. But remember, before he said that, he was taking his grandkids to school, passing walls painted with graffiti saying, 'Martin McGuinness – traitor'. So his remark was also a play on 'dissident' terminology and what they'd been saying about him. He was also emphasising in a big way, with dramatic language, that the dissident campaign was going nowhere, would lead to no gains and that the fight had already been fought at huge human cost.

Look, if the IRA – with the extraordinary organisation that it had at the peak of its powers, where it could import arms internationally, do this, do that – if the IRA reached the conclusion in the 1990s that there was a military stalemate, then no modern organisation was going to change the situation. I supported the ceasefire and it took very strong people at the top to make it happen. I think credit has to be given that Martin was persistent in his commitment to reconciliation.

When the queen first visited Ireland, I wrote a piece – I think for *The Guardian* – and the title was 'The Arrival of the Queen of Sheep'. It was aimed at the Free Staters and the fawning nature of not just the establishment but many of the public in the south. But when she came and went to Croke Park, used Irish, went to the Garden of Remembrance – I went on TV and said I was wrong. The fact is that the IRA inflicted a lot of hurt and death on its enemies. We can't just pretend that that did not happen and that only our side experienced death and suffering.

I thought Martin got a lot of grief for how he acted during her visit. That was undoubtedly a difficult situation for a republican to be in since it was her country – even though she's only a figurehead – which enacted internment and all the other repressive laws. But I understood why Martin had to do it. He could with conviction and honesty state, 'We stretched ourselves with our base who'd been hurt by these people, stretched ourselves in order to be able to strive for reconciliation.'

It's also important to remember that it wasn't all unionists who threw these gestures back in his face. For example, I didn't believe in IRA decommissioning. That was personal – in August 1969 people were burned out of their houses and the IRA weren't there to defend them. That has always haunted me. But in order to push the thing forward, there are certain things you have to do which earlier you wouldn't have contemplated. To survive, to win, you have to be flexible and pragmatic and leave fundamentalism behind.

When the Brits realised how important our electoral strategy of involvement had become to the struggle, they began erecting obstacles that they thought would limit our political development – like their introduction of the oath forswearing the use of political violence following the council elections in the north in 1985. Some republicans at the time said, 'We can't take that. How can we do this? This is a denial of my cousin who's in the IRA,' etc. I said, a little tongue in cheek, 'The IRA doesn't use violence; it uses force. Take the oath.' The Brits hoped that by not taking the oath we would exclude ourselves from the councils. Our attitude was, 'We're getting into these councils.'

David Trimble also misread us and got it wrong when in 1998, possibly being misadvised by the informer Seán O'Callaghan, he said, 'Sinn Féin have an exit strategy' [i.e. they have a plan other than political involvement]. He couldn't have been more wrong! Sinn Féin had an entrance strategy.

Being pragmatic wasn't simple or easy. The SDLP was still the dominant force in nationalist electoral politics at the time of the negotiations leading up to the Good Friday Agreement in 1998. That meant that republican demands, which were more ambitious and imaginative than the SDLP's, were circumscribed by the demands and the negotiating skills of the SDLP and the Irish government. But still, going into a flawed – perhaps even doomed – political system in order to push and popularise republican demands and consolidate and expand one's electoral base was the right thing to do. Of course the strategy also called for compromise, and compromising is a delicate balancing act. If you don't give enough, the process is stalled. If you give too much, your opponents mistakenly view you as a softie, a pushover, and your base becomes insecure and disillusioned.

Often we didn't appreciate the effect Martin's efforts were having. A friend of mine, an ex-prisoner from south Derry, was fitting windows in the house of a Presbyterian minister and eventually got talking to the minister. My name came up and the minister said he 'wouldn't mind meeting Danny Morrison'. So I agreed to meet him for lunch in the Linenhall Library. This was October or November 2016. We were both frank with each other. I explained how exasperated republicans had become. I said, 'We're fed up turning the other cheek, sticking out the hand and no response.' He said, 'Let me urge you, don't adopt that attitude. You've no idea, among Protestants that I know ... What Martin McGuinness has done in outreach is extraordinary and has been recognised, and please do not abandon this.' This was before Martin became sick.

The disillusionment so prevalent in 2017 has been years in the making. In 2015, just before the Sinn Féin Ard-Fheis was held in Derry, the party thought it had reached an accommodation with the DUP on the mitigation of welfare cuts and the protection of benefits. A figure for the cost of covering the mitigation had been given by the DUP and agreed upon by Sinn Féin. However, a paper was leaked to Sinn Féin showing that the true cost was much more. Therefore, it was clear that the DUP's intentions were less than genuine; instead, in the event of Sinn Féin agreeing to the DUP's wording, they knew that down the line when the money ran out and it was a fait accompli, Sinn Féin would be depicted by the DUP and the media as idiots for not understanding the meaning of the figures.

So Martin telephoned Peter Robinson and said, 'We need to talk. You're trying to pull the wool over our eyes. I thought we were dealing with honest people.' Robinson said, 'OK, I'll see you at Stormont Castle.' So Martin drove down from Derry, on a Sunday afternoon, goes to Stormont Castle, waits for several hours. Robinson doesn't show nor does he phone. That's just one example of the disrespect that was shown.

Here is another. Martin was up in Donegal near his mother's old place, fishing. And he gets a call, informing him that Peter Robinson had sent a letter from Florida saying the Maze/Long Kesh Peace Project wasn't going ahead. This despite the fact that Martin and Peter Robinson had already been photographed cutting the first turf for the project. Robinson hadn't the courtesy to inform Martin that he was reneging.

So the cumulative effect of all those things – Martin going to the Somme commemorations, then being rebuffed by Arlene Foster when he suggested that they attend two matches being played by the Republic of Ireland and Northern Ireland soccer teams together and she said she'd only go to the Northern

Ireland one! – meant that things were bound to come to the boil. The contempt and arrogance shown by the DUP – I mean, it's pitiful. It has to do with self-righteousness, supremacy, that mentality, that mindset. It would have been easier for her to go to that Republic match with Martin than go to Martin's funeral.

The jury is still out on whether Martin's policy of reconciliation was successful. What it did do was convince many nationalists, 'We're the good guys here. If it brings unionists and us closer together, we'll be nice to the queen.'

***

Gerry Adams was the first one to tell me of Martin's illness. He told me it wasn't cancer. I was aware Martin's father had died young. When we were up in Derry, Martin's mother, a lovely woman, used to feed us, and I knew she was a widow. Anyway, Gerry said, 'Martin's not well.' I wondered what it was.

Gerry was in our house on the Sunday before Martin died and he said there'd been a slight improvement. Clearly that wasn't the case. One paper had a story about the condition being genetic and being peculiar to the part of Donegal from which Martin's mother came.

When I switched on the radio on the morning after Martin's death I heard BBC Northern Ireland's political correspondent Mark Devenport, on BBC Radio 5 Live, saying 'he was' several times before he actually mentioned Martin's name. I didn't want to say anything to my wife, Leslie; then Mark Devenport made the announcement and I was shattered. This irreplaceable person was gone.

Subsequently, I was really glad that Michelle O'Neill was the one to succeed him; that Sinn Féin took the risk with someone younger, a woman, someone not from Belfast or Derry but from Tyrone.

You couldn't imagine the republican movement without Martin, because of the longevity, the service to it, the importance of having someone like that with all the experience behind him, the judgements respected. You'd be concerned because it was like a ship losing its captain. Is it going to lurch to the left or right? It also brought to attention the fact that Gerry's term is also coming to an end. But the movement is in a very strong place at the moment. I would just hand over to young people right, left and centre and take the risk. After all, that's what happened in the 1970s.

I was at Martin's funeral. Clearly he had affected many people. It says something about what he achieved, the reverence he was held in, when the British queen sends a personal letter to the family, when the former president of the US comes over, when the first minister goes to it, the taoiseach – all these political leaders. That is testimony to an achievement of international standing. He was also involved in Sri Lanka and he went out to East Timor and the Basque country. He was trying to export ideas, help other places. It's so sad because he was intending to stand down in May anyway, and hoping to have some time with his family. It's sad, but none of us in this life knows what's going to happen next.

Martin was a soldier and a peacemaker. And both those roles were connected through politics. His contribution to the armed struggle was political in that he wanted to bring about a political end. Besides, people who don't understand the IRA will attribute everything to Gerry Adams or Martin McGuinness, without realising one of the reasons the IRA remained impenetrable is that there was a lot of autonomy within the army so, while in a corporate sense leadership personnel are morally responsible, they certainly did not know every detail of every republican action. But it is true to say that Martin was powerful, he was fearless, he had foresight. Here was a guy from the Bogside, up against people who'd gone through Sandhurst, with all that theory and thinking, with centuries of diplomacy behind them. They'd every possible scenario covered – except ours.

9

Jonathan Powell

The Northern Ireland Office advised Tony Blair, Alastair Campbell [Tony Blair's spokesman and campaign director] and I to have our first meeting in 1997 with Martin McGuinness and Gerry Adams in a small room with no windows inside Castle Buildings. It was pretty remarkable as it was the first time a prime minister had met a republican since Lloyd George.

They came into the room and I remember Tony shook them both by the hand. Alastair Campbell and I stayed at the far side of the table and avoided shaking hands. They for their part didn't make any effort to shake our hands – they could see it wasn't going to happen, so they walked round and sat down.

The reason I didn't shake hands was that my father had lived in Northern Ireland during the war. He was in the Royal Air Force and had been injured in an IRA ambush in 1940. He wasn't hurt badly – in fact, hardly at all. Besides that, my brother, who worked for Mrs Thatcher, was for a long time on a death list of people to be assassinated by the IRA, so he felt pretty unfriendly towards them. There was also the fact that I'd been in Washington in the embassy there, where my job had been to stop Gerry Adams getting a visa to come over – this was before the ceasefire but after the 1993 Downing Street Declaration. I worked pretty hard and I thought I'd it all sorted out with the state department, FBI, CIA – everyone on side. Then Teddy Kennedy and Nancy Soderberg [the deputy national security advisor at the time] appealed directly to President Clinton and he got the visa. Which, in retrospect, was exactly the right thing to do. But I felt pretty sore at the time and pretty unfriendly.

I mean, someone like Peter Sheridan [former RUC assistant chief constable] had real reason to hate them, considering what happened to him [a planned assassination by the IRA]. I'm not in that category at all. I'm more of a conventional British civil servant establishment figure: I didn't like terrorists.

Later on I realised it was a silly and childish thing, not shaking hands. All over the world, the handshake is a big issue in nearly every conflict I work on. If those people can shake hands, the way Peter Sheridan did in Number 10 when he first met Martin, Gerry Kelly and others when I brought them in in 2004 – that in my view is the sensible way to deal with these things and not to do what I did.

So we had the meeting and at the end of the meeting they gave Tony a little sculpture made out of bogwood and said they hoped this was the only bit of Ireland he'd hold on to. The meeting was more symbolic than anything else. That was in October and we had a subsequent meeting in Downing Street in December.

I can't really remember the impact Martin made on me in that first meeting. I remember more the impact in the second meeting in December. Alastair Campbell sent me a memo saying we should move the Christmas tree because we didn't want terrorists in front of our Christmas tree. We didn't move it in the end.

I got a better impression of Martin as a human being then – and Gerry too, actually. But it was more a cumulative impression. And I was struck by the contrast between him and Gerry. As I got to know Martin he was much more human, warmer, much more voluble – he would talk and talk and Gerry would cut him off. So yes – Martin was a friendly guy. In principle he wanted to be your friend even if you were coming from the other side, whereas with Gerry it was never quite as emotional or open as that.

Gerry rather than Martin would assert things that I would know were untrue. That's not unique to republicans – you get quite a lot of that. Ian Paisley would assert things that I also knew to be completely untrue, and he seemed to think he had a dispensation from God to lie in those circumstances. In the case of Martin and Gerry I didn't take it very personally because I imagine in a covert movement you have to spend a considerable part of your life not entirely telling the truth when you're asked questions.

Some people asked me if it was hard to negotiate with Martin because I knew they were lying. My reply was that it wasn't particularly. Everyone you negotiate with lies to you on one thing or another, but that's not the point of the negotiation – the point is to get to the settlement. Although it's always a bit of a mistake to tell people a lie that they may know is a lie because then you've undermined the confidence the other party can take in the things you are saying.

Martin told me in a private conversation that Bloody Sunday would have been better dealt with in an apology rather than an inquiry: I took that from my diaries, and I'm not swearing that my diary was true, but it's obviously what I thought he said to me at the time. I suspect it may have been more of a throwaway remark. He had quite a good sense of humour and very often was teasing. So it may have been more of a teasing thing. At that stage we were tied up in getting the Bloody Sunday inquiry going, which was costing us money but apparently serving no purpose, people were getting more and more cross about it, and he may have been more teasing than anything else when he said you didn't need to go through all that, an apology would have done.

And it was actually true at the beginning, when we were being pushed for an inquiry: the Irish government in particular was saying an inquiry wasn't really necessary, an apology would do. It was Mo Mowlam who came to us and told us we should have a full inquiry. I don't want to suggest that Martin was making light of Bloody Sunday – obviously to him it was a big issue. At the time the inquiry seemed like a problem, but in the end it did have a good effect, a cathartic effect and was worth it.

***

There was one occasion when Martin called us on the telephone, rather unexpectedly, when things were getting a bit difficult. He suggested I come over and meet him without telling anyone, particularly the police and the army. It was after the Good Friday Agreement, when we were having trouble implementing it. The call was unexpected – basically I'd been the friend of the unionists; that was my role. I looked after them in Washington when they were there. Mo had a good relationship with the republicans and nationalists. Anyway, I asked Tony what he thought and he said, 'Go and do it.'

I got a very talkative taxi driver from Belfast airport to Derry, who'd been a professional cyclist and who told me a very long story about being a professional cyclist. He didn't know who I was. In fact, that was the advantage I had – no one knew who I was. That really was the point of me.

Anyway, I got to Derry, stood outside this hotel and two guys turned up, pushed me into a taxi and said Martin had sent them. I was in the back seat on the phone to Paddy Ashdown [leader of the Liberal Democrats at the time] because we were trying to organise something between the Liberals and ourselves. But the drive seemed to go on forever and I began to think, 'This is very odd.' We were going round in circles. Eventually we got to a little estate, somewhere near the Bogside, to a modern house on the edge of the estate. I knocked and Martin came to the door on crutches. In my diary I made a note that he made some joke about kneecapping – a throwaway comment.

Someone – I assumed it was a lady – had made tea and sandwiches. So we sat before the fire and had tea and sandwiches. We sat there for three hours or so, talking. We didn't make any sort of breakthrough. But what did come home to me was that, if you're going to do something like this, it was important not to demand that they come to Downing Street or castles in Belfast at all times – instead it was important to take a few shared risks. That way you get a frank conversation. After that we had lots of meetings in houses in Belfast and hotels in Dublin and so on. It was the first of a series of meetings.

Later on, when it became public that I was meeting with Gerry and Martin, I mentioned it to my mother. She was quite old and every time I'd go over to Northern Ireland she'd say, 'I'm so sorry, dear.' She came from a real Anglo-Irish family, the Ascendancy, and thought *The Irish RM* [a TV series based on humorous books by Anglo-Irish writers Somerville and Ross] was a documentary rather than fiction. So, for her, talking to republicans was the worst thing of all. She definitely didn't think it was a good thing to do.

A bit later on, when I told people, the reaction was as if I'd seen a unicorn. They'd ask you, 'What's it really like? What's it like meeting a killer?' I got some of that sort of stuff. My response was that people are human. It was the point Tony made at the first meeting we had. Humans have very similar needs, wants and natures, no matter what their background may be. And if you treat someone as a human being you're more likely to get a decent reaction out of them than if you treat them as an enemy or subhuman or anything else. So basically I'd say, 'It's like meeting anyone else involved in politics when you try to achieve something. They're very insistent on their point – you're talking to someone who has a strong point of view.' There's a need to demystify.

That's a point with work I do around the world – you have to make peace with your enemies, start talking to them, possibly find some way of understanding them. The first time I met Martin McGuinness and Gerry Adams the image was of those people you saw on television whose voices were spoken by actors; the perceived image was that they were mass murderers.

We didn't do personal stuff early on. However, I remember when my mother died, Martin very kindly sent a condolence card. He knew my mother had been sick and that I'd gone to say goodbye to her. He was a very human and humane person from that point of view, very concerned about those sorts of issues. Family issues. So those were the sorts of things we'd talk about when there were issues for him at home. He'd talk a little bit about that – obviously not completely unguardedly; I don't want to pretend we were best buddies – but yes, he would certainly be more inclined to talk about personal and family matters than some other of the interlocutors. Particularly when I was meeting him with Tim Dalton from the Department of Justice down in Ireland, Martin would talk about fly-fishing. Tim was very close to Martin. Martin presented him with a fly-fishing rod at the end of talks at Leeds Castle, disguised as an aerial for a bug.

My mother used to spend her summers at an estate outside London, which was her great-aunt's. And her great-aunt's sister was Kitty O'Shea, who lived on the estate. She used to see her in the park in the summer holidays. I mentioned that to McGuinness one time, so he'd know where I was coming from.

**

I work all round the world on similar issues and it's quite often the case that people engaged in violence are deeply religious, so I didn't see a contradiction between Martin McGuinness's Catholicism and his engagement in political violence. I talk to people in what you might call the more modern terrorist movements who have very strong religious convictions. So I didn't ever see that as a contradiction in Martin. Gerry was also a practising Catholic, as far as I could establish, but Martin's Catholicism was worn more on his sleeve.

His meetings with the queen, etc., were after I'd left government, so I wasn't involved in any of that. It struck me as very much a part of Martin McGuinness – that he was prepared to do these things. Someone had to do the difficult thing and he was prepared to be the one to go and do it. I don't think anyone could accuse him of lacking in courage. He was willing to do it even though he knew it would cost him in terms of supporters.

He quite often talked about threats to his life during the talks. Things daubed on the walls round his house, and how someone could give a gun to a kid to go and do something stupid.

He was very aware of that, but it never stopped him doing what he wanted to do. There was a good deal of courage in the man. That is why doing things like meeting the queen didn't surprise me. He didn't talk about the threats to his life in a complaining way; it was more matter-of-fact. Maybe he was making the point that he was serious about this. That he was prepared to take risks to do something he really believed in.

Another risk was of course his relationship with Ian Paisley. Like everyone else I was amazed at the 'Chuckle Brothers' [as McGuinness and Paisley were dubbed during their time as first and deputy first minister, when they were often seen laughing together]. I remember a day in Paisley's office with the four of them (McGuinness, Paisley, Bertie Ahern and Tony Blair) squeezed on the sofa and the rest of us sitting round the room. I was absolutely not expecting that at all. And the fact that they were able to do that on both sides was extraordinary. It was a very interesting symbol around the world of what can happen to two people who are at daggers drawn for so long, how they can make it work if they are determined to make it work. Some people complained about the Chuckle Brothers, but actually it was the best possible way in which you could make it clear to people that there was reconciliation. Although it did come as a big surprise to me.

I talked to Ian Paisley Junior about this and he confirmed that Martin and his father did have a genuine personal human relationship and he stuck to it. And to be fair to Paisley, he also was determined to make this work and be a friend. That was impressive, I thought – the sticking with it.

I remember asking Martin about his move from violence to politics. Probably in Martin's head, it wasn't such a big move. In his head he probably had the same objectives but was pursuing them in different ways, starting with violence and then going to politics. Of course the transition from one to the other was fairly gradual. I think if you were asking him to justify what he did he'd have said it was an issue of continuity. You had to get the British attention, you had to force them to negotiate seriously and then, when they were ready to negotiate seriously, he negotiated seriously. I think he would see it as a sequence rather than a breakaway, where he suddenly went from one to the other.

At the time it did seem an extraordinary thing that he would have been a young man quite so engaged in violence. But then if I'd grown up in Derry, there's no knowing what I would have done. It was easier to understand after ten years of talking with him, to see what the journey had been. And from his point of view there was continuity. For him it wasn't such a big break.

He did see, more than other people, why the meeting with the queen was important. What he saw was, if you're going to have a proper reconciliation, you do need to apologise, to show grief and understanding of the suffering of the other side as well as your own side, and I think he did grasp that very clearly and I think that was very important. Again if I compare it with other conflicts around the world, you need someone who is prepared to stand up and do that, who's a very prominent figure among the guerrillas, and if that doesn't happen there's a problem. So I'm not sure he'd see himself as having had a conversion on the road to Damascus, but he understood that if you're going to have reconciliation you have to show that you understand the suffering you've caused, and I think he tried to do that.

**

I learned about his illness rather late in the day. I went over with President Santos of Colombia to visit Northern Ireland in November 2016. Santos came on a state visit to the UK and wanted to go to Northern Ireland – he asked me to go along with him. Martin was there and did a speech for him along with Arlene Foster. Arlene wasn't particularly friendly, but Martin was extremely friendly. He was very friendly to Santos and said some very nice things about me in his speech. At that time he seemed fine – slightly thinner than usual but friendly and all the rest of it. I had no inkling he was sick; then someone told me on that visit that he was ill, although we didn't realise it was so serious. Some time after, I was told it was serious and it came as a big shock to me.

Tony Blair wasn't at Martin's funeral, I assume, because he was travelling around. He has a schedule booked almost a year ahead so he would have been on the road, I guess – I don't work with him any more so I'm not sure. Tony liked Martin and he respected him. Alastair Campbell went and sort of represented him and very kindly passed on some messages from me to the family. I said how much I respected him and certainly a seminal moment in my life had been working on that negotiation with him.

Broadly speaking, he was a man of his word. If I put a deal to him and he couldn't do it, he'd say, 'I don't know, I've got to go away and consult.' If he did do a deal, he'd then deliver on it. That made life a hell of a lot easier as a negotiator but also gave you some reassurance that the man had fixed positions, that he was not one who was constantly changing. There was a solidity and centeredness to him that was unusual among the people I negotiate with.

I didn't see any contradiction between that and instances of lying during negotiations. That was more at the beginning of the negotiations, when there was a tendency to do that. When I say he was a man of his word, I don't mean a man who's necessarily always telling you the truth about what happened. What was important to me during the negotiations was that he was someone who when he said he was going to deliver on a particular deal, he actually then did deliver on it – he didn't sort of wimp out halfway through.

His greatest strength of all was obviously the leadership that he provided. He was clearly a very strong leader in the republican movement, both in the armed wing and then later politically. I think that was his greatest strength – his charisma, his ability to lead, but for me it was that centeredness. He knew what he thought and would stick to what he said.

I'm sure I have many more weaknesses than he had, but he was inclined, once he got going, not to stop. When we were talking, he would sometimes just go off into a complete diatribe about something and then Gerry would stop him. The passion he had about things would sometimes tip over into too much. It could be anything – it could be a historical point, but not knowing when enough was enough – going on and on with great passion and noise and all the rest of it. It was a very mild fault, but it certainly was a fault.

I did like him. I never forgot what his past was and for me that was always an issue because I wouldn't agree with what he did in his early life in any shape or form. But I did like him. And when I left government I did invite him and Gerry – and David Trimble – to a party when my wife and I finally got married. I invited both of them to it; they didn't come. But I felt he was a friend.

I don't think I'd say I admired him. If you admire someone you tend to have someone who is admirable in all of his or her virtues. And I think because of Martin's past and the violence, I'd find it quite hard to say I admired him. I admired many aspects of him – his leadership, his solidity in terms of being able to trust when he said he would do something that he'd do it. But I can't say I admired his past. And yes, states can certainly engage in terrorism, as well as individuals and groups. But on the whole I disapprove of states doing it. There's a difference between using terror and using armed force. You might use armed force against other people with armed forces. But when civilians begin being blown up, in my definition that tips into terrorism. As I say, governments do it too, so I wouldn't exempt governments from it. But what Martin was responsible for in his younger years is not something I would ever relate to or find I could justify.

If I'd grown up in Palestine or somewhere else I might well have taken up violence, but that wouldn't mean it's right. I encounter this frequently in the work I do around the world. But I never think it's right. I can understand why they do it, but I don't necessarily think it's right.

I've been asked if he was a figure comparable with Michael Collins. I talk in my book about when he came into the Cabinet Office at No. 10 and said, 'So this was where the damage was done!' [It was assumed at first that McGuinness was referring to the mortar attack on 10 Downing Street during a cabinet meeting in 1991; however, McGuinness explained that he was referring to the 1921 Treaty, which had led to the Irish Civil War and confirmed partition in Ireland.] Being sold a pup by the British in Downing Street – I'm not sure he'd like that comparison.

I think there are some interesting correlations between the two men but not so much as military men and all the rest of it. It's quite clear, as they got into negotiations, that it was Michael Collins who did the negotiations. Before they went to Downing Street there were covert negotiations while the IRA was still fighting, with Michael Collins popping up in places like Belfast and talking to agents of Lloyd George to try to get negotiations going. So when you think of Martin and his role in the secret back channel, I think there are some interesting comparisons with Michael Collins.

But I think Martin will be remembered for being the man who was able to finish what Michael Collins was unable to finish. In the end, Michael Collins's treaty led to a civil war. What Martin was doing was ending that civil war, if you like. In a way, it's a bigger tribute even than the Michael Collins tribute. Will people be making movies about Martin McGuinness in a hundred years' time? I don't know. History tends to move on in these things. But I am sure of one thing: he will be remembered as a leader of republicans in the Troubles, for negotiating the peace and also, maybe even more importantly, for implementing it.

If you hadn't had a Martin McGuinness as deputy first minister building a relationship with Paisley, I'm not sure that the Good Friday Agreement would necessarily have worked as well as it did. If you look now at the generation who came after the Troubles and can't seem to make it work, it's a striking tribute to Martin that he didn't just fight the war and make the peace, he also made the peace work. And I think when people remember him in a hundred years, that'll be one of the biggest things they'll remember.

Martina Anderson

In 1972 I was a ten-year-old whose brother was imprisoned in Portlaoise. Martin was imprisoned there too at the time. His mother and my mother and Martin's then girlfriend, Bernie, and my sister's boyfriend, Frankie McFeely, used to all travel together to Portlaoise to visit them, leaving in the middle of the night. And even in the jail Martin gave leadership. There was always that air about him.

Growing up, everybody knew Martin – he lived round the corner. And everyone loved him. If he talked to anyone, or came into their home, or passed someone and said 'Hello!' – as a child you would whisper, 'There's Martin McGuinness!' He always had time for you. He was somebody that everyone looked up to; he had that leadership quality.

I went on the run around 1980 when I was eighteen, nineteen years of age, ending up in Buncrana – a place everyone went to on their holidays. There was a number of us there who were on the run. Martin and Bernie spent time out there too. When we were in Buncrana, Martin was always taking care of us. He would tell us to remember who we were, what we represented.

I got to know him personally over the years. He was so reflective – he reflected on every situation before he responded to it. I never heard or saw Martin react to a situation with aggression or in a knee-jerk fashion. I used to think he must have a pause button in his head. A number of us, in contrast, would have been quicker to react. But Martin stopped you in your tracks and made you think. I believe that's the legacy he left us. He always thought things through. That's something he took with him all his life and it made him different from the rest of us. He was a strategic thinker before the term was invented. He thought about every situation and the need to be long-headed. Where do you want to be and how do you want to get there? Are you going to use this route or that route? He forced you to think. He was absolutely focused, committed. And his energy – God Almighty, his energy!

I became his junior minister in 2011 – it was probably the biggest privilege of my life – and so I travelled with him a lot. It often meant being up early in the morning. With Martin it wouldn't matter if he had only arrived home at 4 a.m., he'd still be up again at 6 a.m.

Through all his political life, he always went home to Bernie and the wains, no matter the time or distance. We might have been in Dublin, and Martin might have to be in Dublin again the next day – so it made more sense for him to stay in Dublin – but he'd still always go home. I don't think he ever needed to say why he was going home – everybody understood – Martin goes home. He'd often talk of his children and you just knew they were at the heart of everything he was doing. They were the core for him. The only time he didn't go home, from what I remember, was during the negotiations for the Good Friday Agreement.

***

People sometimes talk about there being two Martin McGuinnesses – the fighter and peacemaker. That makes no sense. The

Martin McGuinness who died was the same Martin McGuinness who fought in the streets of Derry. He always stood up for the people. And he fought for them during the negotiations. Through it all he was the same principled man who fought all of his adult life in one sort of struggle or another.

During the time of putting arms beyond use, Martin and the Sinn Féin leadership took the republican family to a place that some struggled with, didn't want to go to, but he knew that was where the republican family needed to be.

His beliefs and his conduct and personality were why people respected him – there was nothing false about Martin's engagement with anyone. He was totally sincere throughout all his life. Once he gave his word, he never stood away from it. And he was a good listener. They often say that a politician should remember that they've two ears and one mouth.

I remember at a commemoration in Derry in 2006, he walked with me the whole way – just talking to me, hearing my views. He empowered you. He never tried to ram his view down your throat. Instead he would get you to talk your views out with him, and then you had to stand over your views. You couldn't just have an opinion and not back it up. If you couldn't back it up with Martin, you were beaten before you started.

I learned a lot from him. I feel that because his passing was so sudden, we're all still feeling very raw and hurt. And you can only imagine what Bernie and the children must be feeling. But that pause button of his has been transferred into my head, and I'm sure it's been left in the heads of hundreds of thousands of the public. When I've had issues that called for a decision since he's been gone, I've stopped and reflected on them, whereas in the past I maybe would have made spontaneous decisions. Now

I ask myself, 'What would Martin have done?' The answer is often very different from what I'd been planning to do. So he's changed me in that way.

He had so much personal courage, as well as a strongly held belief in the pathway we needed to go down. You knew by listening to him that it wasn't a pathway somebody else brought him to – it was his vision, his belief, and he felt it was his job to get as many of us as possible walking down that pathway of peace with him.

And he was respectful to political opponents like John Hume. Martin didn't like the way the SDLP sometimes treated John in later years. At counts, for example, when John would be walking about and might be in need of a little care and attention, Martin was the one that gave it. Martin looked after Ian Paisley as well. He wouldn't ignore anyone, even if he had a political difference with them – he would look after and care for anyone in any situation that arose.

***

During Martin's Irish presidential bid in 2011 the southern media acted in a way that was disgraceful, absolutely disgraceful. The Martin McGuinness who grew up in the Bogside and stood up against the British state was no different to any southern people's family members who stood up against the British state at the time of the Easter Rising. Terrible things happen in war. It's how you get out of it, how you build conflict resolution that counts. Martin did more than anyone I know to build reconciliation on this island, especially this part of the island.

The south had a bloody civil war. To the media in the south, the 'good old IRA' was different. They fought differently. They killed differently. There was a difference between the 'good old IRA' and the version of the IRA personified by Martin McGuinness. And I thought that, for any of us watching some of those interviews during his presidential candidacy, the sheer hypocrisy of the state was appalling.

Take the RTÉ news item during the presidential election in 2011 involving David Kelly [whose father Patrick, an Irish Army private, was killed in 1983 in the course of the rescue of supermarket executive Don Tidey, who had been kidnapped by the IRA]. Kelly confronted Martin on TV about knowing who killed his father. Whether it was set up or not, I don't know. Maybe the man wanted to have that confrontation. Maybe it was done to try to provoke a different kind of reaction in Martin, but I think the way he responded to it epitomised Martin. He stood there, he engaged with David Kelly, he told him he didn't know. I think when people are hurt, it's wrong for them to be used in a stage-managed media ambush or whatever. Especially when those people are victims and they're hurting.

Martin was a decent human being to his core, in everything that he did and everything he represented, and that's what the media struggled with. They wanted to present this other image of Martin McGuinness, but nobody who knew Martin recognises the image the media portrayed. They presented him in a negative way because, if they hadn't, they'd have had to present our struggle in a completely different light. Our right to resist was valid. We didn't start the war – the war came to us. They could have analysed what happened here accurately, told the truth. But it suited them not to.

There was more to Martin than you'd expect. For example, he loved fishing. He'd be on the phone talking about what he caught and what he didn't catch. Or telling how somebody landed up to his house with a salmon. He had a friend – James Quinn – and the two went fishing a lot. I met a man recently who was out fishing in Donegal and he said, 'Do you know, Martin was there. And I didn't know if I should talk to him.' He also loved Gaelic sports – he loved going to county finals, All-Ireland finals. But out fishing was probably the only time he got space to himself. If he walked down the town with Bernie during the All-Ireland Fleadh, he was surrounded. If he went out for a meal, the same thing happened. People meant well, but it left him little space.

When he was education minister, I worked closely with him. I've been into schools with him, and they would ask him questions of all kinds. If a school came up to Stormont, especially a school from Derry city, they'd get Martin in to talk to them. They loved that. When he went into schools, the children just seemed to flock round him. This city – Derry – had one of the worst school estates. And Martin McGuinness turned it into one of the best school estates, one of which any city could be proud. A new school at St Mary's, another at St Cecilia's – new schools, new buildings. And it was Martin brought all that to this city.

Of course we live in a society where not everyone will see a person for who they are. The media will paint a false image and that's what some people will use to decide whether or not they like the individual. Maybe it's because of all the things they have heard, or because they don't have the belief system. So I'm sure there were people who didn't like him, but that didn't prevent most people from engaging with him to get the outcome that both they and Martin wanted.

***

He told me when he started to feel ill. He'd just come back from the doctor. He'd had a cough and he was getting different antibiotics for it. Soon after we were at a funeral and Martin told me that he had been to the doctor the day before and how it hadn't gone well. At that funeral one of the family members came up to Martin and asked him to help carry the coffin. And he did.

I often texted him during his illness. Once it was out there, no matter where I was – and I travelled all round the north – people came up to me in their droves. So I'd tell Martin, 'You don't have to answer these texts I'm sending you, but this one was asking for you and that one was asking for you.' He'd come back with thumbs up or he'd let me know how he was.

When you think back to before his illness – every time Martin was on the TV and people would try to present him in a negative way, you just would burst with pride at the way he responded. He was amazing. That is the kind of person he was. I remember texting him one time he was on *The View*, telling him how proud I was of him. And he came back with thumbs up and *go raibh mile maith agat*, and then he said, 'And I'm proud of you too.' That was Martin. Even when he was in the hospital, he'd be trying to communicate with you.

I didn't visit Martin in the hospital. I left for Brussels – in the course of my work as an MEP – on the Sunday that he took ill. I texted him and told him that. We as republicans in Derry would have taken over that hospital and I would have been over in a heartbeat if I could have been of any assistance. But this was a time for Bernie and the children.

Later, at the Bloody Sunday Commemoration Service in January 2017, it was quite evident he was having a reaction to the treatment. I remember seeing him that Sunday when he came out of the car. God, I could have screamed; he looked so ill. But they thought that the treatment was going to help. Everybody was coming up to him – they just wanted to take him away to rest. He looked so ill, so sick, and yet he believed that this was his place to be, to be there with the families, to take part in the service. I remember I went home afterwards and cried for hours.

It was in Brussels in the early hours of the morning that I got the call from my husband telling me that Martin had died. I was floored. Absolutely floored. That was one of the worst journeys, going back. I remember years ago when I was in Strasbourg as part of my MEP work at a time when my mother was very ill. The doctor was put on the phone to me and he said, 'You just need to say your goodbyes.' Christ, I'd a hell of a journey. But it was Martin who contacted me throughout that journey – 'Where are you now?', 'I'll be here when you get home' – supporting me. Now, while that journey was bad, I was in bits coming back after Martin died.

The funeral certainly was fitting. The entire wake we stood outside the house trying to get people in and out. I thought, 'I'll never get this crowd in.' Because the crowd was lined up seemingly forever. At one time we thought we'd get the house clear at midnight, have it for just the family. I went in to Bernie and his brothers and I said, 'Look, the crowd's out here, I'm never going to get them through.' I was trying to get people to not stay talking too long. 'Just go in and then out immediately.' But the family said, 'Should it be four o'clock in the morning, there'll be nobody turned away from this door. Everyone will get in.' And they came in their hundreds and thousands to the wake.

I thought Gerry Adams's oration was also fitting. Martin was

Gerry's best friend and vice versa. Gerry's heart was obviously aching and yet I thought he gave one of the best orations I've ever heard. How he managed to do it as he did – I thought it was as absolutely desired.

Martin was an amazing, decent human being who loved people and his country. He was someone who simply refused to allow his people to be subjected to injustice and inequality. He was our Nelson Mandela.

II

John McCallister

I first met Martin McGuinness when I was elected to the Assembly in March 2007. In September of that year I was over at a British–Irish event in Oxford. I remember meeting him at that event – he was the main speaker. I introduced myself and he said, 'I know who you are, John', and we shook hands. That was the first time I'd spoken to him on a person-to-person basis, rather than through an Assembly question along the lines of 'Could I ask the deputy first minister …?'

When I was elected as an Ulster Unionist MLA one very common question I got from the unionist electorate was, 'What are Martin and Gerry like? What are they like to talk to?' I got this from a range of people. There'd be those who'd say, 'I don't know how you speak to those people', and those who'd encourage speaking with them.

I, personally, had no qualms about it whatsoever. I never viewed myself as a victim in the Northern Ireland context – thankfully – and I have always taken people as I find them. I've no doubt I could Google and find out lots of baggage for everybody I meet.

I remember, shortly before I was elected, I was taking part in a constituency debate and Caitríona Ruane [a Sinn Féin MLA] seemed quite surprised that I'd walked up to her and offered my hand. I always thought it strange that people had such a reticence. Particularly people who were in politics and who were elected and in government, or their party colleagues were in government.

I found Martin McGuinness, on the occasions we met, to be very personable. But if someone had asked me then, 'Do you think you'd ever be at Martin McGuinness's funeral?', I'd have said, 'Don't be ridiculous. What would I be doing there, even if I were in the Assembly?' Yet when the time came I felt a very strong reason to be present.

I think what made the difference was working with Martin on different issues and getting to know him. I always say the Assembly has maybe not set the world on fire, but the one big success it has had is that it got people talking. When you look at the very early days, even before my time, people would hardly get into a lift with members of other political parties. When I first went, Jim Wells – a constituency colleague – wouldn't be in the same photograph as Sinn Féin, wouldn't shake hands and wouldn't acknowledge them. Now, you and I end up chatting and the next thing you know, we're asking about your children or your grandchildren or how has your mother been since that fall. Before people realise it they're not talking politics but enquiring how your mother's hip joint is doing. The Assembly may not have achieved much in legislative terms, but it achieved that.

I didn't worry about losing votes because I always believed the people voting for me would be in the same place as I was. I voted Yes in 1998 for the Good Friday Agreement and by the time I left the Assembly I felt like I was the only unionist politician left who would get up and freely admit they'd voted Yes. And I've never changed my mind about the agreement. I always took the view, 'Look, two completely opposing political viewpoints have made an agreement. This is as good as it gets.' All of my time growing up, unionism wanted Sinn Féin to act democratically and now they were doing just that. By 2007 they'd entered the Policing Board, devolution was back – what more did we want?

***

Martin McGuinness's personal affability came through in public as well as in private. If you remember back in 1999 when he was nominated education minister, there was this great gasp went round the Assembly chamber. I wasn't a member of the Assembly at the time, but the general thought then was of this awful man who'd brought such destruction to Northern Ireland: in some unionist circles, you might as well have been nominating the devil himself to be in charge of our children. But change happened and each year that passed Martin McGuinness became less of the bogeyman to unionism that he once was.

I think that largely was due to Martin himself, because you couldn't say the same of Gerry Adams. We've come through a year [2017] with two elections. Gerry was a key player, the bogeyman that was used to try to frighten broad unionism in the March elections. I think that was probably testament to Martin's taking people at their own level, not trying to force himself on people or trying to say, 'I'm the deputy first minister, I have to have this.'

Even the way he worked with Ian Paisley from the start, there was a kind of deference and almost respect because Paisley was twenty years or more his senior. I'm quite sure that angered some in republican circles.

There were also times when you saw incredibly strong leadership from Martin McGuinness. Take that awful murder of a PSNI police constable: for him to use a term like 'traitors to Ireland'. As a unionist, I probably don't feel it as much, but I know it's hard to get a much stronger phrase in Irish republican terms. It doesn't get much more hard-hitting than that.

There was also the fact that he was able to lead and hold the broad republican constituency together. There was going to be no young whippersnapper coming up and asking Martin McGuinness, 'Well, where did you earn your stripes?' If there had been, he would have got short shrift.

So Martin could balance the political and the more historic baggage he brought with him. This was proven by the very fact that even before his illness he wasn't the bogeyman that he once was in unionist politics – although I'm not saying he was going to be invited to every Orange Order event. In 2007 people would ask me how I could meet such a person. By 2013, when I left the UUP, there was not that same level of animosity. There are people who would never forgive Martin McGuinness and that's fine, that's their view, but there wasn't the same number who held that view.

If you even look at the polling – Martin McGuinness's poll ratings tended to be better as a party leader. There was a broad unionist constituency that might never vote for him, but there was a respect: he was doing a decent job, he was leading. He effected change in unionist politicians and in the wider unionist electorate. When he would have first set out as education minister, far from every school would have wanted Martin McGuinness through their door. But by the end he was getting closer to the point where there were no longer places that were no-go areas for him.

I did come across cases where people didn't want to shake hands with him. I've seen people trying to make sure they weren't forced into an embarrassing situation. I noticed it more with people in the DUP, who'd have made great efforts to avoid sitting beside a Sinn Féin member. But with Martin – and that was one of his strengths – he wouldn't have been out to corner somebody so they'd either have to snub the deputy first minister or else shake his hand. He always preferred to avoid that. If you needed another two years to get to that point, he would give it.

I look at the way things are now. I look at the fact that Martin McGuinness was at Dr Paisley's funeral. Or the fact that Ian Paisley Junior paid tribute to Martin after he resigned and was clearly in ill health, and after he died. He acknowledged the work that Martin had done; he acknowledged that relationship between Martin and his father. It wasn't like some other DUP people who would go, 'Look, we don't want to talk about it.' Ian Paisley Junior was very open. If you check with the BBC, that appearance by Ian Paisley Junior to discuss Martin McGuinness shortly after his death was one of the highest ratings they ever had for the BBC's *The View*. I know, because I previously held the highest rating for the night I resigned from the UUP. Ian Paisley Junior beat me, so I had much to be annoyed about!

Looking back ten years later at the relationship between McGuinness and Paisley, there was a warmth between them that wasn't faked for the cameras, even if people at the time thought it was a bit overdone. When I was a newly elected MLA in 2007, I remember watching them walk down the stairs, with Blair and Ahern there too, and I thought, 'What was it all for?' At the same time I was glad that at least we were here. I was born in 1972. The Troubles were our normal – growing up and going to school and college and farming. If someone had told me even ten years before that Martin McGuinness and Ian Paisley would be deputy first minister and first minister of Northern Ireland and would get on so well, I'd have found it incredible.

But I think Paisley learned from the Trimble–Mallon partnership. It had looked like some really tetchy family feud constantly going on – a battle a day. So Paisley warmed up and got on instead. The advantage of looking as though you're enjoying it is that it gives confidence to the unionist electorate.

Martin also gave the impression that he was enjoying it. I rarely saw him lose his cool. The only incident I can think of was when Reg Empey was party leader of the UUP and Fred Cobain was chief whip – they had a full stand-up row in McGuinness's office with him one time. I think he threw them out, or at least asked them to leave. But they bore this as a badge of honour – they were quite pleased: 'He told us where to go and we told him where to go.' But I'm struggling to remember another time when he lost his cool, even in the Assembly chamber.

Looking back at Martin's early life, I suspect he had a whole other life that I may never know fully about. I imagine a lot of it wasn't good and I'd be opposed to and incredibly critical of it. I tend to think of his change from violence to politics as a slow realisation that the only way to solve this thing was to start to talk and come to some sort of agreement. Looking at it as an outsider, one who was never involved in paramilitary activities or in the security forces, I think there was probably a realisation on all sides – on Martin McGuinness's part, on Ian Paisley's part – that we couldn't go on the way we were. I think there was a pragmatic waking up on all sides.

With the start of the Troubles, we didn't just press a button. We ambled into it somewhat and, once in, we couldn't get ourselves out of it. Probably no one would have thought when I was born that I'd be a thirty-five-year-old member of the Assembly by the time devolution came back in a stable form. There was a realisation that this was at best a messy 0–0 draw and nobody was going to win. We just needed to stop sacrificing so many people to the Troubles.

***

I became aware of Martin's illness when there was something announced about him not going on the China trip with the first minister. I knew from being in politics – I was out of politics at this stage – that his not going was a pretty big thing because the joint office really required the two of them. And I knew from a few friends up in Derry that the rumour was that it was quite serious, whatever it was. And then like most people, the night he resigned there was quite a shock at how much he had failed physically in such a short space of time.

I felt the need to go to his funeral because I knew him, I enjoyed working with him and I felt incredibly strongly that – even though I wasn't an elected politician at this stage – I still was recognised as a former unionist politician and unionist politicians should be seen there. At the time there was some debate about whether Arlene Foster was going to attend. I felt that the point should have been made to her: 'You've had weeks when you knew he was ill, you've had weeks from his last appearance to plan and think about this.'

So I was very supportive of Arlene's decision when she did decide to go, and I was pleased to see Peter Robinson there as well. I think the hurt and offence in broader republicanism and nationalism would have been enormous had the senior unionist politicians not been there.

I just wanted to go. I'd worked with Martin on numerous occasions. We didn't always agree on everything, but it was good to deal with somebody in work and be respectful and courteous and enjoy working with that person.

I'd like to share a personal story: back in March 2012 Mike Nesbitt and I were going for the leadership of the UUP. On 29 March 2012 my wife, Jane, went into labour and we had a wee boy, Harry. He was born at home on the luxury of our bathroom floor and I delivered him. Wendy Austin interviewed me afterwards for *Talkback* – she was presenting the programme at the time. A while later, a message came through on my phone: 'Martin here – I heard it on *Talkback*, wishing Jane and you and baby Harry well, delighted to hear the news.' He'd heard my wife's name on the radio, but he'd made a point of going and getting my mobile number and taking time to send a message. I thought it was a very human, very nice thing to do.

So that was part of our connection – I got on with him, though our politics are poles apart – Martin was a left-wing republican with a huge amount of baggage; I would be at best a centre-right fiscal conservative in those terms, which were all of the things that he might absolutely loathe. But did we both want to see something very positive for Northern Ireland – or as he would have called it 'the north of Ireland'? The answer is yes. And that's why I thought it important to go there for his funeral.

The warmth of the greeting? I met a guy that day – I call him Terry from Derry – a former Ulster Unionist, Terry Wright. Terry got me a parking space and brought me down to the church. And that day – it was quite a pleasant March day – I was talking to the great and the good. Bill Clinton came out of the church, Simon Coveney, my old friend Joe McHugh, now government chief whip in the Dáil, people like that. But even walking back down the street, the number of people who recognised me and said, 'It is great to see you up here in Derry today.' There was just something quite special in being there. It reinforced my view so much. If I was hesitant about going on the way up, it convinced me on the way home that I'd done absolutely the right thing.

***

Back in 2011 when I was the deputy leader of the UUP I'd been asked by the very affable Mickey Brady to speak at a Sinn Féin event. I'd agreed, not really thinking much about it: if Mickey was running it, it'd probably be about welfare reform and I'd get to expose my hard Tory credentials or something. But I agreed to do it – it was actually part of their Uniting Ireland series. Tom Elliott [UUP party leader 2010–12] was not happy when this leaked. I hadn't asked Tom, as I was working on the old Irish idea of better to seek forgiveness than ask permission. But I went down anyway, and it turned out that Martin was also speaking. I was under a bit of pressure in the constituency: 'Oh you need to have a hard message.'

I worked at it and put together what I thought was a pretty good speech – including some hard lines about confronting their bloody past. And to be fair to Sinn Féin as a political party, they are good at bringing in people and saying, 'As long as this debate is done in a respectful way, we'll sit and listen to a point of view, even though we totally oppose it.'

It was actually a good event to do and be at, and I was probably relieved that I'd done it. And I know my constituency party at that time was 100 per cent behind me, even the wider party too. One of the guys who liked to write poetry wrote a wee poem about me going to speak at this Sinn Féin event. But by 2011 appearing with Martin McGuinness wasn't a major problem for south Down unionists. In 2007 or 2002 that might have been different. There had been a definite move forward, and that came about by Martin making the institutions work, his personality in how he got along with people and getting on with the job in hand.

This was also evident one night in Londonderry at a Young Farmers event in the Millennium Theatre. There were four of us there: my wife, Jane, and I, as well as Jane's sister and her husband. We were coming out of the restaurant and there was Martin and his wife, Bernie. We went over to speak to them – they might have had one or two grandkids with them. There was just that feeling of broadened understanding, when you see someone in a personal circumstance.

When he died, I'd a sense of loss the way you'd feel when someone you know dies. Not maybe a personal sense of loss, but I certainly knew I'd lost someone that I'd worked with, that I had respect for, and with the way our politics have played out since his passing it's clear that we're missing Martin McGuinness.

I had been expecting him to resign and I'd guessed he'd go on his tenth anniversary. He went before that and wasn't spared to see that tenth anniversary as deputy first minister. But I think the loss was felt as much in the political realm. We've lost all sense of a spirit of generosity in our politics and I think we're now in a place that we wouldn't be in were Martin still alive.

In time, I think there'll be a recognition of the journey he undertook from the 1970s Martin McGuinness to the 2017 Martin McGuinness. He was going to see Willie Whitelaw when I was a babe in arms, yet he was still in politics until the year of his death. During that time he moved from paramilitary terrorist to peacemaker. I know there are some people sceptical about how real any of that change was. But look at the difference, at how Northern Ireland is now when compared with how it was twenty, twenty-five, thirty years ago.

I admired the way he dealt with people, even people who were obviously uncomfortable with his past. He could put people at their ease – I've no doubt in the Sinn Féin party machine you had to lay things down a bit firmer – but dealing with the public he had that quality and it's a quality not everybody has. To be able to deal with all walks of life – from somebody maybe lower down in the social order to sitting with President Bush or Obama or Clinton. In fact, Martin probably disliked most of what President Bush ever stood for. But that's a quality I think he had and it's a quality I admired about him.

12

Joe McVeigh

I'd see Martin in Mitchel McLaughlin's house often during the 1970s, where he'd be coming in and out. Every time I visited Mitchel he was there. He'd go in and talk to Mitchel for a few minutes and then disappear – he was like a man in a hurry all the time. Although he was very polite and personable, he didn't seem to hang around. You got the impression of a man on a mission.

Then, at the end of 1981 or start of 1982, Mitchel arranged a meeting with a friend of mine, Carolyn Forché [American poet, teacher and rights activist]. She wanted to meet Martin more than anybody else. She'd been to El Salvador; she'd experienced the war there and spent a year there working closely with Archbishop Romero. So we had this prearranged meeting – myself, Carolyn, Mitchel, Seán Keenan and Martin. That was my first up-close meeting with Martin.

It was in the Sinn Féin office in Capel Street in Derry. Somebody made tea. I was struck by the fact that here was a serious man, interested in the bigger picture, interested in hearing what Carolyn had to say, interested in El Salvador and international politics. My assessment was of a serious political person.

He was very fit-looking, around six feet, looking down a bit on me when we stood up. And he was very fresh looking – he had the Art Garfunkel look about him, with curly hair. No matter how serious the conversation was, Martin always ended up with a bit of a joke, a laugh. You always went away feeling good having met him.

Carolyn found him warm and welcoming. She was greatly impressed and thought, 'A good-looking man too!' I found him friendly and personable. But I also got the serious side of him. He wasn't into small talk.

On that occasion a patrol of the British Army arrived at the door of the Sinn Féin office. Whether they knew he was having visitors or not I don't know. But I could hear Carolyn's cup rattling on the saucer. She got such a fright, she thought, 'We're all done for!' That's what would have happened in El Salvador – a group of soldiers coming around there meant real danger.

Anyway, the door was being banged on and someone said, 'The Brits are at the door!' Martin got up and went to the door and said, 'What do youse boys want?' They said they just wanted to check out who was there. Martin said, 'Would youse ever fuck off!' He banged the door in their face and came back in, sat down and continued the conversation as if nothing had happened.

Carolyn was white as a ghost, and I wasn't used to that kind of up-front stuff either, even though I'd had lots of encounters with the Brits. But Martin had nerves of steel obviously – he was one tough guy. Carolyn was really impressed with how he handled the situation. I kept a note of the meeting and commented in it on how Martin was obviously a good listener as well. There were signs that here was a man who was serious about politics and about making peace.

He was also very intelligent – that came across. He understood Irish history. He was a good speaker, whether in a public speech or one-to-one conversations. He would have made a mark early on as an intelligent guy from the Bogside with leadership qualities – disciplined, very cool – nerves didn't show. I mean when you think of it: around ten Brits, heavily armed, and he tells them to fuck off! So courage and intelligence stood out early in his life.

People often talk about the two lives of Martin McGuinness. Of course he was in the IRA, like many young fellas after Bloody Sunday or around that time, who saw the IRA as their only defence in the working-class areas against the RUC, the Brits and the loyalist death squads. So it was an automatic choice for many young fellas at the time. But Martin's real goal was to make peace in Ireland. He was a peacemaker. He thought, 'If we can work towards an honourable settlement with the British, then we can make our own peace.'

***

I picked up from the media that this was a hard man, highly thought of within the republican movement. He had been brought over to Cheyne Walk to meet the British government along with Gerry Adams and others. A young fella of twenty-one or twenty-two, to be lifted out of the Bogside and flown over to England had to be well thought of by the Brits as well as his own people. He had to be seen as a serious spokesperson.

The southern media had a caricature of Martin. They had their preconceived ideas of this hard man from the Bogside, ruthless, blah blah blah. In my experience and my dealings with him, he was anything but that. The southern media, RTÉ and those, treated him very badly. They wanted to project this image of the obdurate man who wanted to continue the war, whereas the opposite was the truth. Martin was a man interested in making peace from the very beginning. But for him, if he was going to make a settlement, it had to be an honourable settlement. It had to be worthwhile. But the media were only interested in painting a bad picture of him.

Of course much of that changed somewhat once he got into partnership with Dr Paisley. These two men having the jokes, the craic – this presented a whole new image. But there were those in the media who persisted with this image of Martin as the bad boy who was anti-Protestant and so on. Nothing was further from the truth, in my experience.

I was shocked when I heard Miriam O'Callaghan ask him in an interview when he'd last been to Confession. It's such a personal question. I never heard anyone else being asked that question on television. When people go to Confession or Communion it's a personal matter – his faith and its practice are his business, not something that should be of interest to anybody else. Miriam was, of course, primed to make life as difficult as possible for him in that interview. That was during the presidential election and they were trying to paint Martin as this guy who was responsible for all these deaths and killings.

A case in point was David Kelly, who confronted Martin in Athlone. I was quite annoyed about that. The media, of course, made great work of it. This man Kelly was demanding that Martin tell him who killed his father. Martin said he honestly didn't know. But the man persisted, 'You do know!' If David Kelly was concerned to find out about his father – and I'm sure he was – he should have gone privately, had a private talk with Martin, if he believed he or any of the other leaders had information. As it was, the thing was set up at that time to do as much harm as possible to Martin's bid to be president.

The media and the whole political establishment feel very threatened by the rise of Sinn Féin. Martin represented a crucial part of the party, was part of the whole revival and renewal of interest down south. So they were trying to undermine Sinn Féin and undermine Martin as a person, undermine his credibility as they've done with Gerry Adams down the years. There's this fear of republicans getting power in the south, so they're going to do everything possible to destroy their reputations, make them out to be men of violence, without remembering that the politicians in the south also had previous histories – Éamon de Valera and all the old leaders of the southern establishment. But that was the 'good old IRA'.

During the presidential campaign Martin came over from Belcoo to Blacklion, even though we didn't have a vote. I think he wanted to make the point that we in the north should have a vote. He was very strong on that issue too. He was on top of so many issues – progressive political issues. I remember he invited me to join a movement to get the vote on this side of the border in presidential campaigns.

I didn't detect any hostility to him when he came down here in the border areas. He had risen to be a leading politician, the minister for education, and I found that, in general, people respected his position.

***

I noticed there was a mixed reaction to my friendship with Martin and other Sinn Féin people. Those who were attached to the UDR, B Men and all that, regarded me as their enemy. I used to be told that by them at the roadblocks. One guy said, 'You want us killed, don't you?' I said, 'No, I don't.' He said, 'You wrote that in *The Impartial Reporter* newspaper.' I said, 'Show me that report.' He said, 'We know what you're about.'

That particular row started with the man calling me 'Mr McVeigh'. I said, 'I'm a clergyman – you call me either "Reverend" or "Father".' He wouldn't call me 'Father'. He said, 'You're not my father. And I wouldn't call you Reverend either.' They kept me for half an hour. That was just one of my many encounters with that crowd. But anybody attached to the 'security', as they called themselves, was generally hostile, at roadblocks and such. I was asked to produce my licence at the RUC station all the time. 'Where are you coming from, where are you going?' – all that kind of thing.

In the Catholic community, people have always treated me with a certain amount of suspicion. Especially in the 1980s and 1990s, my bishop used to get letters complaining about me being pro-IRA, pro-republican. I was even accused of making sermons in support of the IRA, which was total nonsense. Within the Catholic community, there are people who used to belong to the SDLP who would think I was promoting a republican Sinn Féin position when they expected me to be promoting their political position – as most priests were expected to do and did. They supported the SDLP publicly and privately and every other way. But from the beginning – 1971, when I was ordained – I got a sharp lesson about the British intentions here when they introduced internment without trial, imprisoning my friends and my cousin. From that day on, my mind was made up. There was no compromise; I was not going to be an SDLP supporter. I didn't see them as having any future in resolving this situation.

With Martin, talk was always related to something that was happening. Even when I met him at a film premiere about the hunger strike one time, we had a discussion afterwards. It was all to do with the political position. I don't remember him ever talking about his family.

One occasion when I felt close to him was in 1989, when two IRA men were accidentally blown up – Eddie McSheffrey and Paddy Deery. It was shortly after the bishop of Derry made a statement that there would be no more republican funerals in any Catholic church. This happened a month or two after that declaration. It had been the custom to bring in the coffin with the tricolour, gloves and beret.

Martin was very concerned. These were two highly regarded men in their movement. So Martin phoned me to come down. I did. Martin said, 'Would you be prepared to say the Mass outside the church, in the cathedral grounds, if we're stopped?' I said, 'Yes.' So he said, 'Get your stuff down here and be ready.' Somebody leaked this to the papers and the headline was 'Rebel Priest to Say Mass' – that was in the Sunday paper.

So anyway, I was all set. They took the coffin to the front of the church and, as far as I remember, they let them have the tricolour but not the gloves and beret. So they went straight on in. Neil McGolderick, who had been a classmate of mine, said the Mass. He made very little reference to the circumstances of their deaths. It happened to be 1 November, the Feast of All Souls, so he had an opportunity to speak about All Souls and death generally.

There was an awful scene afterwards, when the RUC attacked the cortege. The tricolour and beret and gloves had been put back on the coffins just as they came out of the church gates. The RUC were waiting to take them off and knocked one of the coffins to the ground. Martin was there – I vaguely remember him being very upset and very angry. But there were so many people; it was very hard to control the situation. There was nothing he could do. Eventually the coffin was righted and they marched up to the City Cemetery from the cathedral. A very sad day.

***

The best and most enduring memory I have of Martin is from just after the windows of my house were broken on 13 November 2016. It was Remembrance Sunday and it would seem some people were a bit high that evening. I had gone to Pettigo that afternoon to my cousin Regina Moss's wake. When I came back I saw one window broken. I thought, 'Someone's broken in to steal my computer.' Then I saw another window broken and another – three big windows round the front of the house. I was a bit shocked.

I remember the next morning, before lunchtime, receiving a phone call from him. 'This is Martin. I'm just after hearing about what happened. It is shocking. It is shocking!' I could hear his sense of outrage for me personally, because it went against the whole spirit of reconciliation and peace, which he'd been working so hard at with Dr Paisley and Peter Robinson. He was really angry but at the same time sympathetic and supportive. He said, 'Anything I can do, let me know.' But he was really shocked. I was very grateful for that support. It really lifted my spirits at that point.

At the funeral of Paddy Doherty [early January 2016] I had one of my longest chats with Martin. After the funeral he was up at the graveside and we stood there chatting about Paddy. I asked him how he thought he'd get along with Arlene Foster. He said, 'Well, I got along with Dr Ian, and I managed all right with Peter, so I imagine I'll be able to handle her too.'

I said, 'I don't think you know this woman.' She's from around here, a few miles from me. She's married and they live on the main road here to Fivemiletown. I thought Martin was underestimating her qualities. He was going to be dealing with a different person from Dr Paisley or Peter Robinson. I didn't say as much because I didn't want to discourage him. I think he realised it wasn't going to be easy, but he didn't expect her to take the approach she did, and get involved in that Renewable Heating Initiative [RHI], which was going to discredit the lot of them. [The RHI scheme was established during the time that Arlene Foster was the minister for enterprise – the department that set tariffs for the scheme. The initiative overspent massively amid internal DUP charges of corruption.]

Despite all the trouble, however, I don't think his policy of reconciliation was a mistake. Martin was deeply anti-sectarian. It was a core principle for him. His notion of republicanism was the unity of Catholic, Protestant and Dissenter – it was at the core of everything he believed in. I think he was really disappointed with some of the actions of the IRA – the more sectarian actions. For him the enemy was the Brits. And Mitchel McLaughlin was of the same way of thinking: to get involved in a local war with the UDR or local loyalism was not smart politically and not sustainable.

I don't think he gave up on the process when he resigned in January 2017. I think he gave up on working alongside people who were not prepared to honour agreements and were not prepared to be open and transparent. He was calling a halt to that, but he was also prepared to work at it. I think, if he'd had his health, he'd have got the thing working again. As he himself said frequently, it was the only show in town.

He took a very hard line on the dissidents. He didn't want them to have any excuse or opportunity to start. He kept saying, 'The war is over, there's no future in the use of arms, that day is done, it's over and gone.'

As for his illness, I didn't know he was unwell until after Christmas. You'd have put your life on him beating it: he was so active, and boy, did he spend himself in the whole thing. In his commitment to his work – up early every day, the way he travelled all over the place; every republican funeral, he was there. He always added to the occasion by being present. I remember once in Castlederg, at a particularly difficult funeral, and Martin came over to me and said, 'Fair play to you, you're always there where you're needed.' Words to that effect. Martin made it his business to be at all these funerals. No matter how busy he was.

He had great energy for getting to all these events. The time I asked him to launch my book, it was no bother to him: 'Oh, I'll be there!' I was so honoured.

I went down to Mitchel at the time of Martin's illness and I got the sense that he didn't want people calling, so I decided I'd definitely not bother him. He obviously had his own spiritual sustenance worked out with the priest who celebrated his funeral and was closer to him. I didn't say I wanted to see him or anything, and Mitchel said, 'He's very, very ill and very weak, and just needs quiet and rest.' So I accepted that.

I think he was a strong man in himself, able to face the future, face the illness, face his impending death. He had tremendous inner strength and courage. So I decided I'd pray for him quietly, and privately send my good wishes to him. I wrote to him, told him my thoughts and prayers were with him.

I wrote to him on other occasions, in fact, such as after his mother's death. I wanted to show my support – I had nothing but admiration for him as a human being, as a leader. I think he made such a huge contribution; I don't know if anyone else could have done it, bringing republicans along – most of them – with the peace process. He was the man.

I miss bumping into him here, there and everywhere. We didn't have long conversations, but it was always pleasant. He'd crack a joke – I can't remember any of them. There's a photograph of me with him and I'm splitting my sides laughing – I don't know what the joke was. But I do miss that.

His love of the Irish people was what I admired most about him. His solidarity with the people, with the poor. He belonged to the people. I saw him as a liberation Christian, the type that concerns itself with the liberation of the oppressed.

The younger Martin that I used to bump into was a bit uptight and tense, whereas in later years he was much more relaxed – always joking, engaging. He felt that what he set out to do had been largely achieved, I think. But in the early days there was a lot of tension in his life – you could see it in his expression. He took on leadership and that must have meant having to deal with a lot of difficult situations. He had a lot of huge responsibilities. To it all he brought the quality of determination – it was a big thing; you could see it in him. He loved the people. I don't like the idea of there being a bad Martin McGuinness and then a good one. There was always a good one.

13

David Latimer

Martin and I first met in June 2006. The occasion was that paint had been splashed onto the pillars and the sandstone of my church. It was a common occurrence but we just kept our heads low because we didn't want to draw attention to ourselves. I heard about this particular incident when I was over on the Waterside with a couple I once married: one Catholic, the other Protestant. A lady who'd heard the news said to me, 'David, your church has been hit with paint again.' I said, 'You're joking', because it hadn't happened for a while.

I went across and had a wee look and I thought, 'Ach, we'll do what we've always done.' So I went home, but then I wakened in the middle of the night and I thought, 'No!' With the heavy footfall of people on the city walls by the church, we simply had to do something about stuff being destroyed by paint.

So early the next morning I got up and went over to BBC Radio Foyle and said, 'Guys, a wee story.' So they opened up the mics and I went in and they said, 'Reverend, what's wrong?', I said, 'My church has been hit by paint.' They said, 'What are you going to do about it?' I replied, 'I think I can only appeal to the one person in this city who can resolve it.' And they said, 'Who might that be?' And I said, 'Well it's a man who in the past wore a hat that gave him a lot of authority, and I don't think he's lost any of it.' And they said again, 'Who might that be?' And I says, 'Martin McGuinness.'

Twenty minutes later my phone was ringing: 'David, Sinn Féin office in the Creggan here. We've heard what you were saying on the radio this morning. Martin would like to meet you. Would you be willing?'

So we agreed to meet the next morning. He arrived at the front steps of the church. My first impression of him when he got out of the car was that he was taller than me. He just came over with his hand out, shook my hand and said, 'David, how are you?' And I said, 'Martin, I'm all right.'

Then we made our way up onto the steps and we shook hands in front of the cameras. And I remember saying to him, 'You're a busy man. I don't want to take up much of your time.' And he says, 'David, I've as much time as you need.'

So we went into the kitchen and the kitchen was a mess. You see, the church was closed at the time because of an outbreak of dry rot, which had been discovered in 2002. For four years this place was dank, it was dreadful, nobody in it – you wouldn't have brought a dead animal into it. Yet here I was bringing Martin in. I'd brought a flask of tea and some scones – but I'd forgotten the butter, so I'd earlier gone to the Tower Hotel and said, 'Look, I need some wee blocks of butter.' They took them out of the deep freeze and they were like concrete! And so in the kitchen I'm struggling with putting the tea in the cups, trying at the same time to butter one of the scones, and they're falling apart.

Then I hear this voice saying, 'David, would you like to look after the scones and I'll do the tea?' And I thought, 'Gosh, this man knows how to make tea!' That was an ice-breaker and it was the beginning of something at the time I couldn't have known would go anywhere.

I remember saying to him as we were having the cup of tea, 'Martin, I was maybe a wee bit strong on the radio, the way I put things.' He says, 'My people think you handled that very well.'

So this was the kind of early conversation we had. At the end of the conversation – there was a colleague with him, Raymond McCartney – Martin said, 'David, I'm going to give you a phone number here. If you need me at any time, don't hesitate to ring.' And he gave me a number. Raymond McCartney said, 'You're privileged. That's a number I don't even have!'

So there was something there that really took me by surprise. I'd met government people before. It can be a clinical experience; it can be just very straightforward. But this was not a businessman. This was a man with humanity.

I never could have imagined that that meeting would lead to an association that really became a friendship that extended over ten years. I just reckoned I would talk to somebody who was going to try to do something that would allow us to exercise our worship and our religious observances in peace. But it became something different.

**

I was aware of the kind of man Martin was and what he'd been doing – I'd heard all these stories. And having been in the British Army myself as a chaplain, I picked up stuff. People would be saying stuff about his hands not being clean. And, I have to tell you, this church paid a very heavy price over the years during the conflict. In 2003 there was a section of the church burned. But while the paint was bad and the burning was bad, worse than anything else was the loss of five people from this congregation. People who, because of the uniforms they wore – whether it be the uniforms of the RUC or UDR – were killed. The steps that Martin and I had been standing on were the same steps where five coffins of servicemen who had been killed by republicans were carried up. So it wasn't an easy thing that we were doing.

My congregation knew we'd met – they saw the pictures in the papers. There was no negative response in the beginning – although I got plenty of that later! My way of trying to take the people here with me – those who'd been hurt during the Troubles and who believed their church was not wanted – was to remind my congregation of the facts when I was preaching on Sundays. 'Folks, we're not in the middle of Ballymena. Nor are we in the middle of Bangor, surrounded by Prods and Presbyterians. We are a Presbyterian church virtually in the Bogside. So either we reach out and try to make friends with people who we perceive as our enemy, or I don't know where this church goes.'

That message got into people's minds and they'd have said to me, 'David, you know, it's helpful you telling us we're not in Ballymena and not in Bangor – we're in a different place here.'

Very few of my clerical colleagues would ever mention my friendship with Martin. But when the news of his illness became public – with shots of him at Stormont looking very ill in the back of the car, the rain on the car window – I started receiving messages from ordinary clergymen and former moderators. They'd ask, 'David, how's Martin? You're his friend, you would have the inside track on things.' I knew very little, but I said, 'You know, I'm very pleased you're asking and I'm going to pass on your good wishes to him.'

On one occasion I was sitting on a train going from Lisburn to Portadown, where my brother is in a nursing home. I'm just sitting reading the paper or a wee book or something. Then I feel someone at my shoulder. I look round and he tells me who he is. He had been the moderator of the Presbyterian Church maybe fifteen or more years ago. He said, 'David, I'm sorry to hear about your friend Martin. How is he? We're thinking about him.'

I remember saying this to Declan, Martin's brother, about these clergymen – senior churchmen, former moderators from all over Northern Ireland, people ringing me up, sending little text messages about him, and Declan said, 'David, there are clearly a lot of closet Martin fans.' They'd kept so quiet. I could count on one hand the number of Presbyterian ministers that would have made contact with me earlier on to say, 'David, we're quietly supporting what you do, it has to be done.' Very few. So I felt quite lonely. And I lost some church members as a result of my friendship with Martin.

The way in which our friendship shaped itself, there were occasions where I'd say, 'Martin, I'd like to say a prayer with you.' I still remember saying my first prayer with him – not the wording but the act of praying itself. We stood up in the living room of my house and held hands. I said the prayer. And when I'd finished he said, 'David, I can agree with every word you said.' It was incredible. I've shared that story with people and it's brought tears to their eyes. A teacher down in Bangor, for example. A principal in Coleraine. And other people. Then he bought me a book of prayers and I've used some of those prayers in my church.

***

I was the first Protestant minister to be invited to a Sinn Féin Ard-Fheis. That was 2011 – five years after our meeting. Some people thought going to the Ard-Fheis was just a daft thing to do. At the Ard-Fheis he welcomed me onto the stage and I described him as a true, great leader of modern times.

I came back the next morning from Belfast and I stopped at Tesco's in Antrim to buy a paper. And I saw the *News Letter* – a Belfast morning newspaper. The headline was 'Latimer Walks On Victims' Graves'. I can remember being glued to that headline. As I stared at it a woman came along, obviously wanting to buy a *News Letter*. I said to her, 'Here – take this. Read what they're saying about me!'

It hurt to see that some people thought that I'd behaved in a way that was just beyond recovery.

I don't know where those words I used at the Ard-Fheis came from. They weren't off-the-cuff words; they weren't naïve words. I am very happy with what I said, when I look back on it. I was looking at the kind of change in this man's life. I still marvel at it. I think of how we all struggle with New Year's resolutions – for a week, a fortnight, a month at the most. And here was a man who put his hand to the plough and didn't look back. He didn't fluctuate; he didn't hesitate. He was on a journey.

I was particularly impressed by Martin's friendship with Ian Paisley. I would have used this unlikely story to try to allow my tradition to appreciate that something extraordinary was happening here. Two enemies – Sinn Féin at one stage even had to be in a different room from the DUP when they were interviewed by the media! – but something was now happening here. They were maligned for the Chuckle Brothers thing, but my goodness, how I would like to see more of that relaxation amongst leaders now. Because it was sending ripples out into the community, causing people at least to stop and look and listen.

And then Martin showed his willingness to meet the queen – that was outstanding. We talked about that. He knew it wasn't going to be easy for him. He knew he'd have to convince his people. I said to him, 'If this doesn't happen, it's going to pull the blind down really on all that progress that we've been making.'

Afterwards, he said that the speech which the queen made should be read by everybody. The part where the queen talked about how, with historical hindsight, we can all see things that we would do differently – or not at all. So here were very powerful examples showing us that maybe bombs or bullets are not the most powerful weapon we have in society – it's talking to people, it's meeting people.

Martin had a very generous side to his nature. One Saturday morning – it was one of his last visits – he arrived at our house. Just bounced in through the door – it was lovely simply to have him around. And he had a lovely big colourful bunch of flowers for Margaret, my wife. Even the last time I saw him – which was a week before he died – he said, 'David, give my love to Margaret.' Powerful.

He visited once when my daughter was home. She's married to a Nigerian fella. They produced this lovely wee brown girl – gorgeous – she's called Gracie, she would have been about a year at the time. And Martin arrived this Friday afternoon to see me, because that's where we mostly met, at my house. Before we went into the room for a wee chat, I said, 'Martin, come on, you must meet my daughter and my wee grandchild.'

So he came in the door and there's Joanne, my daughter – she hadn't met him before – and she's sitting holding Gracie and Gracie sees this stranger come in. Martin takes one look and he says to the baby, 'Would you come to me?' And the baby went into his arms. And the baby did not cry. And we got photographs taken. It was wonderful.

Now I tell you that wee story because we had Martin Luther King III over here in 2013. Martin McGuinness was totally behind the initiative, which was to give young people a voice, and we're still at that. Anyway, there was a lady accompanying Martin Luther King III called Bennie – I can't recall her second name. But Bennie was a confidante of Dr King's wife, Coretta Scott King. And one of the things we did, when Martin Luther King III and his team came into Belfast, we took them to meet the first and deputy first ministers – Peter and Martin – down at the Castle. And they had croissants and we all had a chat.

And in the car on the way back, Bennie was in the back seat and she said, 'You know, I got a great feeling about Martin McGuinness. David, that man has got a good heart, a great heart!' I said, 'Bennie, I'd love you to tell him that, because we need each other.' She got the chance, a couple of days later, to share her feelings with Martin – and we're talking here about a woman who knows how to separate the wheat from the chaff. She got this lovely feeling having spent about an hour in Martin's company.

Martin enjoyed a wee laugh. When he relaxed he could engage in a bit of small talk. Our conversations were light-hearted on occasion: you'd have thought we were just two neighbours talking. On other occasions things would be happening and I would draw attention to things Sinn Féin were saying or how things were done or how they needed to be done. He was tuned in.

He never took a note. But if he promised me something, I didn't have to ring a second time. On one occasion there were a couple of Orangemen from North Belfast here. One of them said he knew Ian Paisley well. This was the burning question they asked about Martin: 'Can you trust him?' I said, 'I can.' And then I said, 'I'm going to tell you why I say that. Whenever he is with me, and no matter how trivial it is, if he says he's going to do things, he gets back. Or one of his staff gets back. It's done. In the Good Book that you guys and I would read, we're told that if somebody can be trusted with the little things, they can be trusted with the big things. Well, that's where I am with Martin.' And the big Orangeman who knew Paisley said, 'You make your point well.'

It's true, you know. That man was full of integrity. But I have to try to balance all this with people in here who've lost loved ones. And my only explanation is, I had the opportunity to discover that the man had another side to him. That was the side of Martin McGuinness I got to know and like.

On one occasion when he was leaving my house – our relationship was so informal and friendly and real – I said, 'Martin, I really value our friendship.' And, standing inside the front door of our house, he held onto my hand and said, 'David, I treasure our friendship.' It was powerful. He was a man who listened. He listened to Ian Paisley and he listened to people who were different to him. I honestly think one day somebody who controls everything put his hand on Martin's shoulder, and that was the beginning of a different direction that enabled Martin to do in the present what he knew was going to influence and shape the future.

I don't think I could have continued to be the minister of a church if I'd done this in any other place. This place is very unique, First Derry Presbyterian church. I think it's because of what they have experienced coming through the Troubles: the pain that has been visited here.

Some of my people who had remained quite quiet are now a little more vocal because we're having a presbytery visitation, which is a sort of church inspection. And the question is: What is our mission? What is our role? How can you justify a Protestant church in the Bogside? Rationally you can't. But yet it has a role. We've lost members – it's got smaller because of my reaching out. And I'm saying, 'Guys, maybe if I hadn't done what I have done, First Derry might be stronger.' And one man who lives out in New Buildings [a village a few miles from Derry] said, 'David, if you hadn't done what you did, hadn't reached out, First Derry would be closed.'

Other people have also said that the style of ministry, the outreach, the willingness to step out of our comfort zone is a necessity here. In other places there's maybe a greater comfort of having more of your own around you. We're here and really there aren't many churches like this.

Over the course of time, since my friendship with Martin became public, people have reacted to that. Those who were a wee bit shaky have either gone or they have steadied, recognising that David Latimer has done what's necessary to keep First Derry open, to keep it alive. I think some clergymen are probably a little worried what their congregation might think if they were to be open and supportive of me.

Being at the funeral and delivering my eulogy there re-opened some of the concerns that people had. There are people that told me I got the right balance in what I was saying, because I wanted to speak about Martin, but I was setting that within the context of the pain that many people experienced because of the IRA. Unfortunately there are some people who just cannot accept that Martin McGuinness could now be in a better place, as I suggested he was in my eulogy.

I had a lady come to see me from Newtownstewart – a lovely lady whose husband was killed by the IRA over twenty years ago. She was held by the group as they shot her husband and blew the air out of the four tyres of their car, with an eighteen-month-old and a four-year-old in the back of it. She said to me, 'David Latimer, are you playing God?'

So there are some people who find it hard to accept. But I was simply saying that by God's grace one day I will be with Martin McGuinness. I wouldn't say that if I didn't believe it was true, because Martin and I had some very personal and private conversations.

And my goodness, when I reflect on his funeral – I was speaking recently to a lady who was listening to it as it was streamed live into her kitchen in England. She said, 'David, I had to stop working. There was something about that funeral.' And I said, 'You felt that in your kitchen? I tell you, sitting in that church, there was an energy.' She says to me, 'It was the Spirit. It was God.' I do believe that the seeds of something were planted at that funeral and we will see the results of that at some point in the future.

***

People say there were two Martin McGuinnesses – the bad one and the good one. I think that however somebody starts off in life, it is not the end of their story. Only dead men and fools don't change. Dead men can't, fools won't. And Martin was neither. So change came about, but it was the same person in the same frame in the same city. He came to a point where he realised – and of course people can be cynical as to the reasons why the guns were decommissioned and all the rest of it – but there clearly came a day when it was seen that there was no need for these things any more. It was going to be language, it was going to be dialogue; it wasn't going to be bombs and bullets.

All through, it was the same man. His moral compass may have gotten lost at some stage, but I think he found it again. He made that change. Because every weed is a potential rose and every sinner is a potential saint.

I'm always invited down to the Bloody Sunday prayer service. For the 2017 prayer service I also had a service in Donegal that day, so I arrived a wee bit late. But I parked the car and weaved my way through the crowd. And unexpectedly, I saw Martin in front of me, so I tapped him on the shoulder. He turned round and his face lit up and we just embraced for quite a long time. He was looking good that day, though he was in the middle of his illness.

Back before Christmas 2016 I had been getting information that he wasn't well. Then I would have been sending him information. One of the texts I sent him – I was struggling to find something to encourage him and I wanted something from the Bible – said, 'Blessed are the peacemakers for they shall be called sons of God.'

I was with Eileen Paisley a month before Martin died and we were sharing our stories about him. She was showing me some of the texts she was sending Martin during his illness and I was sharing some of what I'd been sending him.

A week before he died, I sent a text to his phone and the reply came from his wife, thanking me for it and saying Martin was not answering his messages. Then I thought, 'I need to go up.'

So I went up to Altnagelvin hospital and into intensive care. I thought I'd see somebody in the wee waiting room but there was no one there. I wandered about and I didn't want to intrude. A nurse came along and I said, 'Would Mr McGuinness be in one of the wards?', and she says, 'I'll go and check.' I said, 'If there's some of his family there or his wife, just send her out – I just want to convey my good wishes.' So eventually this nurse said, 'Mr McGuinness is in a side ward. I'll go and talk to his brother who is there.' She came back out and said, 'They want you to come in.'

So I went in and Martin was in his bed with the trolley up and the little computer screen, and he was reading what the *Irish News* was saying about him. I went down the side by him and we held hands tightly and we talked. I shared with him my visit to Eileen Paisley and he said, 'David, they are good people.' I said, 'And Martin, you are a good man. Together you did wonderful things.' He asked about Margaret and we talked about some other things. Then I said, 'Martin, I want to pray with you.'

I don't think he knew he was going to die. I talked to him as if he was – I thought he was a very sick man. He said to me during the conversation, 'David, there is more still to do – more peace-building work, more political work, more still to do.' I was talking to him as I'd talk to anyone who was close to the end.

His brother afterwards took me to the door and said, 'David, there was no hesitation about Martin letting you in. You know, no one is getting in here outside of family. Not even Gerry Adams, and they were like brothers. But I wish I'd had my phone switched on, because that was a very special moment you had with Martin.'

I was emotional when I came out. I was shocked, I think, and disappointed. But where there's life there's hope. I continued, through Declan his brother, sending little updates and messages until the day before he died. The last text message I got was, 'David, the stats are good.' So it was all the greater the shock, him being gobbled up by that illness. His wife – I've been over to see her. I spent a lovely hour with her and Grainne and Fionnuala.

***

I remember when our church re-opened here in May 2011. Martin was a guest, along with Matt Baggott [chief constable of the PSNI between 2009 and 2014] and Seamus Hegarty, the bishop of Derry, as well as the Bloody Sunday people and the Claudy families. I invited Martin up to speak, then after him Matt Baggott. Everybody who heard them thought they must have been together writing those speeches, as their sentiments were so similar.

Afterwards, I'm out there talking to Martin. He's about to go when a man whose brother was shot by the IRA – a major in the UDR – walks towards us. I sort of went, 'Oh.' But there was no time to develop the 'oh', or do anything but watch what happened. This man whose brother had been killed by the IRA stretched his hand out and Martin stretched his hand out, and the guy from my church said, 'Martin, you spoke very well in church.'

And that same man, after the Ard-Fheis, when I was taking a fair bit of flak for going and speaking, the following morning that man threw his arms round me and said, 'David, if somebody forty years ago had done what you're doing, my brother Peter might still be alive.'

So those wee things, on a bad day – even in 2017 I hear of people being unhappy with things I've said – wee things like that give you a bit of wind for your sail to keep going.

I think Arlene Foster summed things up: we might never see the likes of him again. That was a very accurate statement and I was delighted it came from her lips. We may never see the likes of him again. He was a gift to peace-building. Once he embarked on that journey he did it so completely and fully that perhaps he himself came second. His job came first and his health suffered as a result of that.

I miss him – I can't believe he's gone. The election campaign is on right now and Sinn Féin's broadcast was on television the other night. At the end of it, there was a lovely picture of Martin with his date of coming into the world and his date of leaving the world. I could never have imagined the friendship that would evolve between us.

Mother and son: Peggy and Martin McGuinness, on Derry's walls, above the Bogside. *Courtesy of Mandy Harrison*

Wallflowers: Martin with all his siblings, in ascending age order. *Left to right*: John, Declan, William, Geraldine, Paul, Martin and Thomas. *Courtesy of the McGuinness family*

Hello in there: Martin campaigning in Derry for the Assembly elections in 1982. *Courtesy of Sinn Féin*

Protest: Martin confronts an RUC man at the funeral of IRA volunteer Henry Hogan in 1984. *Courtesy of Pacemaker*

Exit: Martin leaving Crumlin Road Prison in 1985.
Courtesy of Pacemaker

Would you look at this: Martin and Gerry Adams at the Sinn Féin
Ard-Fheis in 1986. *Courtesy of Sinn Féin*

Poster girls: the campaign for the 1987 Assembly election. *Front left*: Martina Given; *front right*: Patricia Carlin; *behind Patricia*: Caitriona O'Doherty; *holding the poster*: Monica McColgan – all from Gobnascale, Derry. *Courtesy of Jim Collins, Camerawork Darkrooms, Derry*

Serious talk: Gerry Adams and Martin at the funeral of IRA volunteer Patrick Kelly in 1987. *Courtesy of the Press Association (PA)*

Seeing eye to eye? Martin challenges an RUC officer during the 1997
Apprentice Boys march in Derry. *Courtesy of Hugh Gallagher*

A distinguished guest. Martin and wife Bernie with Nelson Mandela
during his visit to Ireland in 2003. *Courtesy of Sinn Féin*

Happy Together: Martin and Senator George Mitchell at Queen's University Belfast in 2015. *Courtesy of Queen's University Belfast*

The People's Parade: Gerry and Martin at a commemoration for the hundredth anniversary of the Easter Rising in Dublin. *Courtesy of Charlie McMenamin*

High Society: Martin with President Bill Clinton and John and Pat Hume on the Peace Bridge, Derry. *Courtesy of the Derry Journal*

Friendship: the Rev. David Latimer and Martin.
Courtesy of PressEye

The Past: Deputy First Minister Martin McGuinness and First Minister Ian Paisley return to their offices in Stormont in Belfast, 2007. *Courtesy of the Press Association (PA)*

The Future: Martin and Michelle O'Neill in January 2017.
Courtesy of Sinn Féin

14

Eileen Paisley

The two of them – Ian and Martin – were at loggerheads, the two parties were at loggerheads because of the situation that prevailed. But when the DUP became the largest party, Ian had already talked to John Hume. Some years ago he'd invited John Hume to our home and he came. Ian said to him, 'You know, John, you and I could run this country the very best, because you have the voice of the Catholic people and I would speak on behalf of the Protestant people.' And they did – they worked so closely together, the three in Europe [MEPs Hume, Paisley and James Nicholson, an Ulster Unionist]. John and him were always on good terms. John had an arrangement to meet with Sinn Féin and I remember Ian saying to him, 'John, if you do that, Sinn Féin will swallow you up.' And sadly, that's exactly what happened.

Ian said on his dealing with Sinn Féin that there were certain things they would have to agree on as a basis. These were support for the police, the courts of the country and law and order. If they signed up to that, they could start.

Tony Blair was meeting with Sinn Féin in America. He rang here several times in early 2007 and wanted to change the wording in relation to the three principles which Ian had laid down before agreement could be reached – support of the rule of law, support of the police and support of the courts. Tony Blair said, 'It still means the same thing.' Ian said, 'No it doesn't. That change makes a difference. The way I have it put, it safeguards everybody. And if they don't agree to that, the deal's off.' So they did agree to it.

When Martin McGuinness was minister for education, Ian wouldn't have met with him directly. As far as I remember we all met for the St Andrews talks in Scotland in October 2006. I wasn't involved with the talks, but I always went with Ian – I took notes and things like that, to help him. We met there but there wasn't much conversation – it was just meeting round the table with the other people involved.

The first time I spoke to Martin was when we were in New York in late November/early December 2007. We were in the Fitzpatrick Hotel. Martin came over to me in the lobby of the hotel. As he came over towards me I wondered, 'What's going to happen here?' I wasn't apprehensive, but I saw that he had taken the first step.

He asked, 'Do you mind flying?' That was his first question.

I said, 'No, I used to, but I realised I would never be out of Northern Ireland if I didn't get on a plane.' I said I happened to be reading in the Psalms one morning and I came across this verse – 'He shall cover thee with his feathers, and with his wings thou shall trust.' I said, 'Now it wasn't written about aeroplanes, away in David's time. But it was like God's message to me. Wherever you are, feathers speak of birds and flight. So if I'm in a flight, I'm as safe there as I am on the ground.'

He said his wife didn't like flying, and I said, 'Tell her to read that Psalm.'

I thought to myself at the time, 'This is a man and we're all the same in God's sight. We're all the same value to him. He doesn't value people because they are Protestants or Catholics or

Jews or Hindus or whatever. We're all the same – Christ died for everybody. This man is just the same as me. He's another human being, and I can't say I'm better than you are. Therefore, we need to talk.'

I was brought up along with Roman Catholic people. During the [Second World] war years, I was just a child. My father came from Lurgan and we'd Roman Catholic people who lived in the adjoining house. And our next neighbours round the lane were also Roman Catholics. When that lady next door was going into hospital to have a baby, my mother looked after her other wee boy – and looked after her husband, gave him his dinner every night. So they weren't any different to us – they were simply our neighbours. No matter who we are, we are each other's neighbours. Think of the story of the Good Samaritan and the two religious people who passed him by.

It did grieve me and still grieves me, the people who'd have been hurt in the conflict. There were wicked deeds done on both sides. People calling themselves Protestants and people calling themselves Catholics or whatever they were. Human nature is the same – we've all got that thing in us, if we are in a certain situation and brought up with a certain mentality of hatred. Although speaking for myself and I know speaking for Ian, we weren't brought up to hate people – but you hate what they did.

Martin McGuinness was just another person and if Ian was going to go into government with him, well, we had to do what was right. Ian knew it had to be done, and he thought along the same lines as I did. We've got an opportunity to save the country, to save lives. He hadn't the power before that, the power base. Once he got that, he knew he could do something.

If they signed on the dotted line regarding those three

principles, Ian had no difficulty. From the word go, they got on very well. Ian said to Martin the first morning they met, 'You and I could sit in here and fight it out. But that's not what I want.' And Martin said, 'That's not what I want either.' They both said, 'We want peace for all our people. Peace and prosperity for everybody in Northern Ireland, and to get back what we had.' They were both motivated to bring peace to the community, and every matter that came up they discussed it, talked around it, whatever differences they had they smoothed them out and came with a bright face to the people.

Of course they got called the Chuckle Brothers. We laughed at that – we thought it was hilarious. My reaction was, 'You've got a lot to chuckle about, really.' To bring the country from what it was – such opposites, north and south poles – to bring it together. I got more letters from people – businessmen from the south of Ireland who said it was such a joy to come to Northern Ireland now. Before when they came, there was that awful feeling and there was a depression, but now there was brightness.

***

In 2007 a young person, a friend of Martin and his family, took ill with cancer. Martin came in one morning and Ian said, 'You're very glum, Martin – is there something wrong?' And he said yes and told Ian the story. And Ian said, 'We'll just pray for her.' She was a young girl and she'd taken cancer and was to be married within the next year. And he did pray for her and Martin was very touched about that. Ian stood there and put his arm round Martin's shoulders and prayed for the girl.

Martin went home and told his family and the family of the girl. He came in the next day and said, 'Ian, my family and the people I told about it, they couldn't believe that you would pray for somebody you didn't even know.'

'I pray for scores of people I don't know and have never even met. But I just know that God can answer prayers,' Ian said.

I met Martin shortly after that and I was asking him about the girl and he said, 'Oh, she's coming on very well, but she's afraid that she might lose her hair.'

I said, 'Well that is a fear, and especially when she's planning to get married. But God can do more than you ask for.'

Some time later, I met Martin again at Stormont and he said this time, 'Do you remember I said about the girl being worried about her hair? Well, she hasn't lost one hair!'

I said, 'I told you what God can do.' And you know, she had a tremendous recovery, she was able to go ahead with her marriage and everything.

I met the whole family of the McGuinnesses at a function in Hillsborough Castle when a man from America presented the two of them and Peter Robinson with Peace Medals for achieving something. Normally they're given out to people from America and in America. But he thought these three people were worthy of it, and he came over and they had the ceremony here. It was a great night. I met Martin's wife and family then. It was no problem at all, because I remember when Martin's mother died Ian and I were in London and somebody phoned us and told us. Ian got on the phone to Martin and prayed with him on the phone. Then I spoke to him and gave him my sympathy as well. He said he was very touched and the family were very touched and it meant a lot to them.

The relationship was unique. It was something I would never have dreamed could have happened. And I don't think Ian would have thought it could happen either. The party was all right at Stormont and Westminster. There were some people in the party who were totally opposed to it, but the majority gave him their backing because what alternative do you have? Whenever you saw Martin as a terrorist, there wasn't any way you would have thought of coming in touch with him or being friends with him. But when you saw him as an ordinary man – who saw, I think, the destruction that was being done, and then realised that he could remedy it – it was different.

They worked together and I think working together brought them together. Martin was always very cooperative with Ian. And on that trip to America, I must say he was very solicitous towards Ian. It was very icy weather there – snow and ice – and he'd say, 'Just be careful, don't fall.' And he would hold his coat for him and do things like that. It was just bringing out the good in people, that's what Ian did. I've seen it in the church with young people. Young fellows getting a bit wild. You know the way.

There was one lady who came and said, 'My wee boy is a bit unruly.' Somebody caught him one day taking a penknife and carving something on one of the pews. So after church one morning, Ian went to him and said, 'Son, I have a wee job and I think you could do it for me – would you like to help me?'

'Oh yes, Mr Paisley – oh yes!' That changed his life – he became a prison officer.

And another fellow who was really wild, Ian said to his father, 'Send him up to our house at nine o'clock tomorrow morning.' And he sent him up and that fellow became a totally different fellow through contact with Ian – it changed his life.

But young people got so easily caught up in trouble. There

were people who came from otherwise good, working families, they just got caught up by older people who thought that this was just very adventurous, and before they knew it they were caught up in the Troubles. I think that's what happened to an awful lot of people – including Martin.

***

I think there was a quietness and shyness about Martin. He was good company – interesting to talk to. I don't know – I think they saw each other as they really were, underneath, beyond what was on the outside. I think some Protestant people saw Ian and Martin's friendship as somehow giving in to the IRA. But Martin lost a lot of friends on his side and Ian lost a lot of friends too. Ian believed your country is the people who live in it and we have to share it. We go into the same shops – you don't walk in and see somebody with a label saying 'I'm a Catholic' or 'I'm a Protestant'. They're just people. I think Martin realised he had been misled and had taken a wrong path.

I do think some people in the party thought they were too close as friends – the friendship was too much for them to take. I don't know why, because Ian was never opposed to people for their religion. He would have been opposed to people on both sides for being involved in terrorism – he had no time for that. But I expect some people did think it was too close. Some people in the party and in the church just couldn't take it. They couldn't see what Ian saw.

Not everybody sees things the same way. But then maybe they're not talking to people from across the board – they're keeping in the same wee clique. It's like the man who Christ touched his eyes and asked him what did he see, and he said, 'I see men as trees.' And he touched him again to make him see clearly. I think a lot of people need to be touched again. They don't see others as human beings like themselves, with the same wants, the same anxieties and everything else.

Martin rang here one day. I think he just missed Ian's company in Stormont. There wasn't the same rapport between Peter Robinson and Martin as there was between Ian and Martin. So he phoned one day and asked if it'd be all right if he came to visit. And I said that certainly it would. So he came up here, saw Ian and they had a very nice chat together. Ian wasn't too well at that point – though he was not in his last illness at that stage. Martin wasn't uneasy at all – he came in and I welcomed him and made him some tea or coffee, and they had a great chat. They talked about a lot of things. They had the country in common, and people in common. And Martin, despite everything else, was a family man. And Ian was a family man, so they had that as well. And I had no difficulty talking to Martin's sons and daughters and wife – they were very friendly. They were just people to me and I was glad to meet them.

When Ian died, Martin phoned me. He said, 'I know the funeral is in your house and strictly private, but I would love to come up and see you. Would that be all right?' So I said, 'Yes, Martin, that would be all right – come on up.'

Ian died on Friday 12 September 2014 and Martin came up on Saturday. Ian's coffin was in the dining room. He came in and saw us and then he went over there and stood over the coffin and bowed his head and said a prayer – he had tears in his eyes. I wouldn't have turned him away because I knew his friendship was genuine. He listened to what Ian said – from a spiritual point of view as well. But I think what brought them together was the fact that every day, every morning as soon as they met, Ian prayed with him. There was no particular prayer – Ian would have prayed a practical prayer. Whatever was the problem for that day, they would ask for God's guidance and His wisdom. I think Martin saw that he was genuine, that it wasn't just from the lips out; he was talking to God personally. Ian would stand and pray and Martin would listen.

A niece of mine and her husband were here when Martin called after Ian's death. I said to them, 'If you would like to meet with Martin McGuinness, he's here – I just wanted to let you know.' So they said they would like to meet him and they did.

***

One night my daughter Rhonda and I were watching the news on television and I said to her, 'Martin McGuinness – he doesn't look too good.' And she said, 'I was thinking that too. He's failed and he's not as bright as he was.' A week or two later the news broke about him having to get treatment.

I contacted him and sent him a text. And throughout his illness we kept in touch. I sent him texts and he sent me texts. My first was to say we were all very sorry to hear of his illness and we would pray for him. And he'd text me back and tell me how he was and about the treatment he was receiving. And if I sent him a text and hadn't heard from him in a few days, we'd know there was something wrong. We'd send him nice wee lines that I'd come across in my own spiritual reading, and he was always very grateful, said that was lovely and very encouraging. So we kept in touch. In the last wee while we knew he couldn't respond.

Just before he stepped down from Stormont, Martin and a

few others were down in the basement in Stormont – coming from the restaurant, maybe. And there was a reporter – I think he was from the BBC – and Martin was walking along and this guy caught up with him and went to speak to him. And he heard a voice saying, 'Leave him alone!' And he looked round and it was Ian Junior. And Ian said, 'Leave him alone – the man's not well. Don't be pushing to interview him.'

All our family had the same warmth towards Martin – including my son Kyle in England. And my two elder girls – they talked to him normally as well. In fact, he came to the library one day [a library housing Ian Paisley's personal collection of 55,000 books] – and we took him on a tour. It wasn't open before Ian died, but it was set up – Ian saw the beginnings of it before he took ill. He was very pleased. He said to me years ago, 'When anything happens to me, I don't want all my books scattered to the four winds. I would like them to be available to other people who can't afford books or who would like to read books.'

***

I think he was always the same Martin McGuinness, but his life was changed. You can only speak of people as you find them. People say things about other people and you think, 'Is that really true?' But before you ask 'Is that really true?', you sort of believe what they tell you. People tell you, 'Don't have anything to do with that man' – and then when you meet them you find they're completely different.

Martin was always well-mannered and courteous. He could reach out to people in a way that not everybody could do. When people see a different side of a person – I mean people would have seen Ian as all sorts of things, but whenever they saw the real person, what he really was, what motivated him, then their attitude changed. And I think that's what happened between Martin and Ian. They saw each other as they really were.

I don't think either man could have acted and pretended a friendship – you'd see through that. I've seen too much of it – people acting for their own ends. I really don't think Martin acted the part – I really don't. Of course there were people thought he was doing an act for his own ends. People who didn't know him or never got to meet him. And of course they'd say the same about Ian, that he'd done what he did for his own ends. But Ian wasn't interested in his own ends. If he'd been interested in his own ends, he wouldn't have done a lot of the things he did. And I think Martin McGuinness was just fed up with all the bloodshed and the awful atmosphere it was causing. I think he saw it wasn't doing anyone any good, it was only causing chaos and mayhem and broken hearts and broken homes. And I think Ian's influence on him was a thing that brought out the best in him – just a kind word or a kind deed can make all the difference to another person.

I think your life is enriched when you open your mind and heart to see other people as they really are. People do enrich your life one way or the other. If you are kind to somebody else and they respond, it does enrich your life. Some people don't appreciate friendship, but I think Martin McGuinness did.

People can say what they like after death, but you can't judge a dead person – you can only judge them by what they did in their life. You see it all the time in church life – what people were and what they can be. I just saw Martin differently when we got to know him.

At the bottom of it all, he must have had regrets about what had happened in the past. It's not by their words that you know another person; it's by their deeds, their actions. And his actions certainly changed. I was just glad to see the difference in him that the friendship made. I think Ian made a difference with his friendship, praying for him and praying with him and all that. Martin's appreciation of that was genuine.

The BBC interviewed me the day Martin died. Some people weren't pleased, although most of the messages I got, and Kyle and Ian and the rest of the family received, said they were very pleased and happy with what I said. At the bottom of it all is the fact that it's your responsibility to do your best for other people, no matter who they are or how deeply they've fallen.

We keep in mind the families that suffered and will always suffer. And that follows generations – children and grandchildren. But despite that I can only speak of a person as I find them. And that's how I found Martin McGuinness.

Just as Martin said on Ian's death that he'd lost a friend, I would say the same at Martin's death. He was friendly, he showed friendship and he returned friendship, and I think that was a quality. You can show friendship to some people but they're still not friendly. Martin showed friendship.

15

James T. Walsh

I met Martin first on a trip to Belfast in 1995. We met with all of the parties at Queen's University when President Clinton spoke and the congressional delegation of which I was a member met with the UUP, the SDLP and Sinn Féin. Martin participated in that. I think it was Gerry Adams, Martin and Pat Doherty who attended the meeting for Sinn Féin. Subsequently, when we went to Belfast, we'd meet at Sinn Féin headquarters or at the Europa Hotel. But we met first in Queen's University.

I was learning rapidly at the time about the politics of Northern Ireland – you could say I was drinking from a fire-hose. I'd never been to Ireland before and was really a novice as far as Irish affairs were concerned. I'd heard of John Hume and I'd heard of Gerry Adams because we'd backed President Clinton granting him a visa to come to the United States, but I hadn't met Martin until then.

What struck me first was – superficially – his good looks. Here was this handsome, curly-haired young guy. Of course I was a relatively young guy at the time too. But he struck me at first as just a likeable, handsome Irish politician.

When we sat down to talk, what impressed me was the discipline of thought that he had. His job was to go round and smile and win over the Americans, but then we sat down and talked about what would happen next and what they really wanted. The answer was 'Peace with justice.' It was Gerry said that. I remember asking Trimble what he wanted to get out of the peace process and he said, 'Peace.' But with the Shinners, it was 'Peace with justice.' A very clear divide.

What I always knew about Martin revolved around Bloody Sunday and his alleged involvement in the IRA as Derry commander. So when I met him I expected a harder demeanour. Instead, I was struck by his common touch; however, there was also a feeling that beneath the velvet glove there was a steely discipline. When he was talking about what republicans wanted from the agreement, it was clear there was a military discipline there.

That first meeting wasn't lengthy. He was just going round the room, shaking everybody's hand and making introductions. If he had some experience in common with any of the figures, he would say something about it. Typically if he heard you were from New York, he would ask about some certain individual from New York who was known to him – that sort of thing. Always trying to make creative links with the other person.

He had a unique way about him. In contrast, Gerry is sterner. His voice is serious, his face is serious, his demeanour is serious. Martin could be in the middle of a very tight engagement and he would sort of chuckle or laugh and make some sort of off-handed comment or mention a story that broke the tension a little bit. He was really good at that.

***

Martin didn't talk about his childhood or his time in the IRA. I met with him many, many times, but it was usually business with a few pleasantries. We had a common bond in that we both enjoyed fishing and would almost always start with that.

I probably was the one who initiated the fishing link. I told him how on my visits to Ireland I always looked for opportunities to find a stream, get half a day when I could break away. I told him about an experience I had when I fished one time up in Donegal and it was a stream he knew in the Buncrana area. So that was a bond. We would trade stories. Fishermen tell stories – that's what they do. And we had that in common – we'd swap stories, places to go and so on. There's something magical about standing in a stream and hearing nothing but the flow of the river. We shared that; there was an affinity.

When you're a politician, everyone is looking for answers or has criticism or whatever. But you can find rest and peace in the middle of a stream or a river. There's a wonderful sense when you feel the water swirling round you, when you can't hear anything but the water. The only thing that matters is what is happening at the end of that line.

My fishing trip with him was a kind of coincidence, really. We'd talked about it for years. When I was in Ireland, he was always busy with politics, and when he came over to the US, he never came to upstate New York. But this one time he was going to address the national Ancient Order of Hibernians [AOH] in Rome, New York, which is very close to Syracuse. So when Rita O'Hare [the Sinn Féin representative in the US] told me Martin was going to be in New York in July 2012, I asked if I could have half a day with him. Rita was travelling with him and she said, 'Of course.'

So he gave his address to the AOH, I drove down from Syracuse and picked him up in Rome. The two of us drove up through the countryside on the interstate. He wanted to see the countryside, the homes and the towns and the villages – he'd never been there. It was so rural, that's what struck him. We drove up the north side of Oneida Lake, through these small towns and villages to a place called Pulaski. I took him to the fish-hatchery there, which is what they use to stock the stream. I got a guy from the New York State Department of Rural Conservation to give us a tour of the facility and then we went to the fly-fishing section and fished for probably two or three hours. We stood in the middle of the water, just the two of us.

I have a picture of Martin from that day that answers the question about whether fly-fishing for Martin was a social event or a solitary activity. In the photograph he is totally focused on the fly rod and the water. I took the picture myself and I'm not a great photographer, but I captured it: that sense of the solitary.

We fished together and apart that day. I gave him my rod. I had a smaller rod and I wanted him to have the better rod. And this guy from New York state tended to both of us, made sure we were doing the right thing, giving us tips as if it were a sort of coaching environment. So we would fish back and forth – we were within shouting distance of each other most of the time. We fished probably a quarter-mile stretch of the river. We didn't have a whole lot of luck that day. Martin caught one salmon trout – just a small one. At that time the fish weren't migrating so the fishing was very slow.

And after we'd fished we went down to the village where we had lunch. I remember they asked him what he wanted to drink and he ordered pineapple juice. I'd never heard anyone order pineapple juice in my life. I said, 'Does it remind you of home, is pineapple juice a drink in Ireland?' And he said, 'No, it's just something I wanted to try.'

After that I called a fella by the name of Doug, who was a US ambassador to one of the Caribbean countries. He was a big Republican, he was in the Bush administration, he had been a senator and he owned about two and a half miles of this river – from the estuary up to about two miles. We actually didn't fish that part, but I wanted him to meet Martin.

So we drove down to Doug's house. He took us out in a four-wheel vehicle and he gave Martin a turn at driving. I have a picture of Martin driving – a pretty good picture. Doug showed us the grounds and talked about the fishing. Then we drove down to the airport at Syracuse, met Rita and that was it.

But that day, searching for fish, he was in another place, no question. As soon as he was rigged up – he had the rod and a fly, and everything was in order – he was somewhere else.

In addition to being a fisherman, Martin was a poet. I am not a poet (although I've had my attempts), but he was. And he wrote about the fly-fishing experience. I actually have some of his poetry. He wrote one poem that I have somewhere and the title was 'The Last of the Mohicans'. It was interesting to me as an American. It was about trout – his concern was that the sea trout as a species was dying out because of fishing and farming and those sorts of things.

On the trip, he talked about his wife and family, his kids. I'd always heard he was very dedicated to his family. He would go home every single night no matter where he was. If he were in Cork or Belfast, he'd go home to Derry.

***

What I really liked was that, although he was at a much higher level in his government, we had a lot in common. We were both

Roman Catholics and I'm 100 per cent Irish, so I saw myself in him. I often wondered – and we talked a bit about this – how I would have responded to the oppression that he saw. Would I have involved myself in the opposition, if I had lived in Ireland, or would I have stayed away? It was always a quandary for me as to how I would have reacted. So I was always interested in how he got involved in the IRA. He talked about that but only in a marginal way. He just talked about the lack of freedoms available to people and that it was something anyone would have found oppressive.

I always tried, as best I could, to show an even hand. At different times I took unionist politicians like Peter Robinson, Jeffrey Donaldson, Reg Empey and the McGimpseys on tours of the Capitol, or met with them in my offices. I did this because I knew that all Americans are seen as green, so it was really essential. One of the key factors in the peace process was that when we were bringing the Irish politicians over to the United States – the unionists, the nationalists and the republicans – they would all feel a little freer to talk in the US. I really wanted to facilitate that and not build walls between people.

I don't think they had any idea of the depth of my relation-ship with Martin. In fact, it was as deep as relationships can be. I really admired him and I liked him personally, I liked what we had in common and I had respect for him. Here was a man who had dedicated his entire life to his country.

At the same time not everybody liked him. There were several foreign service department people who had no use for him. We met with Michael Portillo one time, John Major's foreign minister or defence minister, I can't remember which. He argued that McGuinness was bloody, he was an IRA fighter, he was a terrorist. Portillo was talking to a group of American members of Congress in Parliament Buildings in London at the time – no Sinn Féiners were around. I don't know if Portillo ever met him or just knew him by reputation. But he was the only person I ever met who really disparaged him. He was strongly opposed to the IRA in general and Martin specifically.

Martin could get frustrated. There were times we would meet in Dublin or Belfast or London and he'd give his thoughts on the positions that the British took. He would have a reaction to those things. Like, 'That is ridiculous!' or 'Is that realistic?' or 'They need to get real with things.' That sort of reaction. I never saw him visibly angry but certainly unsettled and not pleased with some of the things we were hearing back. But he didn't strike me as a man who carried a grudge from losses in the Troubles.

In 2001 Gerry Adams announced in Ireland and Martin announced in the US that the IRA had decommissioned. He asked me to stand next to him at that time and I considered that a real honour. I thought, 'This is a momentous time, and he's doing it in my country and I'm the American politician that's standing next to him.'

He and Gerry were both very strategic in their decisions. Things weren't staged, but they definitely knew how they wanted things to be produced. I think because I had always been supportive of the process he wanted me to be there. I don't know exactly why I was there – perhaps I lent credibility to what they were saying, but either way I was deeply honoured to stand next to him at that time. Maybe it was a reward to me and the other members of Congress who were there, for the time and energy and passion we'd put into that peace process.

***

I heard about his illness first, I think, from Rita O'Hare. He had looked ill, and I don't know if somebody had raised it publicly or not, but he had lost so much weight it was pretty obvious something was wrong. I talked to Gerry a couple of times about it, and while he said Martin was very sick, he also said the prognosis was good and that they were certain he would recover.

It was an emotional blow when I heard of his death. I was in Ireland at the time and I heard it on the radio. I was working with Syracuse Airport, and we were trying to build a bridge to one of the Irish airports – Cork, Dublin, Shannon, Belfast – get flights from Ireland to Syracuse. So we were in a car between Shannon and Dublin, in the middle of a snowstorm – a lot like back home – and I heard it on the radio. I was just dumbstruck. And the driver said, 'Yes – didn't you know? It was announced last night, it happened last night.'

I was devastated by the news. I knew he was getting close to the end of his public life and I knew he was looking forward to his private life – spending time with his family, being in Derry and maybe travelling and talking to people about the peace process. Maybe fishing and getting back to his favourite haunts on the rivers. He wasn't going to have that now.

***

I always thought of Martin as a very pragmatic person. He did what he had to do to meet the goals of the republican movement. What I saw throughout the process was that it was the hardliners, the fighters, who made the difference. Once they decided that the situation would never be resolved militarily, that's when the peace process began. And I think Martin, Gerry, the Sinn Féin leadership and probably the IRA made the calculation that this would never, ever be resolved militarily. No one could win: the Brits couldn't win; the IRA couldn't win. Neither was ever going to end it and the collateral damage to society wasn't worth the fight any more. I really think they came to that conclusion and that's what changed him. Up until then it was, 'We're going to fight and win our freedom.' Once they made that calculation and went from the bullet to the ballot, they were all behind it.

I don't know if religion entered into it – although Martin was a very religious man. War versus peace – all those issues he had to deal with as a soldier. But it was a political calculation that they switched gears and went from the bullet to the ballot. Look at Ecclesiastes: there is 'a time for war, and a time for peace'.

Martin was a man for all seasons, really: I think that's the best way I could describe it. He was excellent in everything that he did. He was a first-rate dad and husband; he was as good a politician as I've ever met. I don't know about his soldiering abilities, but what was really amazing about him was his common touch – his ability to reach across and to connect with Ian Paisley – meet the opposition halfway in a process that took many years. He and Gerry always knew how far they could step forward without alienating their base – it always was a careful assessment.

I feel that my life was enhanced by my friendship with Martin. Absolutely, no question. I've met a lot of important people over the years and I'd say he was one of the most significant people with whom I have ever interacted. I really admired him. It's ironic, given that I consider myself a man of peace, yet I admire someone who was a fighter. But when you consider the commitments that he made for his community and native freedoms, I can't fault him. He ultimately realised that the bullet was not the way to peace and freedom; it was the democratic process.

I have no doubt he will be remembered in history. I consider the Irish peace process one of the most significant foreign policy successes for the US in the last fifty, maybe the last hundred years. I think the role the US played was significant. It was bipartisan, even-handed, clever. We sent our best people over there.

I think what Martin will be remembered for is the turn away from violence towards democratic principles and towards peace. And for his ability to reach across the aisle and make friends and a confidant out of an enemy, as he did with Paisley. Those photos of Paisley and McGuinness together, laughing – there are lessons for the world there.

16

Eamonn MacDermott

My father was a very staunch republican. He was also a doctor here in Derry and he used to treat a lot of IRA men who were injured. He was very conscious that if a republican was shot or injured the automatic reaction would be to take him to Letterkenny hospital, but my father was a doctor first and foremost and didn't want somebody dying because some nineteen- or twenty-year-old had decided to take him to Letterkenny. So in the more serious cases he had to make it very clear that it was his call – if he said it was going to be Altnagelvin hospital in Derry, not Letterkenny in Donegal, then Altnagelvin it was going to be. He went to Martin McGuinness, for whom he had a lot of time, and explained that it had to be his call. Martin's response was 'No problem.'

So my father used to be back and forth to the Bogside and I'd go with him in the car. I would have been about thirteen or fourteen years of age. The house of Barney McFadden [a veteran Derry republican] was the unofficial headquarters and my father would go to Barney's house. I would be sitting there, surrounded by all these IRA men going in and out. I loved it! And Martin would have been around then too – this was during the no-go era: 1971–72.

He stood out in terms of his friendliness. He would always speak to me. I was in the corner overawed by all these big IRA men, but Martin always spoke to me. When he knew I was the doctor's son, he'd chat and ask what I was up to, was I still at school, things like that.

He also stood out in that there was an air about him. He had charisma. You noticed him more than you noticed the others. In all the forty-odd years I knew Martin, he had no airs and graces about him. You never would have thought, 'This is a big IRA man.'

Martin got as much abuse and slagging as anybody else. Nobody bent the knee or anything. I remember years later talking to a prominent Belfast IRA man about the first time he met Martin. He didn't understand Martin's personality. They were talking and Martin said, 'I think this would be a better way to do this' – whatever it was – and the guy said, 'No, no, no!' Then Martin said, 'I really think this would be better.' And it went on about four times, this guy arguing. Eventually someone else said, 'This isn't a discussion – Martin is telling you what to do, but he's doing it in a nice way.' His words would have the force of authority and people responded. But I never found him overbearing.

I'd love to say I saw in him then what he was to become, but the honest answer is that I didn't. You were impressed when you saw him taking part in press conferences with Seán MacStíofáin and others. But it'd be a lie if I claimed I said, 'This boy's going to go far.' To us he was always an ordinary figure and he acted like an ordinary figure. Later on, when I was a republican and would meet him, he was still ordinary. He would almost worry about us. We were sixteen- and seventeen-year-olds, running about. If you ran into Martin or were in the same house, he always was that wee extra bit concerned: 'Now, yis know what you're doing, you know where you're going?' Even though it wasn't his business –

he was way up at a different level – he'd still be concerned for you. Your welfare mattered to him.

The no-go area of the Bogside was totally self-contained and the IRA operated openly. After the no-go area went, he was on the run. He was arrested in Donegal and got six months in prison. Then he came out and was on the run again, up until the ceasefire in 1975. When he was on the run he'd be in different places. He'd be in Buncrana – the Provos had a couple of houses down in Buncrana; he'd be in other parts of the country, in places I wouldn't be privy to, and then he'd be in Derry. He would go up and down, over the border and back.

One of my motivating factors for joining the IRA was the fact that there was a major conflict going on and I felt it wasn't enough to simply watch. You had to take sides. My father was very republican, so it wasn't a major leap. I was slightly different to other volunteers in that I was middle class. It wasn't happening outside our house and if I'd chosen to I could have remained oblivious to it. But I didn't believe in that.

During the no-go area time, Derry was very different, clear-cut – the population versus the state. There was very little sectarianism, in my view. And that's one thing I'd give Martin credit for – he always did what he could to keep the lid on sectarianism. There were very few sectarian killings in Derry. There was a period where there was a UDA man shot and then a Catholic shot, another UDA man shot and a Catholic shot. But the IRA response was measured and Martin would have been behind that. 'No, boys, we're not going to get into that game.' He would hope you would see the point – we're not sectarian, the IRA is not a sectarian organisation, we're not getting into playing sectarian games.

He was at the press conferences around this time and was then brought with the delegation to the Cheyne Walk talks. So people had recognised the qualities of leadership that he had. He inspired great loyalty because of his ordinariness. As things progressed and he became a politician, a lot of stuff that republicans were biting their tongues over, people would say, 'Well, Martin's OK with it', and that gave you a certain amount of reassurance.

Obviously the qualities that I found in Martin, other people saw too. And he had the ability to bring people with him. He was one of the Young Turks of 1975 when the Dublin leadership was discredited [due to the lack of political progress after the IRA ceasefire in January 1975, which resulted in considerable demoralisation within republicanism]. You had the coming together of people like Gerry Adams, Danny Morrison and Martin in Derry, who were basically taking control of the north. Martin was second-in-command in Derry. Nominally there was somebody ahead of him, but I never heard of the guy until years later.

Martin didn't have the Long Kesh experience, of meeting up with others there. But he did have a way with him. After Operation Motorman, he was moving in circles higher than just Derry. He'd be travelling to Belfast, down over the border. He wasn't based in Derry and he wasn't on the Derry Brigade staff.

He had a good brain. When you heard him talking, you knew what he was about. Where there were disputes about what to do, Martin could be very succinct. 'Hold on. If we do this, that'll happen, and would that be worth it?'

When I joined the IRA it was full of very strongly opinionated people – they had to be to make the decision to join the IRA. They used to have fierce arguments – what should we do about this, what do we want to do about that? Martin could cut through the arguments: 'Naw, houl' on a minute, boys,' he'd say. 'Youse are at the wrong end of this thing here. Let's look at this.' And then you'd think, 'Oh, well yes, I suppose.' You could argue with him, but in the end he was probably right.

I have never seen 'Martin the Enforcer'. People talked about the ruthless, cold person, but in all my life I don't think he ever said to me, or to anybody, 'You're going to do this.' He always had a nice way of going about things.

The IRA could have adopted much more brutal tactics than they did. To Martin's credit, with the commercial bombing campaign in Derry, there was nobody killed in that campaign. That was quite some achievement because they blew this town from one end to the other and back again, but no civilian was ever killed. Martin's humanity shone through. If someone said, 'Oh, we could get two soldiers in that house!' Martin would say, 'What about the people in that house?'

I remember talking to a loyalist in jail and he said, 'If we had been you lot, we'd have been twice as bad as you. If there was a bar with one republican in it, we'd have blown up the whole bar.' With the republicans there was the Dropping Well pub bombing – though that was the INLA – and in England there was Guildford and Birmingham – but here the IRA never really got into that as a pattern.

I don't think he was in charge in Derry at the time of Patsy Gillespie. [In 1980 Gillespie, a local man who worked as a cook in a British Army base, was killed along with five British soldiers when the IRA strapped him into a van loaded with explosives and forced him to drive it to an army checkpoint where it detonated.] I think he was at a much higher echelon by that time.

People who talk about incidents like that don't understand how the IRA worked or don't want to understand. The levels Martin was at then – he probably heard about Patsy Gillespie when it came on the news the next morning. Maybe because of the nature of it they might have run it past the higher echelons, but the IRA worked in very autonomous units – you did the job and that was it – the leadership found out about it when it came on the news. It was a Derry Brigade job. And the IRA made it quite clear – you work in an army base, you are a target. You may disagree with that, it's terrible, but it's quite clear.

Following Martin's death, you'd think he knew about every single incident. That's not the way the IRA worked. And at the early stages, there was that much happening, there was no way of keeping track of it. I remember reading things in the paper and asking, 'Was that us?' And the O/C or whoever would say, 'Aye, that was us.' Up until the ceasefire of 1975, there was no real coordination. Yes with big operations, but that was not the case with the day-to-day operations.

***

My typical picture of Martin would be of him coming in the back door of some house I'd be in. We'd be there for some totally different reason and Martin would just appear. This would be in 1976 when he was off the run. Sometimes if he was in to see one specific person, he'd give what they call 'the republican nod', and him and the person would go off and have their confab, then off he'd go again. Other times he'd sit down and ask what we were up to, maybe give his tuppence-ha'pennyworth. But my memory would be of him coming in the back door: oops, there he is.

Conversation wouldn't stop when he came in. The IRA was a very democratic organisation – your stripes didn't matter much on a day-to-day basis. The fact that he was Martin McGuinness didn't really feature.

He always tried to keep his family separate, away from publicity. Martin and Bernie got married in 1974 and had the children fairly soon after. But Martin had this thing about keeping family separate, and there was very little reporting at the time about Bernie and the children. Which I always thought was admirable.

I knew his wife, his family and I knew where he lived. Which used to cause us some concern because it was a vulnerable spot. A couple of years later when I was in jail, we were forcibly being integrated with loyalists and one Derry loyalist told me that the Brits told them on one occasion, 'If youse want to hit his house, the checkpoint on the bridge will be open from six to seven o'clock.' This guy's story was that they didn't do it because Martin had a wife and children. I don't know whether that's true – I'd think they were just too cowardly to do it. He lived just beside the City Cemetery, which was very accessible. He used to be out walking and we'd say to him, 'Martin, what are you doing?'

I was in jail from 1977 to 1992. [MacDermott and Raymond McCartney, both from Derry, were sentenced for killing an RUC officer. In 2011 the UK Supreme Court cleared both men of the charge.] During that time I was watching things from afar. By 1978–79, the northerners had started taking control of the IRA. There was a feeling that the north was fighting the war, so the north should be running the war, rather than somebody in Dublin who was talking about the Second Dáil [which convened in Dublin from 1921–22 and ratified the controversial Anglo-

Irish Treaty, thus agreeing to Irish partition]. The Second Dáil didn't mean a wild lot to republicans in the north – it wasn't top of our agenda. The feeling was, we're the ones doing the fighting, so we're the ones should be making the decisions.

So we watched Adams, McGuinness, Tom Hartley. During the blanket protest, we looked to them to back us up, but we were very rebellious. We were the ones living in those conditions. We would do what they told us if it suited us. And the hunger strike – I don't think Gerry Adams could have stopped the hunger strike, even if he'd wanted to. The old republican tradition is that you can't be ordered on a hunger strike, but equally you can't be ordered off a hunger strike. I think if Gerry Adams had sent a message, 'Call off the hunger strike now', it would have been 'Sorry but no, Gerry.'

Martin was viewed by the prisoners in the same way. We argued bitterly in the jail about the move into politics. You also had the Belfast–Derry thing. The Belfast guys would slag us about Martin when he ran against John Hume in the 1982 Stormont election and won a seat but came second to Hume. I mean, God himself running against John Hume would have had difficulty. But the Belfast ones would say, 'Ach, Adams'll run against him – Adams'll show him!' Of course Adams never did, but that's another story.

But we recognised Martin was going in a particular direction, and it wasn't a direction we were particularly sold on. However, when they did well in 1982 for Jim Prior's Assembly [Sinn Féin won five seats], there was a great feeling of elation. We still weren't 100 per cent happy with the road they were going down, but we were happy that they won seats.

Adams and McGuinness were looked on as co-equals. At

the time they were moving into politics, my brother – who was a reporter – was covering a press conference in the Guildhall. And it was Adams and McGuinness, the two of them. So our Donal – my brother – asked some question of Adams and Adams said, 'That's a question you'd have to ask the IRA.' So Donal, quick as a flash, says, 'OK – Martin?' Everybody there just burst out laughing. That's how it was. Adams was spearheading the political thing, while Martin was attending to the military side.

Martin seemed to have some respect for Hume. You see, Hume never did a Gerry Fitt [the leader of the SDLP before John Hume]. Hume knew that if there was a soldier shot dead at the bottom of some street, that the vast bulk of his constituents weren't particularly upset. So he'd issue a nice bland statement – 'There's no room for violence on our streets', or something like that. But he never alienated the people of the Bogside or Creggan. He annoyed them occasionally, but he never came out with that personal condemnation that Fitt did. So relations between Martin and Hume stayed at the level of civility. Hume could still pick up the phone and ring Martin and Martin could pick up the phone and ring Hume. There was never that breach there was with Fitt. No self-respecting republican spoke to Fitt at the end, while Martin and Hume never closed off the line of communication. Hume never went too far. Eamonn McCann wrote about it when he said that the wee woman who would vote Hume religiously would have the Armalite under the bed.

***

Martin's success as a politician when he moved in that direction wasn't a surprise in that when he set his mind to doing something he did it right – 'OK, we're going to do politics, and we're going to do politics the way politics should be done.' Martin's aim and objective in life was to achieve a united Ireland, and for twenty or thirty years he thought the way to achieve that was, in his own words, through 'the cutting edge of the IRA'. The same man, with the same aims and objectives, said, 'This is no longer working, so let's try something else.' And he moved from a military campaign into a political campaign. The objective never changed, and Martin never changed in his vision of what he wanted. What changed was the means. He put his all into the military campaign until he decided it was no longer working. The whole point of the military campaign was that you always thought it could succeed. When you reached a stage where it was not going to succeed, it was immoral to continue.

Although there were times when, for some republicans, Martin went a bit far. Meeting the queen for example. I said to Martin, 'What the hell?', and he said to me, 'Come on, Eamonn, you can understand.' I said, 'I can understand part of it, but I can't understand why.'

I'd been on radio and somebody asked me if he should meet the queen. And I said he should if he found himself in a situation where not to meet the queen would be bad-mannered, but he shouldn't go out of his way – so he obviously didn't listen to me! I said to him, 'I can understand in some ways, but I find it a wild hard step to take, meeting the British queen.' And he said, 'It's one of the things we have to do.'

That was the way – you would take things from Martin that you wouldn't take from a lesser man. I always found Martin extremely honest. He wouldn't bullshit. I mean, I remember Easter Sunday 1998, two days after the Good Friday Agreement. I said to him, 'Martin, that agreement doesn't look good.' And he said,

'It's crap. But it's the best we can get at the moment. We'll have to see what we can do with it.' He was aware of the limitations of it.

He was also good with people, which helped him as a politician. I remember at Raymond McCartney's wedding, our Donal was eight or ten weeks old, so we couldn't get a babysitter, but they said, 'Aye, bring him to the wedding surely.' He was in a car seat and Martin came over immediately, started getting our Donal all smiles. I said, 'He knew who to smile at!' Or you'd be out shopping and Martin would walk in, or you'd meet him on the street. There were no airs and graces with him.

There was one time him and Adams were canvassing during some election, and they were walking up Shipquay Street. All Adams's minders were in front of him, pushing people aside. Martin looked a wee bit embarrassed about it because you'd never see Martin with an entourage. I was thinking, 'OK, Gerry, you might need your minders in East Belfast, but it's a totally different thing in Derry!'

My brother Donal and Pat McArt had a big interview with Martin around February/March 1994 – my brother was dead from cancer by September that year. After the interview Martin left and Pat said to Donal, 'What do you think?' And Donal said, 'There's going to be a ceasefire.' And the *Journal* ran a headline – 'Ceasefire imminent' or something similar. This was at a time when no one believed there'd be a ceasefire and people said, 'Are yis nuts?' And then the week the ceasefire was declared, our Donal was dying – he was drifting in and out of consciousness in the hospital in Dublin. We said to him that the IRA had declared a ceasefire, and he said, 'I could have told you.'

Martin talked to Pat and Donal enough that they had decided to run the risk of putting it out there. That was where the

Derry Journal was great for Martin – Martin would float things to the *Journal*. If there was an adverse reaction, it wasn't binding any further than Derry, and not even there. Albert Reynolds, the taoiseach, visited the *Journal* and said, 'It's a magnificent use of the local paper – that's what you do. Float your ideas in the local paper. If there's an adverse reaction, you change your ideas.'

***

In later years, it was very hard for republicans to accept everything Martin was doing to appease unionism. But that was the thing: Martin carried people, much more than Adams did. Martin had that respect of people who mightn't have agreed with everything – and still don't agree with everything. At the time of the queen or one of the other controversial times, he would say, not in an arrogant way, 'Do you really think I would do something that would damage the movement?' He brought the whole republican movement with him. He was seen as the IRA, unlike Adams. With the likes of the south Armagh men and the Tyrone men – they would have had a lot more time for Martin.

Thankfully before he died he said, 'That's it. We tried and it didn't work.' Although some of us came to that conclusion years ago, that it wasn't working. But Martin would say, 'No, we've got to keep trying, we must try a bit more.'

I remember in 2005 we were at the funeral of a colleague of my brother, Siobhan Quinn. We were chatting and joking and Martin said, 'Donal and Siobhan are up in heaven now, chatting.' And I said, 'Aye, they're chatting and saying, what about this peace process?' And Martin said, 'What bloody peace process?' When he was talking to the likes of me, he wouldn't say, 'Oh, the peace process is great!'

The Chuckle Brothers act was a shock at the start. I remember arguing with people in Sinn Féin, 'Please tell me how does getting Ian Paisley into government benefit me as a republican?' I think Sinn Féin pushed to get Paisley into government without thinking the whole thing through. But Paisley was in many ways like Martin: when you're going to do something, you do it right. And did we ever think we'd look back and say, 'If only Paisley had stayed in power a bit longer'?

At the start I thought there was a very patronising attitude to Martin coming from Paisley, but I think it changed over time. Initially I was very uncomfortable watching it on TV – it was sort of patronising, pat him on the head. But then I think Martin wore him down. But I'm still not 100 per cent convinced that the DUP are capable of changing. You still have the likes of Gregory Campbell who has never broke breath to a Sinn Féiner – never. But while Martin may have done something that didn't work, the one thing he can't be accused of is not trying.

I've seen Martin confronting the RUC or the British Army. He'd be angry, but he'd never be out of control. He'd be very aggressive, in their face, but it wasn't a temper tantrum.

He always would have had time for you. I remember meeting him during some festival in the city here and he was walking up the river, him and Bernie. He was deputy first minister at the time and must have had a workload up to his eyeballs. I had applied for a visa to visit America – I have a son and grandchildren out there. I met him and we were chatting, and I said, 'Martin, by the way, I'm trying to get a visa.' He said, 'Leave it with me.' He phoned the consulate the next week, and while there's a limited amount you can do with Americans, he made the case to them for me. He could have said, 'Talk to somebody' or 'Give somebody a ring', but he said, 'Leave it with me.' And I wouldn't class myself as a close friend of his or anything. But to have that sort of feeling for the people around you, when you're struggling along with the workload of deputy first minister, and with constant pressure from the DUP, who offer no reciprocation in everything you try to do – even a simple thing like when he suggested to Arlene that they go to a Republic of Ireland match and a Northern Ireland match together and she refused. (By the way, she went to the Glasgow Rangers match on Saturday – and they got stuffed!) That sort of constant pressure, while receiving nothing back, must have been a struggle.

Every issue was a battle. But he had great humility. When Peter Robinson ran into the whole thing with Iris [when the media revealed that his wife, Iris, had had an affair with a nineteen-year-old for whom she'd allegedly procured large sums of money so that he could start up a restaurant], he didn't exploit it. He went in, we're told, and said, 'Anything we can do.'

***

I last saw him probably during the summer of 2016. I had no sense of him being in bad health when we met then. I was in contact with Raymond McCartney, and he was always my first point of contact. Raymond would always tell me the inside story, but in this case he said he didn't know. Martin was that private – he even kept it from the Shinners. And when *The Irish Times* leaked it, that's when they found out. Up to then he just told his own people he wasn't well, would have to take a back seat.

I was at his wake and I have to say I was shocked. You wouldn't have recognised him. He must have had a horrendous time over the last couple of weeks. Raymond went in and he came out and he said, 'It's not Martin. It's not Martin.' I had a chance to prepare myself; I went in and I looked and said, 'Aw Jesus, naw.'

There was great pride in the funeral, and I thought it was very much a people's funeral. We were up at the Long Tower chapel as the coffin came over the flyover. The Sinn Féin leadership was at the front, but the coffin was in the middle of the people. A great image. And it was the people that buried Martin. Sinn Féin played their part, but it was really well organised. There wasn't a cop in sight; the nearest one was about half a mile away. And you had Bill Clinton and Enda Kenny and everybody. It was really well done. But I thought it was the ordinary people.

There was applause as the coffin made its way through the streets and as it came up towards the chapel. People like Arlene, who'd never been to a Catholic funeral, must have been thinking, 'Do these people do nothing but clap?'

I found it very emotional. It was surprisingly emotional. We grew up with Martin – Martin was always there. Like him or hate him.

The burial date was almost to the day that they fired shots, away back, over Gerard Logue's coffin. [A volley fired at IRA man Logue's funeral, within the Long Tower church grounds in 1987 caused great controversy between Catholic clergy and republicans.] The Logue incident reminds me of a story about my mother. She was a very good Catholic and was great friends with Eddie Daly, the bishop, in the 1980s. Then Bishop Daly made a sermon where he said you couldn't be a Catholic and support the IRA. She was a weekly Mass-goer. So she wrote to Bishop Daly and said, 'I won't be able to go to Mass then.' They stayed friends, but she wouldn't go to Mass. But after about a year or two, she bumped into Tommy O'Fee [Cardinal Tomás Ó Fiaich]. And Tommy said, 'Ah, no, no, no – that's only Bishop Daly's view, not the church's view.' So my mother said, 'Great.' She went back to Mass. And two weeks later that incident with Gerard Logue's coffin happened.

It was a war and a nasty war at that. There were things done in the course of that war that were very regrettable and sad, but it was a war. And Michelle O'Neill said it recently: 'The war's over.' So stop fighting it. I think that's our problem – the Brits won't accept that they had a role to play. I think the solution is for everybody – republicans, British, loyalists, all of them to say, 'There was a war. It's over.' But the Brits will never say that. Which is why we're never going to sort out our legacy issues.

Martin had an honourable life. He stayed true to himself. He did what he thought was right. If you talked to him during the armed campaign, he would have said what he was doing was right – as all republicans would have done. When he was in politics, he still did what he thought was right, things that he felt had to be done. So I would say it was an honourable life lived by an honourable man.

17

Terry O'Sullivan

For me, contact with the world of Irish-America started about 1995. I had come back to Washington: my union [the Laborers' International Union of North America] had moved me around the country – it's kind of like the military – and then they brought me back to Washington.

My father had been an Irish activist in San Francisco, but I was too young at that point in time to know what he was doing. By the time I returned to Washington, however, the similarity between the labour movement and those campaigning for a united Ireland was clear to me. James Connolly, for example, came to mind. There's such synergy between human rights and labour rights, worker rights, social rights. And that's how and why I started to become engaged and involved in Sinn Féin activities in the mid-1990s.

I first met Martin when he came to Washington for meetings with the Department of State. From about 1995 union leaders here in Washington DC began hosting a breakfast around St Patrick's Day events. Gerry Adams would come and occasionally Martin would come too. Rita O'Hare would always be there, Richard McAuley and Mary Lou McDonald at times as well. So we would have a fundraiser breakfast and Gerry would tell us what was going on in the north, in the south, throughout the country. And the first time I met Martin was at one of those breakfasts.

If it's possible, the person that I first met exceeded my

expectations. I saw a man – we all know his history – a fighter, a peacemaker, somebody who would help negotiate the Good Friday Agreement in 1998. The person I came to know was a man of real compassion. At the same time he had the qualities of toughness, tenacity and compassion – someone who cared for people, whether Protestant or Catholic. And it showed in the discussions I had with him.

Most of my dealings with Martin were either around Sinn Féin events – whether they were functions in the US or elsewhere – or sitting around and talking about what's going on in Ireland. We also talked about life in general, our families – he was such a family man. None of it surprised me. Knowing the things he had gone through in his life – having read about his past history, how he was involved in war, was involved in peace – I was more than impressed.

If you look at the accomplishments of Martin McGuinness – and I mean no disrespect to the other side of the discussion – Martin was two or three steps ahead of other people. He was a brilliant tactician. And also, as I said, tough and tenacious. That's a rare combination.

Some people who are tough and tenacious are hard to get along with, can sometimes be pompous. He was anything but that. He was a gentleman. He talked about his family, about his love for fishing, about his goal of a free and united Ireland and how important it was. Even after one meeting, I was deeply impressed.

He wasn't really different from Gerry in personality. Everybody is unique, but I'd assign a lot of the same attributes to Gerry as I would to Martin. Those two were similar in more ways than not. Fun-loving and strategically brilliant.

***

President Clinton was phenomenal on Irish issues – probably the best president we ever had in that respect. And God bless George Mitchell and what he contributed to the Irish peace process. I usually go to the White House on St Patrick's Day and during the Clinton administration it was different. The Bush years were a little tougher, that's for sure.

Some American politicians would have been put off by Martin's IRA past. I didn't hear it said publicly, but you could tell when you tried to schedule meetings. We're a big political operation and you found there were people who didn't want to meet us. No one ever insulted me because of my friendship and relationship with Martin or Gerry. They wouldn't say, 'I'm not meeting with those terrorists.' But I knew when we were getting put off on meetings, and I speculated that one of the reasons might be that they didn't want to be seen with or associated with Irish republicans.

During the Clinton years there was more interest. Even in President Obama's time, when Joe Biden was vice-president, there was a small breakfast on St Patrick's Day morning for about forty people and the taoiseach would come along and speak. I got invited every single year. And in the afternoon, the president has the official bowl of shamrock and the rest of it. That's when I would take Gerry over to the White House.

Now, we don't have a champion in the White House any more. Even if you forget about the president, who have they appointed to help? I think that since President Clinton that position has been extinct. I think the progress that has been made in Northern Ireland could be built on, while still dealing with the Middle East and all the rest of it. We've certainly encouraged greater involvement, but we haven't seen many signs of it yet.

***

Martin McGuinness: The Man I Knew

I think that in everything Martin McGuinness went through in his life, his love of his family and his love and joy in life always showed through. He loved to have dinner and be able to talk about something other than politics. Because he was in a powder keg most of his adult life, from when he was eighteen until he unfortunately passed away. His family meant a lot to him. He didn't drink, but he liked to sit down and break bread in a small group.

Martin was also very constant. Some suggest that Martin and Sinn Féin jettisoned their early ideals for a united Ireland, but I don't think that's true. Equality and prosperity for all – that's what my union and American trade unions stand for. We're not necessarily socialist – although where I grew up in San Francisco, there was a very socialist labour movement. But on matters like equality, I don't think Martin conceded on any of those principles in his lifetime fight and I think his body of work reflects that.

I never saw any difference in Martin when he was at an Ard-Fheis or when engaged with those outside the party. I also think Martin's toughness shows in his accomplishments. Against – I won't say all odds, but against strong odds he and Gerry have been able to position Sinn Féin in such a position of strength in the north and south that one day, maybe in our lifetimes, it will bring about a free united Ireland.

The job is not yet over, of course, but we wouldn't be where we are today if he hadn't done the healing things. And Martin did those things. Whether you like somebody or not, you shake their hand. Even people that I don't care for – even some I may end up getting in a fight with – we still extend courtesies. That was never an issue with me.

Martin's years of reaching out was a time of building, not a cul-de-sac. Where were we a few short years before that, after all? Fighting in the streets. Progress has been made – though not enough as far as we're concerned. Martin, along with others, has gotten us to that point. He passed the baton: it may be ten more years before you get to the top, but we'll never say never. So I don't think the ten years were wasted at all. I think he created the foundation with the peace process. To say it was wasted time would be an insult to the man and to the cause, and to what he was trying to accomplish.

I would never speak for Martin, but I would say we haven't achieved reconciliation today. Not today. But there's tomorrow and the next day and next week and next month and next year. He never gave up the fight and at the end of the day – to use an American footballing metaphor – he advanced the ball down the field. Did we get across the end zone? I would say, not yet. But when we do, it'll be patriots like Martin McGuinness and Gerry Adams, along with a whole host of others, who will get the credit for getting us across that line.

I'd have a hard time just picking one quality that Martin had, but I think it was his resolve that stood out the most. His resolve to promote fairness and equality. He would stop at no bounds for fairness and equality. He did that through the other traits that I've already listed – he was tenacious, compassionate, a fierce negotiator. His resolve for the cause and the mission of a free, united Ireland was unshakeable.

I would absolutely say he had the stature of other great Irish patriots – Wolfe Tone, James Connolly. I'd put both him and Gerry up there. I think Martin had that capacity – I mean, who else could have got the IRA to put the guns down? To say, 'We need to do this politically, not just continue with the Troubles.'

That took the courage and the vision he had. I don't think we're overestimating his stature as an Irish patriot in any way by comparing him to those other great names.

***

I talk to Sinn Féin all the time so I knew Martin was sick months before his death. I saw him some six months before he passed away. He showed no signs to me of his illness then. In January 2017 I was told that things were not good and it was one of the saddest times in my life. Martin was somebody who had an impact on me as a patriot, as a leader, as a human being. And there is a strong link between what we do in the labour movement and what he did. I cried like a baby when I went to the house to pay my respects to Bernie and his family. It was an emotional, overwhelming moment. It still is, thinking back on it.

Through our involvement with Sinn Féin, and with Martin and Gerry, I got to carry his coffin for part of the way – just as it passed some murals. It was – I want to use the right word – one of the most *emotional* moments of my life. It was emotional because we'd lost somebody who had fought so hard for his principles and for whom I had the utmost respect.

I don't have to lay my life on the line for what I do. In contrast, Martin and those like him didn't seem to worry about laying their lives on the line for the cause of freedom. To me that is absolutely powerful, absolutely incredible.

When his life ended, did he leave the world better than he found it? Yes, he left it a hell of a lot better off. I'd like to think that knowing him made me wiser – though he might disagree with that. Did knowing him make me even more passionate about what I do? Absolutely. His passion for life and for the cause was infectious, as was his determination. Everyone knew he would stop at nothing to accomplish it. He was never going to back up and he was never going to back down. Quite simply, he was one of the most impressive men I've ever met. It was a privilege for me to interact with him and to be able to call him my friend.

18

Michael McGimpsey

In the 1970s awful things were happening and Martin McGuinness was seen as very much part of that – central to that, in fact. I vividly remember him being elected and coming out and saying, 'Getting elected to politics won't make any difference, it's the cutting edge of the IRA that's going to do the business for us.' I saw him as a hard man.

Among unionists the IRA was seen as cruel, violent, sectarian and steeped in blood. When you become the spokesperson of a movement like that, then it's fair to say there would have been no admirers of Martin among unionist people. Including myself.

I first met him some time in the late 1990s. It would have been post-ceasefire, around 1998. We did an event in the Waterfront Hall where we all – Ulster Unionist, SDLP, Alliance, a former RUC man – were interviewed while sitting on high stools. The joke back then was that Martin McGuinness looked like Art Garfunkel, with his blond, curly hair. I understood that he was very much part of the IRA leadership, whom I regarded as extremely cruel. But we had to end the war, the killing, the whole agony. I believed firmly that if you could get the republicans stopped, the loyalists would stop. The loyalists were always talking about terrorising the terrorists – in fact, they terrified everybody. So stop the IRA and you stop the loyalists and you get peace. And McGuinness and Adams were saying at that time that they wanted to stop.

Very often when you meet people you only know through the media they surprise you. For example, I'd listened to Ian Paisley on TV for years: strong, loud, etc. When I met him I expected him to shout at me. In fact, I met this gentleman who talked to me quietly. McGuinness would have been much the same as that when I met him that night at the Waterfront Hall. He didn't look like a storm trooper nor act like one; in no way was there any sense of an attempt to intimidate or threaten. I take people as they come. My view on McGuinness and Adams – because they always went together – was that they were trying to find a way forward.

People frequently would say to me, 'Anytime you see McGuinness tell him that I said …' The truth is, in years of working with him, I really didn't know him, because there was always a reserve there with him, there was always just a little bit of holding back. I knew him professionally, we were in business together, but on a personal level I can't say that I knew him.

I'm not sure that he understood unionists. I think he was on a route. There was the cutting edge of the IRA; then, sometime in the 1990s he decided that wasn't the way forward, politics was the way forward. I think that just as he was enthusiastic in the armed struggle side, he became enthusiastic in the peace process and that meant doing business with the likes of me. I'm quite sure he had no huge regard for me or other unionists, but he knew that he had to do business with us. I spent hours in his company and I saw him as very enthusiastic about politics.

He left Gerry Adams to do most of the talking; I would have done the same with David Trimble – one talking, one listening. In the exchanges then it was very much about decommissioning, which was a requirement of the agreement and the key to getting unionists fully on board. Our party [UUP] was ripped down the middle with this – we were stretched to breaking point. Sinn Féin was stretched too but never to breaking point, and so they grew stronger and stronger through skilful management. But as far as I was concerned, the point was always, how do we stop the conflict, stop the killing, stop the hurt and pain? And I think we got there.

I'm not sure that Martin had any empathy for unionists. I never sensed that he did. His focus was always very much on his constituency and on bringing them with him. Gerry Adams was the front-of-house man, while McGuinness was the one who actually managed the house.

It was always business: we were there to do business and once the business was over you got up and left. There might have been a bit of small talk, but none of it was particularly revealing. It was always politeness. McGuinness told me at one point that he was going salmon fishing for the summer and how he caught his first salmon, which he was clearly still excited about years later. I did a bit of fishing myself when I was a wee fella; but I was, I suppose, a bit surprised that this was his passion – clearly it gave him relaxation.

The truth is, we were always looking for something from him and he was always looking for something from us. When we went to the US ambassador's home in London in 1999, we were all round a table sitting there with the Yanks, and we tried to just chat. But it was strange.

Martin was never rude. It was always, 'Hello, how are you?' There was a bit of chat, but it never went any deeper than that. We did our business, usually we agreed to disagree, then we got up and away we went.

***

I think the big change that I saw in Martin was over our first Executive, in 1998. I wasn't quite sure what to expect, but all of a sudden, without any real warning, I found myself a minister in the first Executive. I was minister in the Department of Culture, Arts and Leisure [DCAL] and I have to say I enjoyed it very much. Martin was in Education and Bairbre de Brún was in Health. We got huge criticism for sitting down in government before decommissioning was completed.

But clearly Martin was enjoying it. He felt that it was another step forward, an achievement, so he was generally very cheerful and practical round the table. We were under huge pressure from our own party because of the lack of decommissioning, but the SDLP was under pressure too because they had lost some ground. McGuinness was probably the most relaxed at the Executive table, but Bairbre de Brún was under huge pressure. People were merciless with her as minister for health. I always got the sense with Bairbre that she actually cared about the job, but she was slaughtered in the chamber. The crowd that we had round the table wasn't the happiest of groups; we weren't the most sympathetic with each other. But Martin McGuinness seemed to be enjoying himself.

I got the sense that he didn't think he'd get as far as he did, so he felt he'd achieved something. He was fully energetic and energised when it was an armed struggle, and once that changed and it was politics, he gave it 100 per cent.

David Trimble, John Taylor and Reg Empey were the top men in our party, so I wasn't involved in the discussions about what departments we were going to take. We went for Enterprise, Trade and Development, Mark Durkan got Finance; but when it came round to the DUP's turn, the expectation was that

Nigel Dodds would take Education. Instead Robinson took the Department of Regional Development and that left Education. Sinn Féin jumped straight in.

I think there was surprise at that among unionists. We could have had a discussion, I suppose, with the DUP, but then we were so estranged at that time. I think what bothered them was the idea that the education of our children was being led by someone who had played so prominent a part in a terrorist campaign. But that was always the contradiction: someone who came from that background being involved in government, balanced against the need that if you want peace that's what you have to do.

At the time he was minister for education, Martin was a very divisive figure within unionism, so no matter what he said or did it was dismissed. He said he'd abolished the Eleven Plus, which of course wasn't true [the examination was officially discontinued under Caitríona Ruane]. There was a constant criticism within unionism directed at him and, therefore, a constant criticism directed at unionists who were doing business with him. I can't think of anything he did as minister for education that was of note, other than the fact he was the minister. There was money around in those days, so he didn't have the financial constraints, didn't face hard choices. There was always the suspicion that he was leaning towards the Catholic schools sector. I was absorbed in my own DCAL role, but I didn't detect that he was overtly steering resources in one particular direction.

If the minister wants to go to some place, the minister goes; he arranges his own invitations. I would have thought that McGuinness would not have got a good reception at schools in places like Newtownards or Ballyclare, for example. I think things were too raw for Martin to visit state/Protestant secondary schools at that stage. The violence was too fresh in people's minds. There were, and still are, so many people in pain and who have suffered, that attempting such visits would have been a mistake – counter-productive. If he'd done that I'm sure he would have been met with protests.

After the Executive fell in 2002, fruitless discussions were going on about trying to get the decommissioning process into action; then the DUP overtook us and we became very much the junior partner. Eventually in 2006 we all wound up in St Andrews and we got the deal [the St Andrews Agreement, where the DUP and Sinn Féin agreed to be senior partners in a new Stormont Executive] that's haunting everyone at the moment.

Once we got back round the table in 2007 and Martin McGuinness became deputy first minister, he became very diplomatic. He was very much into doing business with Ian Paisley and Paisley was very good at that too. He and Paisley were there to make it work, and I think the two worked well together. I think Paisley decided this was the way forward. He was a bit like McGuinness; he did it enthusiastically. There was a bit of conflict at times round the table: Margaret Ritchie [SDLP social development minister] annoyed Sinn Féin routinely and I annoyed the DUP. But as a general rule, Paisley and McGuinness were able to run the show.

I think it's true that McGuinness and Paisley became friends. I can understand that. I found Ian Paisley a very warm individual, softly spoken and not like the public image that I'd grown up with. I think Paisley was a clergyman first, he had empathy with people, he liked people. I would say that Martin McGuinness was probably the same way.

The expectation was always that the Executive with Paisley

would go for a wee while and collapse – it didn't. He got through with Paisley. Paisley was determined it wasn't going to collapse and Paisley did a good job. It was unfortunate that he ran out of road when he did. If he'd stayed on a while I think things would probably have been better, but his party wanted him out. It lost its humour when Peter Robinson came in – he was going to have a battle a day. I think it was clear that Robinson and McGuinness didn't get on, didn't like each other. But McGuinness still held on to doing good business. He wanted the power-sharing Executive to work.

McGuinness's problem was always his background, his baggage – it was very hard for the average person to get beyond that. It still is today. It was difficult for him because of the reaction he was provoking.

Robinson clearly wanted to make things work. He relished being first minister, relished the whole power thing. But he had a difficult horse to ride as well. It's the old story: you ride the tiger, eventually you fall off and it eats you. But you have to keep on feeding the tiger otherwise you will fall off. The tiger was public opinion within the unionist community, who couldn't see beyond Sinn Féin/IRA, the cutting edge, etc. Every family had someone who was hurting.

I think Sinn Féin made some serious mistakes. Decommissioning didn't come quickly enough. That told of an intent to go back to war. I would have thought McGuinness would have had an important role there, much more important than Gerry Adams. I think they were too concerned about their own constituency, about holding that together. They could have taken more risks. That stretched unionism and created further deep suspicion – and that suspicion is still there.

After the first period of government, you then had in the second half of the 1990s killings by Direct Action Against Drugs [a vigilante organisation which killed several drug dealers], which in fact the IRA carried out, showing they were still active.

Going into the Executive, I think McGuinness did take the important step of standing with Robinson and Hugh Orde. That, I think, took courage. That was off the script, I didn't expect it and I thought it was an important step. Also meeting the queen. He clearly enjoyed it – he loved being deputy first minister. He enjoyed meeting President Obama, enjoyed the trappings. I'm not sure if his head was turned, but I do think he took a pleasure in the duty. There were certain things he did, but to look for reciprocation was a huge stretch for us.

I think Mary McAleese, the queen and so on, these events were clearly choreographed, well planned. Gerry Adams and Martin McGuinness, as with decommissioning, would have been very carefully managing their constituency. So yes, there would have been a number of republicans shocked by McGuinness meeting the queen, etc., but I think most of the constituency was well prepared. Nor would I have thought he was bounced into meeting the queen. I think Mary McAleese and the queen coming to Dublin and laying a wreath, etc. – I think that was very much part of the choreography. It would have been very difficult for McGuinness not to reciprocate in some way. When he went to do that, he did it fully.

I'm not sure that unionism fell short in reciprocation. I think it's hard to encapsulate in a few sentences. The UUP and the DUP were never involved in violence, the SDLP the same, but Sinn Féin was; so it took a huge effort to bring Sinn Féin in. But against that you never get away from the fact they have a mandate and you want peace, normal society, an end to killing. These are the things that have to be done. As far as reciprocation is concerned, unionism is a very fractious constituency. You can have one hundred different opinions.

There were moments, things that Trimble said and did, moments also with Paisley and Robinson, that demonstrated unionist sincerity in the process. I can't think what they were right now – I know that there were occasions where he stood with McGuinness and got criticism.

I think there was unionist reciprocation, but it wasn't by a grand gesture and unionists didn't shout about it. A lot of this has to be done by evolution not revolution. It's quite clear if and when Pope Francis comes here, Arlene Foster and whoever leads the UUP – if they're invited – will be there; that's the type of reciprocation I'm talking about. We'll be there and we'll not be found wanting, but it's not the sort of thing that will be a grand gesture.

I mean if John Hume met the queen, no one thought about it. John met everybody and talked to everybody. It's because of Martin's background that all of a sudden this is a huge gesture, and unionists recognised that, yes, he made a gesture.

***

I was shocked by Martin's illness and death. I had retired by that time, having stepped down in March 2016, and he seemed to be just his usual self then. I think he wished me well. He never passed me in the chamber without saying, 'Hello Michael' – we always kept the formalities of friendliness. Then when I heard that he had cancelled his visit to China on doctor's orders, the rumours were rife. Usually when you hear about someone not able to fly because of doctor's orders you think of a heart issue. Then McGuinness stepped down from being deputy first minister. He always seemed to be in reasonable health, but within a matter of weeks he was gone. It all happened so fast.

And I do think the political process misses him. He had an authority clearly within Sinn Féin that I don't see from any of the other Sinn Féin leaders, including Gerry Adams. That was apparent in the Assembly. He had the authority; he could take the risks. I think they miss him. I don't think Michelle O'Neill, with the best will in the world, has Martin's ability or his authority. I don't think Adams has it without Martin behind him.

I wouldn't say unionism lost its best friend when he died. I wouldn't say that. I think the key thing to remember in this is every generation in Northern Ireland goes back to violence. We're now twenty, twenty-five years into the peace and we're getting ready to do it again if we're not careful. We need to understand there's nothing inevitable about the peace. We can go backwards again.

Martin definitely was a barrier against that sort of slipping back. He had made up his mind – the war was in the past; war was self-defeating; violence wasn't going to do it for republicans or anyone else. Peace and politics was the way forward. He was very firm about that. And you saw that with his ability to lead that constituency – primarily republicans but also later the wider nationalist community – with authority. That was his major strength. I always had the sense there was a degree of affection for him within Sinn Féin. I saw that in City Hall and I saw that in the Assembly. And his funeral showed he was held in very high regard for the journey he had taken.

His greatest weakness, on the other hand, was what had gone

on before and the baggage he carried. The memory of Claudy and Enniskillen and Darkley and La Mon – you can't put it all at his door, but he played a key role in all of that. And that was his greatest weakness. That meant he had no ability to reach across into unionism.

If the peace process works, he'll be remembered in history. You get peace; after you get peace you're looking for understanding. Through that understanding you get tolerance. And then, with a bit of tolerance, you get reconciliation. I think we're a long way behind that – we're barely off first base. And I think that's a problem for us.

So if the process works, then you can say he played an important part in making it work. Putting the gun away forever. He's not the only one – I think Trimble played a huge role in this, took huge chances – I know because I was close to him. I think Paisley played a huge role. I think John Hume, and Adams too, of course, and Tony Blair and Bertie Ahern; they were the facilitators.

Did I like him? I think you have to know somebody to like them. I didn't dislike him. On a personal level I never got to know Martin. I think there was always a reserve there. As there was with Adams. I don't think they were there to be liked or disliked. They were there with a job to do. So, as I said, you have to know somebody to like them. But I didn't dislike him.

19

Aodhán Mac an tSaoir

I started working with Martin on a full-time basis in 1992–93; we were both part of the core Sinn Féin political group, dealing with the then embryonic peace process. I had worked in Gerry Adams's office and moved from there into working on the peace process, developing a negotiations group initially set up for discussions with the SDLP and John Hume. And then there were secret discussions, or confidential discussions with the Irish government when Albert Reynolds replaced Charles Haughey. That opened up a direct dialogue between the Irish government and us. Martin Mansergh was the Irish government representative for that and Martin McGuinness and I had a series of meetings with him.

I was very much a party official, an apparatchik, as opposed to a public figure. Gerry Adams had a small political strategy group round him – probably eight or nine people – managing the attempts to engage in dialogue, break out of isolation and open up some discussions and possibilities around the peace strategy. So I was part of that grouping. Martin was designated as the main contact with the Irish government, to lead that face-to-face engagement. And I was appointed to accompany him on those meetings.

So that's how I started working with Martin. Then, as the peace process negotiations kicked in, I became Martin's political assistant/adviser. Right through the Good Friday negotiations I was working full-time in that position. Later, when Gerry asked Martin to take on the job as minister of education, Martin asked 'Will you come in with me as my adviser?' and I agreed.

It was a daunting prospect to go into Rathgael House [in Bangor, where the Department of Education is based]. There was a bit of apprehension, this idea that we were heading into the unknown. We travelled in Martin's car. I think Gerry McCartney, who was Martin's driver, was there at the time, but I don't remember who else.

Nigel Hamilton was the permanent secretary for education then, and he and all his senior officials were at the door to meet Martin. A small number of other people were also there out of curiosity. Once inside, Nigel brought Martin his first-day brief and formally introduced himself. We'd decided, because it was an entirely new experience for republicans, that I would be with Martin in every engagement, watching, because if you're in the eye of that storm you can't watch everything. So I accompanied him everywhere that day.

There was definitely a frostiness as we moved from the top floor down at Rathgael House. Relations were good at the top – these were long-standing officials who had probably worked with a lot of people. But as you moved down to the canteen, attitudes changed.

I remember one time Martin wanted to talk to the entire staff and we did it in the canteen, which was the biggest room. The canteen staff weren't in the least bit interested – they talked among themselves, had the fans on – every kind of minor disruption they could cause. They were probably from working-class areas in Bangor and so felt hostile about the fact that here was this IRA man coming out to talk to them.

In general, there was a wariness. Nigel Hamilton had made it very clear that Martin was the minister and he was to be treated as the minister. Nigel came at things very professionally. All the senior officials were very good in how they related to Martin – very professional. But within a very short time, Martin had built up an incredible relationship with all the officials, including people who probably had relatives in the police and the British forces. Some of the things Martin did took them by surprise. They wouldn't have expected his decisiveness on some issues.

I remember one particular incident, where we were developing a new element to the religion curriculum. The status quo is that the main churches draw up the curriculum. Martin and I had a discussion and decided it wasn't taking into account the new realities in the society we live in. So we said, 'We want you to look at that again and find a way to give an input from the new religions that are coming in – Islam, etc.' I remember the officials being pleasantly surprised. They were probably anticipating that Martin, as a traditional Catholic, would keep and defend the status quo. But that wasn't Martin's approach at all.

If an issue was clear-cut, Martin would be very decisive. But if it wasn't, he would weigh it up, consider the different sides and possibilities. Sometimes I would get very frustrated by how much he weighed things up; he had much greater patience than I ever had.

He appeared to enjoy himself most when he was engaging with ordinary people. He had a great way with children and related to them, and was very relaxed in that environment. Generally people were very impressed by how personable he was and by his incredible patience. No matter what his own pressures were, he'd never be rushed. Sometimes he used to run badly over schedule and put me under pressure for the rest of the day – but he did like all that a wee bit: giving certificates to primary school kids, getting photographs taken with kids.

Every school did it differently. I suppose any of the staff could, if they wished, have opted out, but most times people were very receptive – whether it was curiosity or whatever. When he went to Methodist College [a largely Protestant grammar school in Belfast], it would have been a very new experience for them and for us. Again, he was treated with absolute courtesy and professionalism – it was a very good engagement. Any of the contentious issues were set aside. He was the education minister as far as they were concerned, so we had a good discussion. I think the issue of the Eleven Plus was beginning to bubble up so they were very anxious to give their perspective on it.

He always went by invitation. Clearly there was less contention around visits to Catholic schools. I don't think I could ever detect any difference in approach and welcome between grammar and secondary schools. I would say perhaps there might have been with some of the staff – his politics would probably have been more aligned with the people who were teaching in the secondary sector, as distinct from the grammar; but for the most part he received very warm welcomes. At Dominican College, Fortwilliam, on the Antrim Road in Belfast, he got an incredibly warm welcome. The choir sang for him. I think he went to all the Derry schools and he had a good relationship with them.

One of the good days we had was the day Martin took the decision to end the Eleven Plus [examinations sat at eleven years of age to determine if a child will attend grammar or secondary school]. That happened about seven o'clock on a

Friday evening because David Trimble had said he was going to bring the institutions down, suspend things from Sunday night. So wherever we were – I think maybe we were in Stormont buildings – Martin said, 'Right. Let's go out to Rathgael House and get some decisions made.' These things were all in a pipeline of decision-making, so we went down on Friday. That was pretty unusual for the officials, but they accepted that. Martin said, 'We're going to run through some of these things.' There were a number of decisions he made that day but the most obviously important of them was to bring the system of the Eleven Plus to an end.

His decision was driven by conviction and party policy. We worked off the Sinn Féin manifesto. That was our starting point when we went in. We all had a sense that Northern Ireland Office ministers had essentially sat on their hands for so long and things had remained the same. Martin was determined and decisive.

***

While Martin was education minister he was also a key negotiator dealing with the British government, David Trimble, the Irish government and the republican constituency and IRA leadership. It was an exhausting period for both Martin and Gerry. They were juggling so many pressures, conflicts and demands.

I remember when the IRA commenced its decommissioning process, Gerry was doing a republican meeting in Conway Mill in West Belfast with a couple of hundred people. It was to explain how this was the next step in the peace process. Meanwhile Martin and I went off to New York to do the same over there.

We did a press conference straight after the IRA made its announcement, in Rosie O'Grady's in New York, I think. There was a massive media turnout for that – it was a big occasion. We were driving back downtown after it and we went through Times Square about twenty minutes after the announcement. The news was already coming up on the news feed in Times Square. I remember saying to Martin, 'There you are. You're making history.'

I think the groundwork was always done in advance. That's one thing that Martin and the Sinn Féin leadership and the IRA leadership were very attentive to – keeping our own people on board, explaining every step we were taking, ensuring that people would have their view expressed rather than something coming as a surprise to them. We had negotiations training with the African National Congress [ANC] in South Africa before our negotiations kicked in. One of the clearest lessons that they said we needed to take on board was: 'The most important negotiation is the negotiation with your own people.' They had been through that process successfully and we probably did that more than any other political party or group emerging from the conflict. We actually said to the DUP at times, 'You are not engaging with your own base – your victims groups are off on a different line.' And they said, 'We don't know how to do that.'

Martin was a very tough negotiator when he needed to straight-talk to anyone – whether it be the British prime minister or another republican activist. He could be very forthright. In his public demeanour he always came across as very friendly and relaxed and calm. But if Martin needed to make a point he could make it very forcefully. And he did that at some points with the Irish government, at some points with the American administration, when he thought their position was wrong, but most commonly he did it with the British government.

He probably had a gentler approach with unionists because anything else wouldn't have worked, but with British officials sometimes it got hot and heavy. He had a particularly fractious relationship with Peter Mandelson, who tried to lecture Martin. I remember a blazing row one time at Hillsborough Castle. Mandelson was – I'm choosing my words carefully here – a very arrogant person. He talked down to everyone and Martin didn't like that at all and would have told him that. It's one of the few times I remember Martin raising his voice. It was heated but obviously controlled.

I had bought Martin tickets to see Tommy Fleming in the Millennium Forum in Derry, and we were talking about this concert at the start, before descending into the row with Mandelson. So afterwards I said to Martin that I'd a Tommy Fleming tape in the car. He said, 'Will you go back and give Mandelson that tape and tell him I hope he enjoys listening to Tommy Fleming.' And I think Mandelson gave Martin, at the end of that row, a tie. So even though it was hot and heavy at the time, Martin would have never carried a grudge or not be on speaking terms with a person. He spoke his mind and that was it.

Normally he would have pointed out, in a very subtle and diplomatic way, if something wasn't done right. Certainly he never challenged me directly. I enjoyed working with him enormously. I never had an argument with him, though I'd disagreements with him, not infrequently. He'd have had one view and I'd have had another. For example, he'd have said, 'I think that's not the right line to put out on that.' And then I would give him my perspective. And he'd say, 'No, I think we should do it this way', and that's how he would have told you he didn't agree with you. But he would listen to what you said. He didn't have a fixed view; he was prepared to listen. If there was a logic to what you said, he'd have accepted it.

Martin was a practising Catholic and I'm an atheist, so there were issues where we disagreed. We'd have discussed religious matters. Most people of religion nowadays, they have their own version of their faith and it isn't as rigid as would have been the case in the past. But Martin believed in the Catholic faith. As a consequence of that he had a great relationship with Rev. Harold Good [the Methodist minister who oversaw the decommissioning of IRA weapons] and other people like that. He also got on OK with John Hume – pleasant. I don't think there'd have been any great affection on John's or Martin's part, just because they had such different perspectives. They'd respect for each other.

***

Martin didn't talk about the past and the Troubles. He might very occasionally make a reference to staying in a house or having a meal when he was on the run, or an encounter with someone. But it wasn't something that occupied his mind. Martin's view was that what happened in the past should never happen again. That's what his entire commitment was to.

He'd have defended to the last the decisions he made in his life. If pushed on it, he'd have said very clearly that people who grew up in the circumstances he grew up in, and witnessed the events he'd witnessed, had an opportunity to do something. And he probably would have viewed those who didn't use that opportunity as the people who had questions to answer, rather than the other way round. He was very proud that he'd stood up when he needed to. But he also believed that when we found a way out of that conflict, we had an obligation to take it. He brought all his energies to doing that. Even for people who are unconvinced about the possibility of achieving peace through politics, Martin would have gone to any lengths to try to persuade them.

He was working hours that no one else would have worked. Sometimes driving home in the evening he must have been fed up and pissed off with the effort that he was making and the reaction to it. But he just kept going. What was amazing about him was that he could not be discouraged. I did see him frustrated at times. The most obvious in recent times was when we became aware of the decision taken on the Líofa bursaries. [In December 2016 Paul Givan, DUP minister for communities, withdrew the Líofa Gaeltacht Bursary for disadvantaged children – then wished everyone Happy Christmas.] To think that these people were engaging in such petty, sectarian politics, and we were stretching ourselves to work with them, trying to reach accommodations.

Martin very rarely swore. Maybe in the privacy of a room with one or two others who were very close to him, he'd have used colourful language. I think he was frustrated at the approach of David Trimble – that it took so long to drag him into the process. He couldn't comprehend why Trimble couldn't take something that was positive and sell it. Rather than recognising the direction of travel, Trimble always said, 'Oh, it's not fast enough.'

I was there on occasions when Martin had to dress formally and he was distinctly uncomfortable doing it. He just thought it was a complete nonsense. He did it, but reluctantly. He was in his own way shy. He was brilliant in public, but he always preferred to get home. If you were travelling, he just wanted to get into his hotel room and probably call Bernie and read a book or watch some sport on television. He was a private man. Whether he enjoyed the public part is impossible to say. He found it easy to do. But once he'd done his job, he wanted to get into a room and close the door.

Martin also had his hobbies, like his photographs. He'd have stopped the car, got out, walked up a lane on the Glenshane Pass [on the road between Belfast and Derry] or somewhere, because he'd seen a flower and wanted to take a photograph of it. He took great pleasure in photography – I don't know if he'd built up a collection or not. Not photographs of people – but photographs of things he thought were unusual. He also liked to talk about sport, GAA – he was interested in any sport. He'd have created a little space for that. He was interested in soccer, and that was a good, non-contentious conversation piece he had with people. I have no interest in sport, so he didn't find an outlet with me – I didn't know what he was talking about. Peter Robinson and Martin talked about football all the time – for five minutes before meetings – maybe longer. Soccer, that is. They'd even have slagged each other.

He was incredibly focused on his children and grandchildren. He loved to get home and spend time with them. That's the tragedy of his death: that he was planning to retire and have that time with his family because he'd so little time with his family in previous years due to his commitments.

***

When he came back from that last trip to America he was very tired. That was in October 2016, I think. He went to an event with Bill Flynn in Houston; then he flew to San Francisco. The trip was shortened because the president of Colombia was coming to London and wanted to come to Belfast to meet Martin. Martin had previously talked to him about our process and he was very taken with Martin. All this meant he had little down time to recover from his travels.

Martin must have been disappointed at the decision he had to make to resign. He made serious efforts to persuade Arlene Foster to step aside temporarily as first minister while the RHI scandal was investigated, but he was put in an impossible position. So he did what he did in the end very reluctantly, and with a very heavy heart, because he didn't want the institutions to come down. He was aware of republican frustration with DUP arrogance for some time, and he was saying that to the DUP. 'There's a problem here. And if we have a problem, you have a problem.' He was basically saying, 'If you don't start doing things differently, we can't sustain this.'

Did I weep at his death? Definitely. Because of how much he had given, because he was robbed of those last few years with his family and because he had been forced to do something that was against his instincts. There was a degree of tragedy in his death, an injustice, I think, which I felt acutely.

When the phone rings now I hear Martin speaking to me. Because he wouldn't say 'Hello' or 'Hi'. He would just say 'Aodhán!' And I hear that in my head all the time, him speaking to me. If he wanted to do something at half-past twelve, he'd ring. And if you didn't answer the phone, he'd say, 'I was ringing you last night!' Like you're not supposed to sleep. And I'd say, 'I saw it was your number – I was asleep!' He actually said to me one time, 'Our people shouldn't be sleeping when there's crises going on.' He said some things like that, which were a bit absurd at times – but were said for the right reasons.

I went to Westminster recently. I'd never been to Westminster without Martin. He was a very big part of my life. Even my kids were heartbroken when he died. He'd been so much a part of their lives as well. He'd be in Belfast and he'd come to our house if he'd something to do or attend – he'd have a shower and a shave. The kids would come in from school and Martin McGuinness would be sitting there. All that has its impact.

As soon as I heard he had passed away, I got in the car and drove to Derry. I thought at first his family had gone to bed – it was 4.30 a.m. and the lights were out. As it happens they were up, but I didn't want to knock on the door. My wife was with me and I said, 'We'll drive out towards Buncrana.' We drove as far as Fahan and the beach. The sun was just rising – day was breaking. We were listening to the radio and at 5 a.m. Tommie Gorman had the news of his death for RTÉ. We were in the car on the beach, with darkness starting to recede and daylight coming. They played this amazing lullaby with Sinéad O'Connor and the RTÉ orchestra – 'Lay Your Head Down'. When it finished they said, 'We're going to the news.' And Tommie Gorman said, 'Martin McGuinness has passed away.' I don't know if the music was coincidence. But it was very hard. Very hard.

He touched so many people. I have met people who were at his funeral because they felt they should go. I saw a guy who lives in Australia – a Sinn Féin supporter – from Perth. As soon as he heard Martin had died he rang the travel agent and said, 'Get me on the next flight.' People from the American Congress – not staffers – came to the funeral. No public occasion and no real need to be there – but they came to Martin's funeral, at their own expense, from halfway across the world. There's a big massive gap in my life, definitely. A close family member's loss – that's the only way I can describe the loss of Martin.

20

Thomas P. DiNapoli

Shortly after I became New York comptroller, I got a phone call asking if I'd entertain a visit from Martin McGuinness and Ian Paisley. Now I know about New York state politics, but back then I didn't know a lot about Irish or Northern Irish politics. I did know the name Martin McGuinness and I certainly knew the name Ian Paisley from over the years. So it was with a sense of surprise and trepidation that I anticipated Ian Paisley coming to see me. This was either at the end of 2007 or the beginning of 2008.

They came to see me and the message was: 'We've gone through the period of the Troubles; we've turned a new page, we now have a different kind of government involving collaboration, and we need investment from overseas. Whatever public investment there is from the UK or Irish investment, it's very important that there be investment from around the globe, especially the US.'

As state comptroller, one of my responsibilities is trustee of the pension fund of New York state public workers. So the message was, it's a new day, it was very important for them as ministers to show on the ground that there's a dividend for peace and a dividend of investment in the economy. I met them in my office. They came in together. I've a picture on the wall of my office of me alongside Ian Paisley and Martin McGuinness.

I knew who Martin was, but I didn't have a predetermined

picture of him. When we met, I got the impression of a very thoughtful man, a very humble man, a very smart man, a very committed man. And in the years I came to know him I considered him a friend.

He always greeted me warmly and he always called me 'Thomas', which is what my family members usually call me. He did it with that beautiful accent and it made me feel very special.

My sense about Martin is that he had really deep commitments and a keen understanding that his role was pivotal in terms of the history of Ireland and the history of the north. Much as there might have been moments where it was very difficult working with Ian Paisley or working with Peter Robinson, and for a short period with Arlene Foster, it was a mission where he was part of a larger goal. He needed to convince people like me as to what was being done, so that we'd make the commitment to be partners to that peace. He was always keenly aware that people on the ground needed to see the benefit. And that's the goal for us – by investment we want to make money for our fund and for our pensioners, but if we can do that by helping to grow the economy, that would give people a new sense of confidence and would keep the peace process together.

I got the impression of the kind of man he was mainly from his manner. When Martin spoke, he had a very deliberate speaking manner. It wasn't impetuous; it wasn't off the cuff. He obviously thought through what he was going to say before he said it – which I appreciated as someone who was looking after investment. You want to feel you're listening to someone who is speaking with authority.

I don't want, at the same time, to give the impression that he wasn't a person of great passion and commitment, because he was. Certainly I learned more about his history from talking to him. He would share stories about his experiences even before he was in government. I mean, the man led an incredible life – a transformative life.

Martin's past IRA history didn't come up in my thinking. I mean, if you're presented with the firebrand Ian Paisley walking in the door with the former IRA partisan Martin McGuinness, clearly this is a unique moment in history. You don't look askance at that. Granted, I had to scratch my head at first.

But when you think of the changes in the leadership within the DUP, whereas Martin was the figure of continuity, if anything his role as statesman only grew. Technically he was junior to Paisley in the beginning, but you didn't get any sense of that. I saw how Paisley interacted with Martin in a room. It was not a sense of 'I'm the top dog and he's not.' Just the opposite, in fact. There really was a sense of a shared role.

From a US perspective, Gerry Adams was more the face of Sinn Féin, and in that sense more of a lightning rod than Martin. Martin wasn't, from a US perspective, as well-known a figure. That worked to his advantage.

He talked about his experience and his real concern for the common man and woman – that the work of government had to be transformative for the lives of everyday people. He had a real sense of neighbourhood. I was invited to come to an investment conference that Invest NI was hosting in Belfast. I agreed. Martin, being connected to Derry, really urged me to stay an extra day and to come to Derry. It wasn't my original plan to do that, but because of his very strong, determined and measured way of requesting the visit, I felt persuaded to spend the extra time to go to Derry.

He hosted a meeting and we had a wonderful session with some of the business leadership there. One of the local choirs sang a musical selection for us. And they asked what were my impressions. So I responded, 'There's no doubt that Belfast is a working city and that Belfast hums. But Derry sings.'

***

When I got my honorary degree in Derry in July 2017 I recounted that story. And it's true. There's a certain beauty and a wonderful warm feeling about Derry. Martin was very proud of the city and of its potential. And now when I go back I see the changes. You see the energy of the young people.

When I visited in 2008 he gave me a tour of the old barracks and some of the ideas he had for transforming it. The Peace Bridge then was just something on paper that he was talking about. Now, we're all able to walk on Martin's Peace Bridge. And he took us to the Bogside. Martina Anderson joined us on that visit.

But to see how far Derry has come now, on this visit in the summer of 2017, was really wonderful. I got to meet his two sons, pay my respects and offer my condolences in person. I said to his sons, 'You know, he will go down in history.'

In my years in elective life – thirty years in public office, or forty if you count my years on the school board – he will always be one of the great heroes to me, because of his willingness to engage in the political process to achieve a positive good. And when you consider where he came from and all that he went through, to make that transformation from being an incredibly fierce advocate to being a thoughtful government leader – without losing any of his core values or his sense of purpose in life – is something I admire tremendously.

Some of that original visit was used by Martin to point out some of the terrible things that had happened there. But the overlay of it was the tremendous pride Martin had in that community, and the appreciation of the fact that I took the time to come to Derry and did not ignore his people, if I can put it that way.

What I've said from the beginning to our investment folks is that – while there's a lot of focus on Belfast for obvious investment reasons – please don't forget the west, please don't forget Derry. And that's my message again. When we next meet with some of our investment partners I'm going to reiterate Martin's vision – that opportunities in the north are not just Belfast-centred. Opportunities can be found through all the regions of the north, with Derry as a centre.

And Derry is also interesting – something I didn't appreciate when I first visited – because of its integration with Donegal and the west. So there has already been such integration in that part of the island between the north and south, and that's something that I think and hope will continue, no matter what happens with Brexit.

***

Martin never forgot his roots, as we say in America. Some people forget their roots; he never did. And of course meeting his two sons this summer, who look so much like him – it was really moving. I lost my dad last year so I can see it's still a painful time for them.

Martin was a good politician because he was genuine. So many people I meet in public life, they develop a persona. They put on a mask; they have a projected personality that's not real.

It may help them get votes or may protect them in some way. Martin, if you were standing with him at a press conference or you heard him speak at an event in the north, or you heard him speak at an event in the US or in New York, or you had a private conversation with him in Stormont or in my office in New York city, it was the same person. So I think there was a purity in his vision, his values and his views; there was a genuineness in his personality. I think he was someone who was totally in touch with who he was, was very comfortable with who he was, didn't want to be anything different from what he was.

He also, I think, was someone who had an incredible sense of history. Others I'm sure could have risen to that important position of being the deputy first minister, but it fell on Martin McGuinness and he rose to the occasion. I think with all of the challenges of today, probably people on the DUP side miss him as well at a moment like this. He had such institutional knowledge and such sensitivity for how far the process has unfolded. He left too soon – his time was too short.

I was fortunate enough to hear him deliver speeches on at least two occasions in the US. He was not the type who bangs a fist on the table, but he spoke with great authority and, given who he was and what his position was, whenever he spoke the room was quiet. He commanded respect. But this was also because he was highly intelligent and an incredibly articulate person. But again I'd stress – with some people their public persona is different from their private self, but there was a consistency with Martin, which I valued. It showed how genuine he was.

When I heard of his illness I sent a note to him to wish him well, and shortly afterwards we had to send a note of condolence to his wife. It came as a shock – although when I heard what his condition was it made more sense, as a good friend of mine had that condition and passed from it. I know it's a very debilitating disease.

Coming to Derry in the summer of 2017, if he were alive he would certainly have been someone whom I would have visited. He was always warm and welcoming, always appreciative of what we were doing in partnership. He was always very kind to me, he always made time for me when he was in New York or on occasions when I have been in Ireland. He never made me feel like he was rushing me when we were having a conversation. He was very patient, very thoughtful, very warm and he had that big smile whenever he would greet me and at the end of a conversation. I never had anything but a wonderful feeling any time I was with him.

We would do small talk too. He was approachable; he was easy. There'd be family stuff, he'd always ask how a visit was going – and we'd get a few laughs on the way too.

I think Ireland north and south, I think the US – even the world – needs more Martin McGuinnesses today. And we should look at his memory as an inspiration for others. He was an advocate not just for his own community but for all sides in the north. And whether you're Protestant or Catholic – especially if you felt deprived because of the troubled history of the north – there is now the opportunity through the peace process to have a new day. That's what he was committed to, and that potential has still not been realised.

To me the leaders are not the loudest people out there. The leaders are the people who really have a focus, have a goal, stick with it, are inclusive in their strategy, bring people together. That was Martin McGuinness.

21

Peter King

My mother's family in Limerick city had been involved in the Irish War of Independence – they were on the de Valera side against Collins during the Civil War. My grand-uncle was in jail for a while during that time. So I knew about it. But to be honest with you, I didn't really know about Ireland until the early 1970s, when the civil rights movement broke out in the north. I just felt that being an American, and seeing for instance the influence that Jewish-America have with Israel, that African-Americans have with South Africa, that we were in a position to exert influence too. Since the British were our closest allies and there was a tremendous personal relationship between the United States and Ireland, we would be in a special position to be honest brokers. Then when I got into electoral politics and won office, I realised that, whether you know what you're talking about or not, once you have a title, people are more inclined to listen to you.

So I became much more involved in the late 1970s, and I went over to Ireland in 1980 during the first hunger strike – I was a councilman then. I remember being there on 8 December 1980 – the Feast of the Immaculate Conception – and the hunger strike was then on. We met with the family of Seán McKenna, who was one of the strikers – he had gone blind that day. Then I was over in the summer of 1981 for the plastic bullet tribunal. I remember the day we arrived was the day Kieran Doherty died. We went up to his house when they brought the body back.

Peter King

In 1983 when I returned to Ireland I was invited by republicans to the supergrass trials, and then I got invited back a few months later by a British TV station that was making a documentary on the trials. At that time I also spent a lot of time with loyalist families, including people who had called for the incineration of Catholics. [In 1984 George Seawright, then a DUP Belfast city councillor, allegedly declared that Catholics/ nationalists who objected to singing the British national anthem were 'just Fenian scum who have been indoctrinated by the Catholic Church. Taxpayers' money would be better spent on an incinerator and burning the lot of them. Their priests should be thrown in and burnt as well.']

I met Martin McGuinness later than I met some others in Sinn Féin. On the occasions I went to Ireland I used to spend most of my time in Belfast. Then, in the autumn of 1995, Martin came to Long Island for an event. He was with Gerry Adams, I believe, whom I'd met in the 1980s. I saw Martin quite a bit after that. Several times I went to the Sinn Féin Ard-Fheis and after 1995–96, I met him on a regular basis.

The real man was very different from the media image. He was very low-key, very unassuming, very – and I mean this in the best sense of the word – ordinary. He made no effort to overwhelm you. Gerry Adams came across as the college professor; Martin McGuinness came across as the guy who lives down the street. He just was a regular guy – very obliging. I'm trying to get the right word … If Martin saw somebody needed the door opened, he would open it for them; he was just very solicitous. I never saw him jump the line on anybody or interrupt anybody when they were speaking. He was a very determined guy, there was no doubt about that, but he was also calm and self-assured in a way that meant he didn't have to try to impress you.

He wasn't getting that much coverage in the US media back then. Gerry Adams was very much the face of Sinn Féin. Although I do remember once, in the late 1990s, I arranged to have Martin appear on the Chris Matthews TV show called *Hardball*. Martin went on and I guess he did a fifteen- to twenty-minute interview. Matthews is Irish-American, but he was very much against the IRA and Sinn Féin – he was pretty much a John Hume guy. But he understood McGuinness.

Anyway, after the interview, which was very friendly, very cordial, Matthews said to me, 'That guy knows how not to give you much!' But he did it in a very polite way. The average person watching wouldn't have realised, but Matthews was trying to get Martin to tip his hand as to what they were looking for, what they were going to do.

Maybe I'm diverging a bit here, but what struck me about that interview – and this also applies to Gerry – is that these were people who had virtually no formal education. Certainly no higher education, no diplomatic training, no political training at all. And he was up against Matthews, who was considered one of the foremost interrogators or questioners, who had some knowledge of the Irish issue; and yet Martin more than held his own. Looking at it, you wouldn't know who had the higher education, which of them had more training.

Martin, when he did start coming to the US, he was always seen by the media, to the extent that they wrote about him as being more the IRA man than Gerry Adams. Adams was the symbol of the republican movement; Martin was looked upon in the American media as the man behind the IRA.

I was receiving flak at the time for my involvement with the whole issue: the fact that I said the republican movement was a legitimate force, that it had to be part of any peace process; the fact that I supported a visa for Adams and also for McGuinness. But I would say I got no more flak for Martin than I did for Gerry and, again, in this country Martin did not get the coverage that he got in the British media. Also he came to the US after Gerry. In fact, Gerry used to say, 'I know I'm getting all this publicity, but I'm just John the Baptist, preparing the way for Martin McGuinness.'

***

I would think Martin's evolution would have been the same as that of Gerry Adams. He felt that the use of force was justified, that it was legitimate; but he also realised the fact that if you could get an agreement that moved everything forward, it was important to accept it. I don't believe his thinking changed so much as the tactics changed. He still wanted a united Ireland, he still wanted an end to discrimination, oppression, etc., which he believed the British were imposing. But when the opportunity came to take part in real negotiations, and he knew that the US was a guarantor in those negotiations, he was able to adapt very quickly.

It was a surprise to us in the US when he became minister for education rather than Gerry. We assumed Gerry would have taken that position. The fact that Martin was able to so easily move into that political role impressed us. During the peace process he had a political role, obviously; but it always seemed Gerry was more up-front in that. Whether he was or not is another matter, but that was the impression we had. I don't know if people realised Martin would be able to move so readily into the role of government.

One thing I was not surprised by was that he was not sectarian when in government. If there was a loyalist or unionist community that needed assistance, he was going to provide it. That may have surprised people like Ian Paisley, but it didn't surprise those of us who knew Martin. I know he could be a hard negotiator when it came to fighting for the rights of republicans, debating with the British and debating with the unionists about where Northern Ireland should be going; but the way he apportioned funding or the way he supported all communities in education, we weren't surprised by that at all.

For a while it seemed like there was a crisis a week or a crisis a month or a crisis every two months. Washington was at the centre of trying to resolve that. So we would have people coming: Trimble one week, then the British government with their version of it, and then Martin and Gerry coming in. Whenever Gerry came here, Martin was always given equal billing. That is where I think John Hume made a mistake. John was the only person in the SDLP anyone knew; Gerry and Martin came together. There was no sense of anyone pulling rank; there was never any sense of division.

People liked Martin – he was a very easy guy. I don't know anyone, including Ian Paisley, who, once they got to know Martin McGuinness, didn't like him. There was nothing not to like. I mean, some guys coming out of a revolutionary movement – where one way or another you'd been fighting your whole life – they've a hard time slowing down. But Martin was always calm, always generous with his time. I met Martin's wife several times and Martin came to know my wife, Rosemary, and he met my son a couple of times. He'd ask how they were doing and we'd exchange enquiries about family. I remember, later on, having dinner with Ian Paisley, who would go on about what a great guy his friend Martin was – he kept calling him 'Martin'.

I remember being at round tables with Martin, along with other American politicians, and some of them would ask him the dumbest questions. They would even use terms like 'Catholics' and 'Protestants' – just headline kind of questions, without knowing anything beyond that. But Martin was always very patient. And not condescending – he would always act as if it was a legitimate question.

In all our meetings I never asked Martin about his military past and I'm only going on news reports about his role with the IRA. I would say he had determination and he knew that the republican movement was in a long, hard fight. To be successful in that you had to have a long-term view. I don't believe Martin was interested in winning day-to-day battles within the movement, nor did he expect any quick victory. So I would think that no matter what was happening from the 1970s on, he was a very cool voice, he was a very calm voice.

When you realise that he was in negotiations back in the early 1970s, he was only in his twenties. And there he was, negotiating with senior diplomats and military leaders. I think that showed the regard people had for him and the esteem he was held in. There's a difference between being determined and headstrong. Martin was determined, but he also realised there was no absolute answer to anything. I never did see him annoyed; he used to banter back and forth with Gerry. It wasn't like guys who tell jokes. His was like a sort of Irish thing: a drop-dead humour.

I think he appreciated the contribution I made – he thanked me a number of times. I guess I saw that when I went over for the Sinn Féin Ard-Fheis in 1998. I attended the afternoon session and then the evening session, and you'd go to dinner somewhere in between, and you'd see his appreciation. I think he was appreciative of Irish-Americans who wanted to help. We weren't trying to impose our views, but we did have some input. He also wanted to know what it would take to get American support.

You know what – I can't think of anything negative I would say about him. In fact, I never heard anybody saying negative things about him. Even the British, when I got to meet them – I mean the British negotiators. People like Tony Lake, for instance, and George Mitchell on the American side, and the British: they trusted Martin McGuinness. There was never any suspicion that he was trying to put one over on them.

***

When I first ran for Congress in 1992, I used to be attacked. John Taylor went on television and said I was an evil man. When I was grand marshal at the St Patrick's Day parade in 1985, the Irish government boycotted the parade and put pressure on Cardinal O'Connor. I got a lot of flak then. One of the British newspapers had a picture of me shaking hands with Cardinal O'Connor and the caption was something about Cardinal O'Connor shaking 'the hand of blood', because I had been speaking on behalf of Sinn Féin.

Now you find Queen Elizabeth met Martin McGuinness, and obviously every recent British prime minister has met Martin McGuinness. Ian Paisley worked with Martin McGuinness. I'm not saying I was ahead of my time, but I knew the Sinn Féin leaders. It was a bit of a gamble, but I had a strong belief that they would honour their word. They wanted negotiations. I felt that if the US went in as a guarantor, we could count on Sinn Féin negotiating honestly and keeping their word.

I never doubted Martin McGuinness would do whatever had to be done in order to keep unity on the republican side, be able to work with the Irish side and also keep his word with the unionists. I also never heard a sectarian word from Martin McGuinness. At least with me, he never took the opportunity to say something about Paisley behind his back – which is something, considering all the things Paisley had said about him over the years.

Nor did I ever hear Martin say anything anti-clerical, which you would hear among a lot of republicans. People around him told me that he was a Catholic, that he took his faith seriously. He never wore it on his sleeve, but he was from all accounts a Catholic, and he tried to live a Catholic life.

As he went forward and saw the extent of the support he was getting – and also I think the extent of international support, particularly from the United States, that the president of the United States was going to be involved – I think that showed him the potential of going down the diplomatic route. And also he and Adams saw how long they were involved, and they thought – judging from my conversations with them – they thought the IRA could never lose, but on the other hand you could have a stalemate going on for thirty or forty years. So they asked themselves was it worth sacrificing generations of young Irish men and women for a stalemate, particularly if you could make real progress and find a diplomatic solution that would, they believed, lead inevitably (this is my term, not theirs) to a united Ireland or a form of united Ireland. Which you are almost at now. The border as a practical matter doesn't exist.

I just think it was a very practical and moral decision to make. If you were offered what they were offered, with international guarantees, then they realised that was the thing to take.

I think Martin did all he could for reconciliation. I think he was able to win over Ian Paisley to the extent that Paisley accepted him as being legitimate – legitimate as being the voice of Irish republicanism and legitimate in the sense that he was concerned with achieving some form of lasting reconciliation. I'm speaking from 3,000 miles away, but I think you're now a lot closer to reconciliation than you would have been if Martin McGuinness had not done what he did.

Of course you still have the centuries of distrust and it's the unionists' position that's being weakened, so I can see how they'd be more begrudging about things, but I just think the tone now has changed. If you went to the rank and file of unionists – maybe not necessarily the activists – I don't think you'd find that animosity towards – let's term them 'Catholics' – that you would have seen back in the 1970s or 1980s. There's a realisation that, for better or worse, we have to somehow deal with each other and, in more positive terms, people realise that so much of the fighting was unnecessary.

***

I didn't know of Martin's illness until my cousin in Limerick contacted me when Martin made a television appearance. She was not necessarily a Sinn Féin supporter; she was more of a southern cynic – basically saying, 'One's as bad as the other.' I'm using her as an example of someone who had come to actually like Martin McGuinness. She phoned me and then emailed me and said, 'My God, Martin McGuinness looks terrible, I hope he's not as sick as he looks.'

When I heard of his death I was really sad. First of all because he was still a comparatively young man. He had done so much and he was never a guy for ego. I never saw him wanting to gain awards or lead the parade. And it wasn't a false modesty. I think he also realised all that people had suffered, including friends of his and people he knew – that there really wasn't that much to celebrate.

And there was his sense of humour. I remember one of the things he said. I guess Gerry Adams had tried to escape from jail a few times and got caught. And there was a construction project somewhere – maybe New York – and he said, with Gerry there: 'I hope they've better luck with that than Gerry had with his tunnel!' I'm not doing it justice – it was said without a smile or anything.

Martin McGuinness was a historic figure of the movement in Ireland, which has led to a bringing together of the whole island. He had to keep a very forceful movement moving forward and, though there were obviously dissenters along the way, he still managed at the same time to make progress. He was doing so many things at one time. He should certainly be remembered.

22

Martin Mansergh

In the autumn of 1991 John Hume brought to then Taoiseach Charles Haughey a document, following discussions with Gerry Adams. This document was the embryonic form of what would eventually end up being [though greatly altered and in much expanded form] the Downing Street Declaration.

I was asked to work it up further. Drafts went backwards and forwards at intervals over the following months, initially to Hume but then through Fr Alec Reid to Sinn Féin, during which time Albert Reynolds replaced Charles Haughey as taoiseach. There came a point when no further progress was possible without the resumption of direct contact with Sinn Féin [which had originally taken place in 1988 but was broken off shortly after the SDLP had terminated their public dialogue with the party]. So, in October 1992, I had a meeting at the Redemptorist monastery in Dundalk at which no colleagues were involved. There was just myself and Fr Reid, with Martin McGuinness and one other person, which was usually but not always Aodhán McAteer. It was the first of several meetings that continued at about six-week intervals up to May 1993. They resumed again in early 1994 up until the IRA ceasefire on 31 August.

McGuinness did virtually all the talking for his side. We were in a relatively small room in the Dundalk monastery, and all the discussions had two phases. The first was where we talked broadly about anything and everything relating to the overall situation. The second part was focused on the text of the document. The room for flexibility was quite limited. Everything had to be checked out on their side. My view is that they did indeed have a collective leadership.

Our meetings were also necessary to support confidence-building. The objective was to enable the republican movement to move from the Armalite and the ballot box to a purely political engagement through the construction of a democratic nationalist consensus. McGuinness was a part of all that.

I did like him from the first meeting. I mean we didn't go off together to the pub, but he was amicable. On substance, progress was slow but methodical, and without sudden breakthroughs, but the potential benefit of an end to violence – if it could be achieved against the odds – was enormous.

In general, I didn't spend time wondering whether the republicans I was meeting at that time represented the IRA or Sinn Féin. My working assumption was that they represented the republican movement. Sometimes I was given a written message to bring back to Albert Reynolds, either purporting to come from the Army Council or signed by Gerry Adams. On one occasion, it was not clear which of the two the message was from, so I asked Martin. He smiled and replied, 'Does it matter?'

Judging from my dealings with him I would say that McGuinness was not a hothead – on occasion, in fact, he could be quite cold. In August 1994, coming up to the ceasefire, the IRA assassinated a leading loyalist strategist. Fr Reid raised it at the beginning of a meeting. McGuinness's reaction was that this man was a killer; he'd been involved in assassination, end of story. So there was that other side to him.

At other times you were quite unsure how he was feeling. An

abiding memory the evening before the Good Friday Agreement was concluded was of Adams and McGuinness coming in with very long faces. There was Bertie Ahern, Mo Mowlam and myself in the room, and there were two sessions for about two hours each. There were detailed issues on sheets of paper, over seventy in number, being raised, mainly by their extensive backroom team, covering various aspects of the negotiations that had not been resolved to their satisfaction, and in reality it was too late to do much about them now. They were not the critical issues, like prisoner release, on which Adams and McGuinness dealt directly with Blair. They left with long faces, to the point where it appeared they would have us believe they were not going to be on board. But we realised you couldn't have a situation where Sinn Féin effectively had a veto on whether the Irish government concluded the agreement or not.

Despite their forlorn appearance, an agreement on Strand 1 or power-sharing followed in the middle of the night and Mitchel McLaughlin, then Sinn Féin Party chairman, sounded an upbeat note on radio the following morning.

***

I went with President Mary McAleese to the unveiling of the Messines Tower in Belgium in November 1998, which was constructed by young people from both loyalist and nationalist communities. Shortly afterwards, I was travelling up to Derry and was a little ahead of my colleagues, which allowed me to have a one-to-one for about twenty minutes with McGuinness. I was recounting the events at the Messines Tower and, a bit to my surprise, he expressed approval of it.

Over the intervening period, Sinn Féin people have revealed

that they had great-uncles who had fought in the First World War, so further gestures could be made, and that could be seen as progress. The second-last time I met McGuinness was the summer of 2016 for one such gesture. He came as deputy first minister down to what remains of Richmond Barracks to unveil a bust of Francis Ledwidge [an Irish soldier and poet who died at Passchendaele, famous for his poem 'A Lament for Thomas MacDonagh']. I think this was part of his belief that we had to broaden our perception of all our traditions. It was a gesture of reconciliation. When McGuinness passed me in the corridor afterwards, he said to me, 'We have a lot to learn.' It was just a comment thrown out, but it indicated that the strong ideological positions held thirty or forty years ago no longer prevailed.

Another area where I found Martin McGuinness very progressive was on the subject of Europe. Another time that I was with him on his own, post-agreement, was after the defeat of the Nice Treaty ratification in the first referendum in the Republic [the treaty was initially rejected by Irish voters in June 2001, but was subsequently accepted in October 2002]. I taxed him with what I considered Sinn Féin's backward ideological hostility to Europe. To my surprise, he expressed sympathy, saying that Sinn Féin had not updated its policy on this since the 1970s.

I, of course, was always aware of his reputation and the various positions he had taken up throughout his life. But positions change over time. In 1998, if you'd been a betting man, the odds would have been 100–1, if not 1,000–1, that Paisley and McGuinness would ever be in government together. The assumption was that the main responsibilities would fall to the Ulster Unionists on one side and the SDLP on the other. Blair did all he could to prop up Trimble; he had a sort of religious objection almost to Paisley for a long time. But he changed that later on – he had to.

McGuinness also held off on decommissioning for a long time. I think Blair didn't really care about decommissioning, as long as the weapons weren't being used. But the unionists did care, and if republicans wanted to be in government they had to accept it, as well as providing support for the police. But for a long time McGuinness was fond of saying, 'If anyone thinks there's going to be any decommissioning, they're living in cloud cuckoo land!' He used that expression quite frequently. But in the final analysis, being in government mattered more. Once asked on radio if I trusted Sinn Féin, I replied that I trusted the necessities they were under.

I think both McGuinness and Adams realised they had to develop and present a strain of moderation. McGuinness managed that well and, I think, actually believed in it.

***

In the 2011 presidential election, he always knew he was going to take a lot of criticism from the media in the south. I think the mistake the republican movement makes with regards to the south is that they don't realise that there's a different ambience. It wasn't so much anything McGuinness did or said but the feeling that, if he were elected, the presidency could be used – coming up to the 1916 centenary – to legitimise the Provisional IRA campaign by trying to equate the two. Where the problem could arise was in any attempt to use the presidency in a party political way to try to validate what had always been rejected by all governments on this side of the border.

Saying that, I do think McGuinness was probably the best candidate republicans could have chosen to run for the presidency. People generally would have a fairly positive view of McGuinness's role from the early 1990s. Whatever happened before that is another matter.

The fact is that Martin McGuinness worked for nearly ten years in government – he sat round a cabinet table and showed it could work. Coming towards the end, there was the Brexit factor, and he was rapidly deteriorating in health. Whether he would have tried longer and harder in other circumstances we don't know. In my last brief conversation with him, at the funeral of Dermot Gallagher [a chief Irish negotiator in the peace process and former ambassador], I remarked that it had been a great achievement to keep the Executive going for nearly ten years, even though at that point it had come down.

My view in long-term projects like this is that you will have setbacks; you have to take a long-term view and have patience. I think the nine years and more spent in government were very good; they were years well spent. McGuinness had the temperament for it.

***

I felt very sorry when I heard of his illness and death. We had a good relationship, which was never broken. We both recognised that he represented one side of things, while I represented another side of things; but yes, I was sorry when he died and I went up to the funeral to pay my respects. I was struck by the community side of the funeral – there were a few PSNI officers observing up on the walls of Derry, but that was it. It was a massive demonstration of community strength in an orderly and dignified way.

How great a loss was he? I believe a big loss. There are many conflict situations around the world that could have used an Adams and McGuinness. What the two of them succeeded in doing – managing to extract their movement from what had at best been a stagnant military campaign, which in my opinion would have eventually imploded – was to convert it into a political currency where they realised gains for the republican community in Northern Ireland and achieved a substantial though not dominant position in the south.

I think that Adams and McGuinness were a more united leader and deputy leader, a more united political pair than any other I can think of in any party, whether in the south or elsewhere. They may have adopted Benjamin Franklin's opinion that if they didn't hang together they would hang separately. And of course they well knew the British would create splits and division where they could. That doesn't mean they always instinctively saw eye to eye, of course, but they presented a united front. I have no doubt there were times when they were at variance, but they weren't on their own; they had a tight collective leadership. They were the two front people, and they had much to offer as a model of conflict resolution to other places of conflict throughout the world.

People face different situations and they have to respond to them. Did McGuinness do his country some service? Yes, he did. I saw in one of his obituaries that he once referred to his discussions with me as friendly and constructive – I would agree with that. I met him the day of Albert Reynolds's funeral, and shortly afterwards on RTÉ television he referred for the first time publicly – and as if he were proud of it – to the secret talks that we had held, which had helped prepare the way for the famous meeting and handshake between Hume, Adams and Reynolds on the steps of Government Buildings on 6 September 1994, a week after the IRA ceasefire, which was meant to seal the peace. While it did subsequently break down temporarily, the course had been set in 1994, and McGuinness helped guide the sequel for more than twenty years.

23

Pat Doherty

The first time I was set to meet Martin I didn't – the whole thing was something of a misadventure. In 1985 I had arranged a meeting with Sinn Féin in Dublin and after that I was going up to Derry to meet with John Hume. Sinn Féin then also arranged for me to meet with Sinn Féin representatives in Derry. I agreed to that, except I wasn't told the address. At that time I was working for the New York city government and we said we'd speak to all representatives of all political parties. We were interested in finding out as much as we could. We had a mandate from our trustees for investment in Ireland, in accordance with fair employment. The state department initially, on our first trip over, seemed to be cautioning us about meeting with Sinn Féin, but we said we needed to meet everybody.

I knew where one of the Sinn Féin representatives lived and so once I arrived in Derry we ended up going to his house and slipping our card into his mailbox, but nothing came of it. I found out subsequently that Martin and a number of other people were waiting for us at the Capel Street office in Derry.

I saw him the following year, either in Derry or Belfast – I'm not honestly sure which. He had a very open face, a very friendly demeanour. Our meeting was the year that programme *At the Edge of the Union* came out, which profiled him and Gregory Campbell, who I also met in Derry. Martin at the time was an elected representative to the Assembly, and over the years I didn't perceive any change in him. We were dealing with him in terms of equal employment opportunities according to the MacBride Principles [nine fair employment principles constituting a corporate code of conduct for United States companies doing business in Northern Ireland], of which he was very supportive. Certainly his commitment to the equality agenda, as his party came to call it, was steadfast from the outset.

In his manner he was extremely friendly, affable, outgoing. In fact, I think we did go for a beer with him. He always had a genial, friendly demeanour when he dealt with us. At the same time his commitment was extremely strong on human rights issues. He was critical of the British government, of the Northern Ireland Office position relating to the equality agenda and other things, but never in a personal way. I never picked up anger from him.

All political figures in Ireland, the first thing they want to know of Americans is, what are your roots, how far back do you go to when your people came to the United States, where were they from, etc.? So I told Martin that my father was born in Derry, in Nelson Street. We chatted about that and I said, 'I have cousins called Doherty.' And eventually he said, 'I think your cousin taught me.' Patrick Doherty was in the Christian Brothers School – he was a teacher there and Martin was a pupil of his. This was my father's cousin – my cousin once removed. He was a very good teacher, Martin said.

I told him my grandfather's history. He was in the old IRA – Derry City Brigade – and fought on the republican side during the Civil War. He was imprisoned in the north by the British and then in Dublin during the Civil War period. My grandfather used to say he was treated worse by his fellow-countrymen. After he got out of jail he went back up north: my father had already been born and my grandmother was up there. He ended up going to New York, earned a little money to buy their passage, and then sent for them. When he left Ireland, my grandfather left the politics behind him. Some people became very active afterwards, but he didn't do that.

So Martin and I traded that kind of information. As I said, he figured we might even have been related – and at the time there was a slight resemblance between us. His family lived on Wellington Street, while my family was on Nelson Street, right next door.

In those early days of coming over to Ireland I didn't meet Martin's family. In fact, during those early days there was an effort – for security reasons – to keep them in the background. So he didn't talk about his family, other than to say that he had two boys.

***

I was with him the first time he came to the States. At that point he was minister for education. I didn't meet him at the airport – we met in town – and eventually we ended up at Francie Gildernew's place. Francie was Michelle Gildernew's brother [Michelle is a prominent Sinn Féin figure and MP for Fermanagh/South Tyrone] and lives in New York. He got a big van, which we rented, and we gave Martin a guided tour through Times Square. He had a childlike quality – he was so excited! It was fun to see him having fun.

Subsequently, when he was in ministerial office and he came over to meet city officials, I would organise the official car. For security reasons we had arranged to close Brooklyn Bridge [of

course there was a concern for his security – there always was].
He came out of the car, I remember, and the police were twenty,
thirty feet away, and he was talking excitedly on his cell phone to
someone: 'Pat stopped the traffic for us!' he said. And once again
it was this almost childlike excitement that was really funny to
see.

I was very impressed when we asked him about the civil
service and the permanent bureaucracy. These people had always
been criticised by Sinn Féin and others because the permanent
civil service would tend to stifle any change or reform. And that
had been our experience, trying to work with them in terms
of trying to promote the MacBride Principles. But Martin
said, 'My civil servants have been outstanding – outstandingly
cooperative.' He was so impressed with them and how helpful
they were. This wasn't expected, I don't think: it was just genuine
surprise at the level of cooperation shown. I'm talking here about
the Education civil servants.

And of course politics had moved on at this stage. It was
post-Good Friday Agreement and there was an air of goodwill.
But it was still impressive. There had been initial suspicion that
if you had a Sinn Féin minister coming into the department,
the permanent civil servants would be extremely uncooperative,
would try to thwart his plans. Martin seemed to be pleasantly
surprised to find that that wasn't the case. In fact, he was moved
by that.

His personality and the demeanour that he brought to the
job also played a part in that, I imagine. I had been going over
a number of times to the north from the mid-1980s and I had
always made a point of speaking to all sides – Sinn Féin and the
DUP and the British government as well. Unionist politicians

would say to us, 'Please pass on this message, we can't speak to Sinn Féin.' I would make the point that there is no substitute for personal contact, as opposed to through intermediaries, because so much of communication is non-verbal.

For example, I had a lot of interaction with DUP officials. And I remember one time being with a couple of Sinn Féin representatives, and I said, 'Look, I think you can do business with the DUP.' And Danny Morrison said, 'No, no – they're impossible to deal with. They can't even bring themselves to condemn attacks on us.' I told them I had been with Peter Robinson and his wife earlier that afternoon – this was when the negotiations were going on – and we were talking about the question of Adams and McGuinness being involved in the peace process, the fact that some unionists didn't like that. And I think it was Peter Robinson's wife – but anyway this woman said, 'Oh, it's going to be like Michael Collins' [she felt Martin and Adams might be killed by former comrades for negotiating with the likes of the DUP]. I was watching Peter Robinson's face at that point and I could see that pained him, the thought of some republicans being prepared to attack Martin.

And that's why I told Martin about Peter's look of concern, of pain. And Martin said, 'How did you know that was really the case?' And I said, 'It was too subtle to be feigned.' I just saw it flash across his face – that look of concern.

I mention that story to indicate the need for face-to-face meetings. Once they were exposed to Martin face to face, I knew it would be different. And the same thing was the case with Gerry Adams.

Martin and Gerry had very different personalities. Out-standing personal skills, obviously, both of them; but they came across as different people, though both were very effective in their own way. Martin might have been – I don't know – a little more touchy-feely. As I got to know Martin better, my appreciation of him and his skills deepened. What he was able to do, the bridges he was able to build. I became more and more of an admirer as the years went on.

Adams came to the US first, and it was very funny. I told people, 'When Adams gets to the States, it'll be like the genie is out of the bottle.' I knew Gerry getting the visa would change things. That's why a lot of effort in the US was focused on getting him a visa. And suddenly in the United States Bill Clinton is in the White House and he reacts and gets the visa sorted.

Adams was given a visa first and then Martin. Clinton said, 'I am doing this to further the peace process. These people are working to promote peace and ceasefires.' So that was the background. The US media knew that something was going on in the republican movement and that peace might be on the way. So here were people who were taking risks for peace. That led to a more favourable coverage of their visits.

During Adams's visit, the media in the US were being criticised for being too friendly and fawning over him. But I told people, 'I was watching that interview. They were very sharp with him.' For American interviews, those were very sharp interviews. They were not like you would have in Ireland and the UK, where some interviewers would say, 'You've got blood on your hands, don't you, don't you?' The US interviews weren't like that, but they were still very sharp.

Both Martin and Gerry were quite literally disarming – they had a disarming demeanour, a way of self-presentation that was very effective. Martin was particularly disarming. I think it may have been his nature. As I said, there was a certain kind of childlike quality to him at times, for want of a better word. He had a childlike enthusiasm and people would pick that up. Some of the unionists, of course, were critical of Adams – they saw everything he said as calculated. Then Martin McGuinness would show up and they wouldn't get the same impression. That said, Gerry could be quite spontaneous as well.

***

Here's a funny story. The first time we went over to Ireland in 1985, we had meetings with the official Unionist Party people. Then we got a call on that trip from Gregory Campbell, saying, 'You know, you should come and meet with the DUP.' So inside the next year I was over in Derry and I made a point of meeting the DUP at the Guildhall. It was to be a twenty-minute meeting: four hours later we were still at it. It was fascinating. The reason for that was, Gregory was only seeing Martin McGuinness on TV or Gerry Adams on TV. He'd never spoken to someone who had nationalist feelings or pro-republican feelings on these issues. So I would say something and then he would give a response. And then I'd say, 'Yes, Gregory, but what about, you know …' and I would take it to the next step in the discussion. And you know something? He had no response. Now why was that? Because he'd been used to talking back to Martin McGuinness on the TV, Gerry Adams on the TV. And the TV never said, 'Hey Gregory, wait a minute, what about X?'

When you had Martin face to face with these people, and Gerry Adams face to face with these people, it was a different dynamic. It was a learning process for them and that was an important aspect of it. But my initial meeting with Gregory was very funny: he had an initial answer or response but nothing beyond that.

***

Martin's public speeches in the US were very direct, very straightforward and extremely forceful. I mean he knew how to rouse people, he knew how to make his points. He had a long history in the republican movement, so obviously he did a lot of public speaking at party events. When he came to the States it was the same. He was extremely effective as a public speaker in the US. He would speak with great force and sincerity, but he was not a shouter. Neither was Gerry Adams. Their presentations were excellent.

Martin knew how to get along with people – whether from a stage or in person – and he was that way with everybody. The unionists and even Ian Paisley found the same. People were exposed to something they hadn't expected. And he was a complete workhorse. The first time that Tom DiNapoli met him, we were both invited over to a conference, and Sinn Féin was having a fundraiser or something in the Europa Hotel the next night, which we were invited to attend. So at the table there was Adams, DiNapoli and then they had me sitting next to Martin. We had a nice conversation and then Martin produced this dossier – all his ministerial papers; and now he's working on his boxes, furiously writing and making notes. And I said, 'This guy takes this very seriously. Shows real dedication to the task.' This was supposed to be a function, a party. He wasn't partying – he was working.

His greatest strength was his humanity and his love of people. I don't think he really judged individuals. His lack of rancour –

that was a great strength. When he ended up negotiating directly with Blair's team, they came to have a great affection for him. It's very obvious – you can read it in the memoirs.

I first heard of his illness by reading about it in the papers. There was speculation that he might be ill when they cancelled his trip to China. Then we got word that he'd stepped down and we read the newspaper reports about the surprising nature of the illness. But no one thought he would go that quickly.

He has indeed been a loss to politics, and his absence in Northern Ireland is very keenly felt in the recent negotiations. I've heard that from numerous people. As for the mock-up coffin and his image that was put on bonfires: that was done by people who obviously had never met him. They didn't know him. They knew the strongman, the scarecrow that some people put together – but they had no interaction with him. People who met him in the flesh and blood ended up interacting with him – even unionists, the British, politicians, government officials and so forth.

His death has left such a gap. But you know, at the same time, with someone like him, he becomes a part of you. Right now, I can hear his voice inside my head.

24

Mary Lou McDonald

Like any kid who grew up in Dublin watching the Troubles, watching the hunger strikes, watching all that politics and all that drama play out in your sitting room, of course I had a strong perception of Gerry Adams and of Martin McGuinness. It was obviously a benign view. But I never could have known – without first-hand exposure to him – how clever Martin McGuinness was. He's always remarked upon for how personable and how decent he was – and he was! – but my God he was astute as well.

You'd see it in simple interactions with people on the street, in friendly situations, but it would also be evident in sometimes hostile situations where he'd have to think on his feet, where an aggrieved person might come across him and where there might even have been media observing. In situations where things could have become stressful for all concerned, he had a way of defusing the situation and sort of deconstructing things. That was the measure of his brilliance, and it allowed him to remain a staunch, committed republican to the very end and yet to take extraordinary initiatives, looking outwards, reaching outwards. You see, he got people; he understood the human condition, the full emotional register.

I started off seeing Martin McGuinness as a hero, a giant of Irish politics, of Irish nationalism, of Irish republicanism. I wouldn't have been intimidated by him – he was never intimidating – but I was certainly overawed by him. Then, over time, the relationship deepened, the friendship deepened and my appreciation of him deepened. So you start out from afar, thinking this person is a wonder. But it was only when you were up close and personal, when you've worked with the person and really appreciated their skills that you realised how incredible a person he was. For all of us, it was a privilege to have had that opportunity to work alongside him.

At one stage the hostility towards him right across the political spectrum north and south was very pronounced. Yet in the south it's very difficult to find a political figure who didn't like Martin McGuinness. They may be there, but they're rare. As for the north, he'd have had his critics. But even those who'd have criticised fairly loudly at some level still had a huge appreciation for his complexity. Because he didn't play to straight stereotypes. He despised laziness, he had a tremendous work ethic, he had very high standards, and he expected very high standards from all of us. He didn't have a lazy mind or slip into lazy assumptions – he always had a capacity to stretch himself.

He didn't need to have a row with people. If you messed up, Martin McGuinness didn't have to raise his voice, he would simply have to give you 'The Look'. The Look told you that something had gone wrong. The Look told you that you had messed up. Never wanting to see that Look again meant that you said to yourself, 'That's not going to happen again.'

He would get annoyed and fed up: anything that was crass or sloppy would irritate him. He worked very hard, as the stakes were very high. So that quality for me was never a negative thing. I would think it extraordinary if anyone in a position such as his, having lived the life he lived, didn't have moments of acute narkiness if people messed up.

He had incredible body language. If you watch for it in the media – shaking his head, his movements – he was a very expressive person. So if he was annoyed, he couldn't just button himself up and contain it. Certainly not working with his close colleagues. He was a human being, he wasn't a saint; but as human beings go he was pretty exceptional.

Depending on the circumstances, Martin was also an instinctive activist, an instinctive politician. His gut mattered to him, and how he would react to a proposition. His sense of the thing, whether or not it sat right with him, whether or not it sat right with the popular mood. Or his sense of how it might sit with unionism, with others. I suppose the modern lingo for it is emotional intelligence – an intuitive sense of things. I don't know, but I'd have put that down to how he was so active in so many ways from such a young age. I always got the feeling that quality got honed in his home, with Peggy and with all his family, but also on the streets of Derry. Sometimes if you have to face danger and come through it, you have to be pretty innovative. And I'd say the same skills served him throughout his life in its different chapters and different tempos and in the different political and economic and social circumstances he inhabited. I don't believe that instinct came to him later in life. It was hard-wired into him.

***

Initially some of my friends and acquaintances would have been cool at the idea that I was a friend of Martin McGuinness. For the most part they'd show it by avoiding the subject. There'd have been very few people who would actually have said out loud, 'What in the name of God are you doing with him/them?' I come from a fairly nationalist family, so it wouldn't have been an issue for the vast majority of my family. As for those for whom it was an issue – feck them!

The interesting thing was that people were sort of intrigued by him: 'What's he like?' And then invariably when people would meet him, it'd be, 'He's very friendly. He's very gentle. He's very funny. He asked me things!' And in later years, when he'd be on the television talking about fishing or things that he loved, people were always very taken with that. Lots of times politicians are seen as being very one-dimensional, and let's be honest, in some cases that's not an unfair perception. Martin was anything but. He occupied very high office and discharged huge public duties, but he wasn't a go-getter or one of these with a big career plan. He was very old school; there was something old-fashioned about him.

I think he loved the work. Declan Kearney [Sinn Féin MLA] and I did a trip to the Somme with him when he was deputy first minister. I had seen Martin in action in different scenarios and on other official trips, but it was at the Somme in May 2016 that I think I really saw writ large Martin McGuinness the statesman. The absolute effortless grace of him at that time. The hospitality was incredible by all of those who greeted us – including unionist people at the Ulster Tower. They couldn't have been happier to see us and they really appreciated our coming. I'm delighted I made that trip with Martin because I got to see him in action.

Sometimes when he made those big stretches it caused annoyance and discomfort in our movement. People felt what we were doing was all one-way traffic. But his instinct as much as his head told him this was the right thing to do. And if there was flak, criticism, OK. He wasn't a people-pleaser.

Though I'm sure it must have been stressful, at times. Stress has an effect on any human being, so I'd be surprised if it didn't take a toll on his health, particularly given the pace he worked at. Having said that, he had the constitution of an ox. We all put in the hard yards in this business, but my God! He could be going to Silicon Valley and the next thing he's in Hong Kong. I remember saying to him, 'God Almighty, how are you managing all of this?' And he said he could get by on very little sleep, but he had to have a time where he could make up for it. He had absolutely amazing stamina. To me he seemed invincible – like the cool, clean hero who sweeps in with that sense of physical invincibility. Then he got sick, and got sicker, and died. And it's still shocking that it all happened so rapidly.

***

I thought his treatment by the media in the south during the presidential election was utterly repulsive. I'm thinking of Miriam O'Callaghan and RTÉ with their 'How do you sleep at night?' I'm thinking of the nonsense of Vincent Browne (though he is a person I personally like). You would swear listening to these people that Martin McGuinness was the trigger that caused the northern Troubles. The utter hypocrisy of it. And the cheek of them to say to him, 'Who are you from Derry to presume that you're Irish enough or that your citizenship is of sufficient standing that you should contest for the position of first citizen?' It was absolutely obnoxious. I'd go so far as to say RTÉ represented a failure of public service broadcasting.

The thing was, they didn't want him to be president. He was an outsider. The establishment in the southern state have had it all their own way for a very long time and they're not going to give up without a struggle. And yes, in part it's to do with class: the hungry streets of Derry meeting the comfortable affluence of Dublin 4. But class is not the only factor. They'd had Mary McAleese, but she'd become part and parcel of life in the south. She didn't always have it easy – she has horrific stories from her time at RTÉ – but then of course she had Fianna Fáil at her back. With Martin, it was the idea that this was a Sinn Féin person. Here he was, coming and debating issues of Ireland; their attitude to Martin McGuinness was, 'Who are you to question us?' That's how it shakes down. It was a partitionist mentality and one that was about protecting the status quo.

Martin knew all that. In fact, one of the most moving speeches I have heard from anyone was made by Martin McGuinness in the Mansion House at a rally for him during his presidential campaign. Colm Meaney, the actor, came home and hosted it. Martin was under fire from the media – all about the IRA, when was he in it, when did he leave it? As a woman in my neighbourhood said, 'We couldn't give a continental curse when he left!' Certainly in working-class areas of Dublin they couldn't have cared less. But he was getting an awful lot of flak. And he made a speech that night that I thought was incredible; I regret to this day that it wasn't recorded.

He talked about joining the IRA in Derry and why he did it; he talked about friends of Bernie's who'd been killed. He talked about being afraid when he joined but knowing he'd have felt deeply ashamed had he not. It was an incredible speech and the most honest account I have ever heard from anybody that participated in armed struggle in the course of that epoch. As he said, his heart was always in the Bogside, but he always had that defiance, that part that says, 'I'm right.' And it wouldn't have mattered ultimately to McGuinness, but he and his family must have found that southern media hostility upsetting. But still there was that defiance in him, and there was a reason at all times for his actions and he could always rationalise them and defend them.

***

At his funeral, I couldn't believe he had died. I had been up to see him a week or ten days previously. I went to visit and we had a great chat. He was quite weak – he was in Altnagelvin hospital in Derry. He was really pleased to see me and I was conscious not to overstay. We were having the craic and I was telling him about the [2017 Stormont Assembly] election. And as you leave, in a typical Irish fashion when someone's in hospital, you say, 'Is there anything you need me to do for you, Martin?' Like, as if. But to my delight he said, 'Yes.' Great, I thought. Now I can be useful. So he said, 'Mary Lou, I want you to go out and win.' And that's the last time I spoke to him.

I felt like a child about to burst into tears at the funeral, listening to Christy Moore sing. I still feel his loss as a friend and as a political leader. But I don't like the way in recent months we've been hearing, 'Oh if Martin were here the institutions would be up' – trying to paint the rest of Martin's friends and colleagues as inept or malicious. Certainly trying to put a bad reflection on Michelle O'Neill. Don't forget, Michelle was categorically Martin's preference to be his successor. And bear in mind Martin ultimately called it, saying, 'We need to walk away from this.'

We're all unique human beings and we all bring our own qualities to bear on things, but there will never be another

Martin McGuinness – or not for a generation, anyway. Someone who brings precisely that blend of what he had – the political alchemy, the magic. So of course at a political level we miss him desperately. When we meet now, even as a political leadership, we still expect him to open the door and walk in. You kind of forget, and then you remember.

I also miss him as a friend. Just simple things. He loved his grandchildren. I remember years ago one of them – he's an older lad now – got burned in the bath. The child was OK, but my God, Martin was beside himself. He took great pride in the fact that Rita O'Hare, one of our great friends, came up with the name for his first grandson and I named his youngest so far – Emmett's daughter Sive – because that's my favourite name. He was tickled pink. He loved other people's kids as well. He'd make a beeline for the kids if they were in the company. He really was a family man.

As well as that, he was resolute. He would assess a situation beforehand, of course, and he would make sure to listen too; but once he was set: resolute. If the brickbats came, if the proverbial hit the fan, so be it. Once Martin McGuinness committed himself to a course of action, that was it.

Do you remember when he went to Windsor Castle in April 2014, and he had to wear a white tux? There was a whole discussion over whether he should or shouldn't wear the white tux. I remember saying at the time, 'For the love of Christ, if you're going to the gig, wear it.' And he looked great in it. But there was a bit of discomfort around all that. And I understand that – it's not our thing. That was the point of it.

He absorbed a huge amount. A lot of people in our party give out about the media, and in many cases we have reasons to do so, but I never remember Martin going on that track. I think he would have regarded it as a terrible waste of time. If he had something to say to one of them he'd say it. He was old school. And I think that's why people latched on to him and were comfortable with him. There was something traditional running through him. And I think that was something to do with coming from Derry. Because I think there's a big difference between Belfast and Derry – two totally different places.

Without question, his name will be alive and fresh a hundred years from now. I think history and reflection will be very kind to Martin McGuinness. And I've no doubt that, as the story moves to the next chapter and the next, we'll get a true sense of the legacy of what he achieved. He moved mountains. He did things that people thought they would never live to see. And I think history will contradict the critics, the naysayers and the establishment bullies who tried to keep him from being seen in his true light.

25

Niall O'Dowd

I first met Martin McGuinness when I was over in Ireland with a delegation of Irish-Americans in 1993. We met Martin and Gerry Adams at the Cultúrlann [an Irish language cultural centre] on the Falls Road. We had come over as emissaries from President Clinton, who had just been elected, and we were putting a proposition to Sinn Féin that we had previously talked to them about, regarding the possibility of President Clinton becoming involved in the situation in Northern Ireland.

We had got a guarantee from Clinton prior to his election that he would intervene and I was very certain that he would do it. Many other people thought it was just a political gesture, but I got to know Clinton's people and Clinton himself, and I thought he was really interested.

There was a lot of media interest in our visit. We ended up in a sort of classroom in the Cultúrlann, and we were sitting at these little desks! It wasn't at all in keeping with our own sense of the seriousness of the occasion. Gerry and Martin arrived separately. Martin arrived in quite a lather. I hadn't met him up to that point, but I had read a lot about him. He had driven from Derry and had been either pulled over or pursued by an RUC police patrol car the whole way – harassment, basically. Clearly they knew he was coming to meet us.

He came in and for the only time in my life I saw him quite indignant and angry at his treatment. He told us, 'You know, this is what we put up with the whole time. They knew I was coming to see you, they made every effort to let me know they knew I was coming to see you, and they were trying to block me from coming to see you.' So I remember it because seeing Martin McGuinness agitated left quite an impression on me.

Eventually we sat down and talked. This was a group of Bruce Morrison, Chuck Feeney, Bill Flynn and myself: a very serious group of Irish-American leaders. What was really remarkable with both Adams and McGuinness was how pragmatic they both were about the whole situation and how they were ready to work with the White House, and how they both held remarkably few grudges against the British authorities. They just saw it all as a continuum; that this was how this thing was developing. There was an American role, there was an Irish government role, there was a British government role and there were intermediaries. We knew all that stuff in the background, but they were very straightforward with us about what they wanted us to do.

Martin had a particularly pleasant way of addressing people. He had these big, bright blue eyes and he'd smile – it was almost an altar-boy look. And he was very interesting. He rarely wasted words. Gerry would argue, go into long tracts about the war of 1846 or some such, whereas Martin would be much more direct, would say, 'Look guys, here's what we want, here's what we're going to do, here's where we are' – very *bup-bup-bup-bup*. I got the sense that if he trusted you, he really trusted you. And if he didn't trust you, you might find him to be very different.

He was very prominent in the media at that time, but I didn't know what to expect. As a journalist you know that no one is like the public image they present of themselves and you don't really know them until you are in private with them. The whole delegation, including myself, found Martin very charming. He was seen by the British media as Public Enemy No. 1 along with Adams, which immediately attracted us to him. If you're a British public enemy and you're an Irishman, you're doing something right! I had a much more filled-out picture of him than I had of Gerry. Gerry was more mysterious, although I'd met Gerry before that meeting and knew him well.

We had a wonderful incident one time – shortly after that first meeting – regarding a bar on the Falls Road. I was with two US congressmen and I said, 'Why don't we go up the Falls Road and meet some Sinn Féin people?' And they panicked about the whole idea, how alien that would be to their entire experience. And it gave me a great insight into how demonised these republican people had become. Two congressmen were still afraid to walk up the Falls Road and meet Gerry Adams and a few other people. So I was very well aware of the demonisation. I felt that the way they could get out of this demonisation was to involve the United States, to bring an outside player in, and that this would give Sinn Féin a more equal footing with everyone else in the debate. And I think both Martin and Gerry – Martin in particular – was very aware of the influence of the American card if it was played.

***

The most amazing moment with Martin McGuinness that I had was the day that President Clinton arrived in Belfast in November 1995. It had been a very tortuous process, first to get him to give Gerry a visa to the US, and then to get him to Ireland. But the view was, within our group, that we had delivered an extraordinary thing: the president of the United States standing before Belfast City Hall. It had been part of our belief that this would change everything.

I remember Martin coming up to me that day, him and Joe Cahill [a veteran Belfast republican], and his eyes were just alive, he was so over the moon. And I remember he gave me a thump – he nearly knocked me out! He was so happy – I'd never seen him so animated. And Joe Cahill was the same.

I was sitting beside Martin when Clinton came on stage and I got this sense of tremendous personal accomplishment coming from him, that he had managed to see this day, which was an extraordinary day in the history of Northern Ireland. It was a huge moment of happiness for him and he wasn't afraid to express it. I mean Gerry wouldn't be the same; Gerry was more reserved – although Gerry could be very congenial and friendly. But Martin was physical, expressed himself physically. That is the day I will always remember because he was so energised. It had been a difficult path getting Clinton there. I think he knew as well as anyone that this was a game-changer.

I saw Martin more often when we started bringing groups over from America. He would sit very quietly and he would perceive people. Then he would ask them very direct questions. He wasn't a guy who was garrulous in his personal behaviour. He would wait for his opportunity and then he would ask the most penetrating question, with those ice-blue eyes looking straight at you, where you'd feel an obligation to answer him.

My experiences with him were always friendly. I don't think I ever had a dispute with him and I interacted with him quite a bit. He rarely talked about his family. He talked about Derry a lot and about cricket and such strange things. You got the sense of a man in full: a family man who was smart enough to keep his family off-limits – I never knew anything about his family – a guy who was deeply involved politically, a guy who carried enormous respect within the movement, it was very evident, because of his own past. And the other fascinating thing to me was the dynamic between him and Adams, which I studied very closely as to how it actually worked and came up with the notion that they really were the perfect complement for each other. I always thought, maybe contrary to what many people thought, that Martin was more the hard man than Gerry – even though they say Gerry was the hardest of the hard men. I always thought Martin was the man who ultimately swayed a lot of the decisions with the IRA. I think he was their No. 1 guy.

I saw Martin with unionist politicians when he was deputy first minister in Stormont. I went over with the Ireland Fund and Martin was incredibly affable. You could see he was born to the microphone. He was the kind of guy who was very much at ease, particularly in small public gatherings. At the time Peter Robinson was his companion minister and it was a stark contrast. Peter was much more stilted. Martin had an effortless charm. It's a very rare quality and I think it beguiled everybody who met him – even opponents. That's probably an indispensable part of what we've lost now that Martin's gone – that ability, not so much about policy or politics, but that human ability to reach out.

And, in ways, he was charmed by other people. I think he got into the whole dynamic with Peter Robinson around that time of Robinson's problems [the scandal with Robinson's wife, Iris]. I saw how well he handled that and how finely tuned he was, that Robinson was a human being going through a dreadful personal problem. I don't think many people would have been as merciful in the same situation. I thought that was an amazing aspect of his personality, that he was able to reach out to Robinson and say, 'You know, whatever time you need to sort out your problems, we're not going to come after you.' It was a pretty dramatic thing that was happening. I thought that was a mark of the man, that he didn't kick the guy when he was down.

I think he was a pragmatist. I think he knew in his own mind, and – I think Adams certainly knew – the limitations of the armed movement. The question I always asked was: How many Brits do we have to kill here – Is it 5,000? Is it 50,000? – before they are going to leave? And I think they asked the same questions. There was a very evident limitation to the armed struggle that was evident from the mid-to-late 1970s. It wasn't going to work. And it was going to transpose another generation into violence. And I think when they became grandparents themselves, it became very obvious to me that they were looking at this very much from the perspective of family. They were saying, 'I don't want my grandson involved in this.' I think Martin was a very big family man in that respect.

People followed him – he was a natural leader. He had the ability to lead even at a very young age. Particularly in a compressed situation like the all-out violence in Derry, that kind of person emerges very quickly. And obviously he was the guy who emerged in Derry.

One of the fascinating things that never got explained to me was how the Hume–McGuinness dynamic worked, because although they were leading rival political parties in Derry, they helped each other in a strange way. One almost depended on the other to happen. I never really knew what their personal relationship was like. I never saw them together.

It was very hard not to get along with Martin McGuinness –

you'd have to be very nasty not to. I found the Chuckle Brothers image not embarrassing but very Martin. Martin would charm the birds off the trees. He charmed Paisley and he charmed Paisley's wife. There's no two ways about it. And that's where the loss of Martin is particularly felt. Not in terms of his theology or his political beliefs but his humanity. He had a way of putting himself in the other person's shoes and that's a very rare gift for a politician – politicians often only see themselves in one-dimensional, this-is-my-point-of-view-and-you're-wrong ways. Martin could see where Paisley was coming from, he could see the journey that he had made and I think he responded to that and I think Paisley responded to him.

***

I believe Sinn Féin were very open and internationalist in their outlook. They were very serious about their convictions. I remember one time Martin and Gerry were staying in a hotel in Manhattan, just down the street from here. It was a Saturday afternoon and I went down to see them and I said, 'Why don't we go for a drink?' Something like that. They said 'No, no, no – we're going to the Indian Cultural Museum.' And that was it. There was a depth in their passion and commitment to issues that rode across everything. The older you become, the more you realise that people with that kind of passion are extremely rare. But when they exist they succeed, because they are so passionate.

I know a lot of Irish-Americans thought Martin had gone over to the other side when he met the queen. That was a huge gamble and I think he carried it off with tremendous aplomb. I think it must have been extremely difficult for him; but it'll go down as one of the most amazing encounters, given the history that they both represented. And I think Martin came out of it very well. I remember talking to him about the queen and he described her in very friendly terms. He wasn't going to start talking about her as being the head of the Parachute Regiment [which shot dead fourteen innocent people in Derry's Bloody Sunday 1972] or something like that. With his innate charm, he had reached out.

It's still hard to believe he's dead, because he was such a larger-than-life figure. I think people like Martin and Gerry, who spend their lives in very dangerous situations where any day could be their last, develop a sense of the importance of humanity, of the importance of contact, of making things happen so that other people don't go through what they went through. And if you think of Martin and Gerry, all those years basically never sleeping at home, constantly in fear not just of the Brits but of dissidents in their own ranks – I think Martin in particular endured that – I think it was an amazing life to live.

I always remember a very significant conversation with Bill Clinton where I asked him what was the difference between the Middle East and Northern Ireland, and he said, 'McGuinness and Adams, as against Arafat.' These guys delivered. Arafat could not deliver. When it came down to it, he could not deliver the Palestine Liberation Organisation. It's a profound insight into what they were able to do.

Yes, US politicians took to him. There's a whiff of cordite off McGuinness, there's a backstory, there's an intelligent, smart human being who's helping bring peace to a land that many people feel incredibly emotional about. So what's not to like? Everybody asked me what he was like, after I met him. Everybody's fascinated by Adams and McGuinness and wants to know what they're really like. And you can only give your own honest summation because you don't know the whole picture of the men. But I think they were two of the most exceptional people I've ever met. With Martin there was a complete directness, coming straight to the point. There was also an absolute integrity in the questions he asked; it was clear he had thought things through. He was just uncomplicated. Very uncomplicated. This is what we want.

I think Adams was more of a bogeyman to the unionists, because Martin obviously made overtures in a more significant way. When you hear about the fragility of the IRA ceasefire and what occurred around that time, there's no question that Martin was the key figure in holding that line, and part of the reason had to be that people were scared of him, that he was still very much the predominant military man within the movement. And yet I saw that scary aspect with Adams but not with McGuinness. There was always a kind of gentle banter with McGuinness before you'd talk to him. I never really saw him lose his temper. With Adams I had a few bust-ups.

The worst I've ever heard people say about McGuinness? I suppose 'killer'. 'IRA bloodthirsty killer' – that'd be the kind of comment some would make when they wanted to paint him in a particular way. I think the general public view of him went from negative to positive pretty fast when he became deputy first minister. I've heard Martin might have clashed with Peter Mandelson and I'm not surprised. Martin could see a fraud and Mandelson is certainly that. I see now that he is swanning round the place saying he was responsible for the peace process.

I remember meeting Martin once in his office in Stormont and we both laughed at the absurdity of things. I mean the ability he had to not take himself too seriously, and the ability to be available to people – that's an amazing ability for a politician. It's not one that's easy to find among politicians. But he understood the absurdity of the former head of the IRA in Derry sitting behind an ornate desk in a very big chamber in Stormont. He understood that journey, but he was able in his own way to laugh about it. It was almost a sense of 'Holy fuck, how did I get here?' I would have said it to him – 'The likes of you, here!' – and he would have laughed and been in total agreement.

***

Human identity mattered in the peace talks. Senator George Mitchell says he knew the day he was making a breakthrough was when Adams – and, I think it was Paisley – began talking about their grandchildren. Those kinds of days are very significant – where you move away from the false image of the person to the real person.

Which is why I fear now that the Stormont Executive has collapsed, these current talks and these discussions aimed at re-establishing it may veer off in a very negative direction without Martin's personality. I think if Martin were there it would be a lot easier. And that's no reflection on those involved.

There's no doubt that he came to the conclusion with the IRA, 'Look, we need to do something else.' I think with parliamentary politics he took it on to an extraordinary extent. The growth of Sinn Féin as the largest nationalist party in the north, the third largest party in the south – I mean, you couldn't have created a more dynamic, politically progressive series of actions than what Sinn Féin accomplished. So I think he would have looked at the non-response of unionist politicians to Sinn Féin concerns as another rock in the road. I don't think it was the final barrier or something he wasn't going to revisit. I think he would have been terribly involved in the current negotiations and he would have found a way. I think he became the ultimate pragmatist.

He got rough treatment by the media in the Irish presidential campaign of 2011, when he was the Sinn Féin candidate, but then so did everybody. That was a particularly rough, nasty race. There was a tremendous amount of violations by the media of ordinary political standards. But I think that Martin would ultimately have thought, *sticks and stones would break my bones*. He'd been through a lot. A few anti-Sinn Féin right-wing columnists were never going to put him off.

My last meeting with him was in the hotel here where he stayed in New York, right on the corner of 31st and 7th. I went down to lunch with him and Bill Flynn was there. Bill at the time was, I guess, eighty-four, eighty-five; he was quite hard of hearing and not in great physical shape. But the attention and the emotion of Martin towards him was extraordinary. Because he knew what Bill had done for them. [Flynn had helped urge President Clinton to grant Gerry Adams a visa to the US and consistently encouraged American investment in Ireland.] And Bill had always been relatively quiet about what he'd done. It was almost touching to see the two of them together because I suppose I never thought it'd be the last time I'd see Martin. I certainly thought there was a possibility I wouldn't see Bill that much. It had the feeling of two old friends telling war stories about what had happened and the way they had forged this path.

An example of this: tomorrow night, as someone who was very involved in facilitating the process that led to peace in Ireland, I'm one of three speakers on conflict resolution at the

Kennedy School of Government here in New York. And that's the level the Irish peace process has reached. And the people who brought it there were the likes of Bill Flynn and Martin McGuinness. Martin was very touching in his concern for Bill that day. He couldn't have been kinder and more engaged with him. That's my abiding last memory of Martin.

I think Martin's funeral told us something very profound: this was a local hero. You can't force people to come out for a funeral. You could see the media very dubiously covering that funeral, trying to downplay the whole aspect of it. I don't know how many thousands were there, but it was amazing. For an American president to fly all the way – that was extraordinary. And I thought Clinton's remarks at the funeral were priceless. They were so short, but they were brilliant.

Knowing Martin added hugely to my life. I lived twenty miles from the border when I was growing up and you saw the pain, hurt, suffering, the deaths and bombs. Then I came to America and I saw the images they were being provided with: 'Why are Catholics killing Protestants? Why are Protestants killing Catholics?' It is amazing to think about the turnaround in my lifetime in the image of Ireland overseas. I think this is primarily due to Martin McGuinness and Gerry Adams more than anybody else, as they took a risk on peace when nobody else was prepared to do so – except maybe for John Hume. A remarkable threesome – a group of three people who transformed not just Ireland, but the world's image of Ireland, and together found a way to make peace.

You think of all the efforts to find peace in the Middle East or wherever that always founder. But something happened in Ireland that was very special. People say to me, 'It's not perfect.'

Of course it's not perfect. It probably won't be perfect until the next generation. But the fact that people aren't getting killed, the fact that there's a political settlement, that there is now an understanding at last that there are two equal groups in Northern Ireland – those are incredible accomplishments.

Martin's whole life was preoccupied with the cause. I can't imagine he had a very normal home life for many years. I've been with Adams in situations where he would change cars and take extraordinary security precautions. So you get a moment's glimpse of what life must have been like – day after day after day, living that kind of existence, looking over your shoulder. Not just at the British, but maybe at some informer in your own ranks who was about to turn you in or something. So I think they came through that in extraordinary fashion.

Martin McGuinness didn't bring the Troubles on himself. Partition brought them on him. He didn't have a choice. Imagine what it must have been like in the Bogside in 1969. And John Hume would be the first to admit that, without McGuinness, he wouldn't have gotten to where he got. It's the old story of Martin Luther King and Malcolm X. King needed Malcolm X, and Malcolm X knew that and was very clear in his role – he would go down and scare the life out of the white triumphalists and then King would come in and say, 'OK, I know a way to solve all this.' I don't believe Gerry or Martin brought it on themselves. There was no other choice.

26

Pat McArt

I'd just become editor of the *Derry Journal* in 1982 and a guy called Paddy Logue, a former priest, told me Martin McGuinness would like to meet me and asked could he bring him down to the *Journal* offices. I agreed, so Martin came down one day. I'd read and heard so much about him. I remember reading *The Eagle Has Landed* by Jack Higgins. Martin McGuinness features in it, along with a Russian spy. This was a guy who was the stuff of legend – you know, the boy general with the curly hair who came from the back streets of Derry and was probably one of the most famous 'terrorists' in the world.

By that time Bloody Sunday and the hunger strikes had come and gone. Adams was the public face of republicanism, but it was almost like a double act with Martin. Adams was Éamon de Valera; McGuinness was Michael Collins. One was a politician who was bendable and you couldn't trust his oath; the other was the unbending warrior chief.

So Paddy brought Martin down and I've got to admit he was not at all what I was expecting. I'd seen him on TV but not in the flesh. There's a doctor here in Derry and he said to me one day, 'I'd love to know who is this two-headed monster I keep reading about in all the British tabloids and in some of the Irish papers. Because McGuinness is a patient of mine in Aberfoyle in Derry, and he comes in and he sits quietly, and sometimes maybe there might be a pregnant woman in the waiting room, and he'll say, "Go on you ahead, I'm in no rush." He's as quiet, modest, respectful and easy to deal with – not in the least bit a thug. But I keep reading about this monster who blows up things and is leading the IRA campaign. I read this and I just don't understand it.' Well, I was similar to that doctor.

I'm a Donegal man and Martin's mother was from Donegal, so I think that formed some sort of a bond – and I'm married to a woman from Inishowen. His mother is from the Illies and my wife is from the Illies. He said to me one time, 'People from the Illies are the best people in the world.' What I didn't realise then was that when he was on the run, they hid him.

In those days, you might say Martin always dressed smart casual. You never saw him badly dressed. He was always thin, he had blond, curly hair, he liked what they'd call chinos nowadays, and a jumper and a polo shirt or a real shirt. He never had a tie. He dressed *cleanly*, I suppose would be the word. He was well brought up. There was no dirty jeans or dirty shirt or that sort of stuff; and his hair was always washed and he always looked presentable, as my mother would have said.

I was the editor then. I was twenty-eight, a young man. *The Derry Journal* was very important because at one stage the *Irish News* wouldn't carry things from an Irish republican perspective. I took a different view and at the time it wasn't wild popular. I remember Martin O'Brien from the *Irish News* rang me and asked could we agree not to carry death notices or those sorts of IRA notices when one of their volunteers had died. I said I didn't agree with that and I was going to publish them. Because I'd thought about it and I'd said to myself, 'Wait a minute – there are two Derrys. There's the Derry of the Culmore Road [middle class] and there's the Derry of the Bogside [working class]. So if we took the side of the guys up the Culmore Road, what would happen to the 30 per cent republican vote in the Bogside? Why shouldn't we cover them? They've got views, they're entitled to give an account of themselves.'

Even from within the *Journal* itself, there were some of the proprietor's family saying, 'You're turning this into *An Phoblacht*.' But we weren't. We had a Tuesday paper, which was a big paper, and a Friday paper, which was a very big paper, and all sides got an opinion. Back in the early days Sinn Féin weren't very politically active, but after the hunger strikes and Bobby Sands, that switched 180 degrees.

It was a wee bit of a fencing match, that first meeting. Martin wanted to know what I was about and I wanted to know what he was about. We sat down and we talked. I let him in on part of my background. I was brought up in a house in Letterkenny and my mother was the ultimate West Brit. She hated violence – as I do. She hated the IRA and she would have hated Martin McGuinness. If she had a triptych up on the wall, it would have been John Hume, the Pope and Jesus Christ. Martin McGuinness would have been down there somewhere with the devil.

Anyway, after I met Martin McGuinness, I found I developed a serious issue regarding him. After a while I found myself genuinely liking this man. Yet this was supposed to be a murderer; or, as my mother would say, 'he had blood on his hands'. And yet I thought it could have been me, if I'd been brought up in the same circumstances. It took me a while to adjust to that, finding that I genuinely liked the man. Had it been just a charm he switched on, I'd have turned off him totally. But Martin was just Martin.

My son, Shane, went to school in Pennyburn [an area in

Derry] – he was a wee fella of eight or nine at the time when Martin used to come down to the *Journal* offices. One day we were driving after Mass and there were election posters up. And Shane said, 'There's Martin!' We said, 'What?' And he said, 'That's Martin!' And Rosie, my wife, said to me, 'He knows Martin McGuinness?' 'He helps me with my homework when he's down in the *Journal* office,' Shane told her. Shane was doing music or something, and he would come down to the office two or three days a week and have half an hour to wait until Rosie picked him up. Martin used to come down at the same time. He'd be sitting out with the reporters and he'd help Shane with his homework. That's how down-to-earth he was – he would chat away. He'd come in and say to the *Journal* reporters, 'That was some match last night!'

He had that ability to talk to everybody at their own level – he never got above himself. Years later, in 1993, Derry won the All-Ireland football final. Martin's brother had played for the team some years earlier. Martin came in and stood at the back of the Guildhall during the homecoming ceremony, while all the other public representatives were up at the front. He stood there, congratulated everyone and left. And yet strictly speaking he should have been up there at the front. That shows the sort of humility there was about him. There was no question of Martin doing the Paisley, making sure everybody saw him. It was almost the other way round.

I imagine some unionists and maybe some Protestant people were frightened of him, but usually it was the opposite. People would come in and say, 'Is that the guy we're reading about, the two-headed monster? Because jeez, he's a wild nice, down-to-earth fella.' I always got the impression that if he'd been brought up in another place, he would have been a very successful member of the Tory party in England. He didn't drink, didn't smoke, there was zero question about his private life. In Belfast there were all sorts of drinking dens, allegations of sleaze and thuggery. In Derry the IRA was run like it was a good Christian boys' society. Everybody abided by the rules.

He also had that sort of persona, that charisma thing. But I want to stress: I don't think for a minute that he was soft. When I met him, he was very much – what would I say – very single-track almost. It was a united Ireland or nothing. And he was very principled: there was no question of bending. I remember the famous remark he made, about the 'cutting edge of the IRA'.

***

He and I had a number of serious rows over the years, and I remember once he said to me, 'It's all right for you, Pat. You were brought up in Letterkenny. Twenty miles up the road from you it was all very different. We were living under oppression. The B Specials, the gerrymandered council, the bigotry, the sectarianism, the discrimination, no jobs. You know, that kind of thing builds a particular sort of society.'

I said, 'Wait a minute. John Hume went one way, why did you go the other?'

He said, 'Pat, did you ever hear about the quislings in Norway? They were certain people who helped the Germans, who acquiesced, and then there were certain people who opposed them. I belong to that group who don't think it's morally right that we should sit back and just let them crap all over us.'

He felt that he was quite entitled to take the stand he did. He told me he had no problem going to Mass on Sunday and he had no problem with going to Holy Communion. His parents were, I believe, daily communicants. He believed that his view on things was morally OK.

Bishop Daly in many ways regarded Martin as an exceptional human being: he was a good father, a good husband and a good member of the community. But the bishop said the big issue he had with him was the use of political violence. Certainly he and Daly fell out after shots were fired in Long Tower chapel grounds [in 1987, at the funeral of IRA man Gerard Logue]. There was a serious amount of tension between McGuinness and the Church then. Martin was well respected within the Catholic community, but I'm not saying for one second that there weren't some members of the Catholic clergy who had serious issues with the IRA, and there were some members of the Catholic community who had some tensions with Martin – and vice versa.

The IRA was regularly condemned from the altar, there's no doubt about that. Fr Mulvey [a senior Catholic priest in Derry] was a regular condemner of the IRA and its actions. And the Catholic Church used to issue regular encyclicals back then condemning IRA violence. But it was the principle or philosophy of violence they condemned, not the individual.

***

In the 1980s Martin walked freely around Derry. A guy I know told me the story that he gave Martin a lift one time and Martin suddenly said to him, 'Turn in!' So they turned in and the guy said, 'What was that for?' Martin said, 'There's a checkpoint ahead.' That's how alert he was. The man hadn't noticed anything, but Martin had noticed the cars backing up. But in general he could walk about quite openly at that time.

He had a certain routine, you see. Every Monday and Thursday for the best part of twenty-five years he'd have come down to the *Derry Journal* offices. If they'd wanted him, all the cops had to do was stand outside the *Derry Journal* offices at about 4 p.m. and they would have got him, no bother. But no, he wasn't on the run then. He had served some time and after that he was free.

I wouldn't go as far as to say he wasn't involved in the IRA then. Martin was in my office one day and Brendan 'Darkie' Hughes said something in Belfast. Martin just said, 'That's not going to happen.' Darkie Hughes was a senior figure in the IRA even then; but a week later there was a statement released by the IRA and it was almost verbatim what Martin had said in my office. So what that said to me was Martin was a major player in the IRA.

There was a man I met, Maurice Johnston. I think he was the last cop to leave the west bank. Anyway, I met him at a dinner one day and we were chatting. Somehow the conversation came round to Dominic McGlinchey [a leading figure in the INLA] and I said, 'Isn't it a good job the IRA was never taken over by a lunatic like Dominic McGlinchey?' And he said, 'I sometimes think maybe the big problem the British government and various others have is the fact that Martin McGuinness is in charge and he's so reasonable. They need to make sure they don't do enough to push people like McGuinness aside. McGlinchey is the enemy; he'd shoot his own mother and all the rest of it. But here's this guy McGuinness, who is logical, reasonable and you can talk to him. It makes things a bit confused and blurred for them.'

Martin, as far as I'm concerned, was never a violent person.

Violence to him was only something that had to be used, not because he liked it or anything like that. I remember talking to a man called Gerry Murray, an accountant. He rang me up and said, 'Pat, do you remember the time up about Portadown – it was either the Drumcree crisis or the Tunnel crisis. Anyway, Martin gave a speech and it was very little recorded. He said, "Look, keep your children at home, there are plastic bullets flying around here. I was over with a young fella who was hit by a plastic bullet and he's unconscious. I don't want other parents going through what his parents are going through." It was the rarest thing. Here's this guy who's supposed to be a thug and a psychopath and all the rest of it, warning people to keep their children at home in case they got injured.'

I'm not sure he was ever a junior member of the IRA. I mean, in 1972 he was taken to the Cheyne Walk talks. How junior are you when you are taken to Cheyne Walk in a six-man delegation? I have no doubt whatsoever he was a senior IRA member. There's a body language you can see when people come into an office. When Martin came into the office and some of those there were IRA guys, you just knew, there was a body language of respect. You could tell it was a case of, 'Whatever Martin says, goes.'

After the hunger strikes, republicans realised there was a second front on which they could open the war and that was politics. The *Journal* in those days sold 27,000 or 28,000 papers every Tuesday and Friday. That paper went into every house in Derry, every house in Inishowen, and a good number of houses in Co. Derry. That gave republicans a massive base. Back then the *Journal* was respected as the paper of record. It was also the voice of the oppressed people of Derry. People knew that this was the one organ where they could get their point of view in print. When I worked in the *Journal*, it was known as 'the Bible'. I remember saying to Bishop Daly at the time, 'Everyone seems to wait until Mondays and Thursdays to make big statements.' He said, 'That's exactly what I do.'

Martin quickly learned to come down about 4 p.m. on a Monday and a Thursday – at that time there'd be a chance of getting included in the paper. He'd bring statements about various incidents. Sometimes he brought statements, sometimes he'd say, 'Look, Pat, you judge it yourself.'

One time he told me to make sure a particular statement appeared in the paper. What I didn't realise until a month later was it was actually a message for the British government. They were getting about ten *Derry Journal*s in Stormont every Tuesday and Friday, and they were going through the nuances. I remember Peter Brooke [secretary of state for Northern Ireland from 1989 to 1992] saying, 'We have no selfish strategic or economic interest in Northern Ireland', and that Britain would accept Irish reunification if the people wanted it. And I only found out afterwards, a lot of preparatory work for that was actually being done through *The Derry Journal* – it was a sort of a back channel.

I remember saying to Martin, 'Sure the British will never talk to you', and he says, 'You never know.' About six months later I found out about the back-channel talks and I says, 'Martin, I asked you.' And he says, 'No, you didn't. You said that the British would never talk to me. Had you asked me "Are you talking to the British?" you might have got a different answer.'

About 1984 or 1985, Martin came down one day and he mentioned 'an agreed Ireland'. He said it once, then he said it a second time and then, when he said it a third time, I said, 'Wait a minute Martin, houl' on, what's happening? Are you trying to steal John Hume's clothes?' And he said, 'What are you on about?' I said, 'That's the third time you've said "an agreed Ireland" and I never heard "agreed Ireland" [which implies unionist acceptance of Irish unity] coming out of your lips before. It used to be always a United Ireland.' They'd issued a peace document about that time so obviously there were some sort of negotiations going on – talks or feelers or whatever.

***

Martin took to politics like a duck to water. Yet I don't think he was a natural politician: he was very much the warrior king and Gerry was the politician. Martin was the man of action and Gerry was the nuts and bolts of the agreement.

Martin accepted that there was a war to be fought on another level – for people's hearts and minds. I said to him one day after it was all over, 'Martin, why all the fighting, why so many people dead, so many in jail? So that you can go into Stormont?'

He said, 'No, Pat. Can I explain it to you this way: the British can say this and we can say something else, but the bottom line is we had fought each other to a standstill. We could keep this war going for another thirty years and they could keep it going for another thirty years. It's like going round up there in Grianan Fort. You walk round it, hitting the wall with your head. It's not moving and you're not moving. But then you come to a door and the question is, if I open that door and go in, am I in more danger in there than out here? But if I go in there, I might make a change. We'd tried the other one and after a lot of discussion we decided we'd go for this option. We're trying the door now, Pat.'

I remember one time Martin said, 'I don't want this life or this sort of society that we're living through for my kids. I want this done and dusted and sorted.' It wasn't about a united Ireland then – I think it was more about an agreed Ireland. Towards the end, in my opinion, he was a bit disillusioned by what was going on in the south – that it hadn't lived up to a lot of things. I think he once thought that partition had failed in the north but succeeded in the south, but now that the south had become very West Brit, very secular, materialistic and all the rest of it, he felt differently. Particularly as the ancient blood of the Celts ran true in the north. People in the north wanted to be Irish, it was important to them. Their cultural identity was important to them, whereas the Brits in the south were busy watching *Coronation Street* and *EastEnders*.

Saying that, he was not an ideologue, not at all, but he loved Irish music. I think his favourite song was 'Raglan Road'. And he loved to go walking in Donegal. He felt that a lot of people in the south forgot that we in the north were not British, we were Irish, and the Dublin 4 set had almost obliterated recognition of that.

***

John Hume's house was attacked one time [by republicans]. Some story appeared in the *Journal* and I think they threw ball-bearings and paint at Hume's house. Martin went up to his house that night to put an end to it. And John Tierney, who was a senior member of the SDLP in Derry, was there, and there was a big meeting in the Corned Beef Tin [a community building in the Creggan Estate] and I think it was hot and heavy. John later told me, 'After the meeting Martin McGuinness waited for me and said, "C'mon John, we'll walk up the road." You know what he was doing, he was making sure I got up the road OK.' John had a lot of time for Martin. He said that was the sort of thing Martin would do.

Hume told me once, 'I agree with a lot of things Martin McGuinness says, but where I fundamentally disagree with him is that the biggest right of all is the right to life and I can't cross that Rubicon and say it's OK. I can't do that.' They would have been respectful of each other. I don't think they were friends, definitely not. But Martin was very respectful of John Hume; he would never have anything said against him. Sometimes maybe some of the more hardline guys would be smart-alecking about Hume, but absolutely not Martin. He reckoned John Hume was trying his best.

In many ways I'd have regarded Martin as a friend. Most times we'd have met in the *Journal* office, but occasionally we'd have gone to a restaurant. I probably got on better with McGuinness than I did with Hume, in the sense that I am from a sort of working-class council house in Letterkenny, so McGuinness was more from my sort of background. In contrast, John went to St Columb's, was in with the professional classes and that sort of stuff. I never quite got that sort of person myself. I could never walk round the golf club and hit a wee white ball, just never.

To my mind, Martin McGuinness made one journey through his life, but it was a significant journey from where he started. He was never the monster he was made out to be; he was never the thug. He stayed true to himself all the way through. I think he was basically a Nelson Mandela figure – I really genuinely believe that. He took the opportunities when they came. Had they been available to him forty years earlier, he wouldn't have gone down the road he went down.

I wasn't in touch with him a lot during his Stormont years. I did meet him one day in 2015 when I was out walking and I think I was wearing headphones. The next thing I heard was, 'Pat, how are you doing?', and there was Martin. We stood chatting for about ten to fifteen minutes.

I retired as the *Journal* editor ten years ago, and I used to do a bit of work for various people. I remember one time I was doing a bit of work for a magazine and I needed something so I rang a fella and asked if he had Martin's number. I rang his number and somebody said, 'He'll ring you back.' Two seconds later, even though he was deputy first minister, he rang me back. It was only a piece for some wee magazine in Donegal. There are some councillors wouldn't ring you back, but that was the type Martin was.

We never fell out. There's a fella, Paul McCauley, he's working for the BBC in London now, but he was the head of BBC Radio Foyle and he was with me one Thursday evening. Martin came down with some sort of statement and it was late and I couldn't get it into the paper. He then rang up and said, 'Pat, this is very important.' I said, 'Martin, you're too late and look, would you ever fuck off.' I remember Paul McCauley saying to me, 'Pat, that was the bravest thing I've ever heard, but I'm not walking behind you after that.' The following Monday Martin was down at the office and he says, 'Ach, sorry about that.'

There was a fella called Kevin Toolis wrote a book, I think it's called *Rebel Hearts*. There's a bit about Martin and it starts off with him saying, 'For fuck's sake, there's the Brits.' And it really annoyed Martin. He said to me, 'Did you read the book? I think

I've got a mention in it somewhere and I didn't say that.' What really annoyed him was not that he was in the IRA or anything like that but the swearing. Martin didn't swear.

That day I met him in 2015 he looked a bit tense. He told me, 'Pat, it's tough going. There are some serious bigots.' I'm paraphrasing now. 'They act like they own the castle and the nationalist community are the butlers. They don't seem to catch on that the days of the old landlord are over and that we are not tenants any more. It's seriously tough going.'

Martin found that very tough to take; I think he bit his tongue and stepped back from going over the top on more than one occasion. And I thought that we were a good bit in by that time; Paisley had come and gone, Robinson was well ensconced. What Martin was suggesting to me at the time was that there was a serious arrogance there, that they thought they were the ruling class.

That's partly why his relationship with Paisley astonished me. I remember years ago, maybe twenty-five years ago, he detested Paisley as a bigot and reckoned Paisley had stirred more sectarian hatred than any other single person. So I never quite got that relationship; I understood it, but I never quite got it.

***

I heard near the end of last year that Martin wasn't well. I hadn't seen him really. The night they pulled the plug on Stormont in January 2017 was the first time I'd really seen him. When I'd been talking to him eighteen months earlier he was absolutely the picture of health. But that day in Stormont I got a shock when I saw him.

Long ago, we had a deal that I was going to write his

biography, but then he went into politics. I said, 'When this is all over I'm going to write the book', and he said, 'Right you're on.' We both knew it probably would never happen, but that was the deal.

You have to deal with people as you find them and I found him decent. You can say, 'How can somebody that was involved in the IRA be decent?' But I found him decent. I can only speak for the man I knew. There were so many characteristics to be admired – he was humble, he was not bombastic, he was as tough as cold steel, you knew he was not a fool. And his private life: you never heard a whisper. He married Bernie and he raised a family.

And his kids are lovely. They came down to the *Journal* offices one time. There was a certain other Sinn Féin/IRA man in this town and I remember his kids came down one time and they were arrogant little shits. Martin's kids were respectful, modest, decent, and you could see they got it from their father. You know, 'How are you doing, Mr McArt, how are you getting on?' Maybe it was the Donegal influence.

I think it was Denis Bradley who said to me about putting people up on a pole and saying, 'Oh he's evil!' He said, 'Wait until you've walked a mile in their shoes. The person who lives next door to you and is normal can do some bloody awful things in certain circumstances. Don't ever think that you're not capable of doing something bloody awful too.'

Martin McGuinness was decent and he was honest; what you saw was what you got.

27

Bill Clinton

EULOGY

I was thinking about it: after all the breath [Martin] expended cursing the British over the years, he worked with two prime ministers and shook hands with the queen, four taoiseachs, navigating the complex politics of the north. ... And I believe the only way a lasting peace can ever take hold and endure is if those who have *legitimate* grief on both sides embrace the future together.

I learned this from Nelson Mandela, who was a great friend of mine, and who called me one day complaining as the president of South Africa that he was getting so much criticism. And I said, 'From the Afrikaners?' He said, 'No, no, from my people. They think I've sold them out.' After all, you know, there he won 63 per cent of the vote; it's inconceivable in a western democracy to do such a thing now. And I said, 'What did you tell them?' He said, 'I spent twenty-seven years in jail, and they took all my best years away and I didn't see my children grow up and it ruined my marriage, and a lot of my friends were killed and if I can get over it, you can too. We've got to build a future.'

Now I want to say something about Martin McGuinness. I came to treasure every encounter. I liked him. They asked me to speak for three minutes; he could do this in thirty seconds. I can just hear him now: 'Here's my eulogy: I fought, I made peace, I made politics, I had a fabulous family that somehow stayed with me and endured it all, I had friends. I was married to Gerry almost as long as I was married to Bernie. It turned out I was pretty good at all this and we got a lot done, but we didn't finish, and if you really want to honour my legacy, go make your own and finish – finish the work of peace so we can all have a future together.'

He was only four years younger than me. He grew up at a time of rage and resentment; not only in Ireland but across the world. And it was pronounced here. One of seven children in a Bogside family without an indoor toilet. (That's a great political story, but I'm the last American president to ever live in a house without an indoor toilet and it's very much overrated except for its political value.) He was part of the rage of his time, he hated the discrimination and he decided to oppose it by whatever means available to the passionate young, including violence.

Somewhere along the way, for whatever reason, he decided to give peace a chance. Some of the reasons were principled, some were practical, but he *decided*. He was good about sticking with something he decided to do, and he succeeded because his word was good, his listening skills were good, he was not afraid to make a compromise and he was strong enough to keep it if he made it.

And finally, he realised that you could have an Ireland that was free and independent and self-governing, and still inclusive. That the dreams of little children were no more or less legitimate, just because of their faith background, or their family's history, or the sins of their parents. In the American law there is a phrase that comes from the eighteenth century called 'corruption of the blood', that the sins of the parents used to be visited on their children, and their grandchildren, and their great-grandchildren, and we specifically prohibited that – easy to say, hard to do. He was trying to do it.

Most of the publicity Martin got as a politician was the very absurd notion that he actually got along with Ian Paisley. I thought it was great that he got a word in edgeways, I never could! But the thing I think he was proudest of that I loved to listen to him talk about, and we talked about it again three years ago this month when we walked across the bridge here with John Hume, was that when he became education minister in the transitional government his first budget recommended a more than generous allocation in aid to the poorest schools in the Protestant neighbourhoods because he thought those children would be just as a crippled by ignorance as Catholic children would, and that the only way out of poverty and the only way to give people the emotional space to learn to live together, work together and share the future together, was if they could have the dignity of a decent job and the empowerment of knowing they can take care of their families and give something more to their children. I could tell he was proud as punch with himself. Normally it's not a good thing to be proud of yourself, but I think if there's a secret category of things you can be proud of, taking care of the children of people with whom you have been at odds is surely on that small list.

So that's what he did, he persevered and he prevailed. He risked the wrath of his comrades and the rejection of his adversaries. He made honourable compromises and was strong enough to keep them, and came to be trusted because his word was good. And he never stopped being who he was; a good husband, a good father, a faithful follower of the faith of his father and mother, and a passionate believer in a free, secure, self-governing Ireland. The only thing that happened was: he expanded the definition of 'us' and shrank the definition of 'them'.

The world at every period of insecurity faces a new wave of tribalism. If you really came here to celebrate his life, and to honour the contribution of the last chapter of it, you have to finish his work – a great son of Derry. And our friend Seamus Heaney, in his Nobel Prize speech, said the secret of his success was deciding 'to walk on air against your better judgement'. Believe me, when the people who made this peace did it, every single one of them decided to take a flying leap into the unknown against their better judgement. It's about the only thing besides your faith and your love that makes life worth living.

Our friend earned this vast crowd today. Even more, he earned the right to ask us to honour his legacy by our living. To finish the work that is there to be done.

28

Gerry Adams

Bill Clinton said at Martin's funeral that I was married to Martin nearly as long as his wife, Bernie. In fact, I was actually married to him longer than her – I said that to Bernie afterwards.

When I was released from Long Kesh in 1972, we had preparatory talks before we went to London. Martin and I met about a fortnight before those Cheyne Walk talks in London. We were around the same age – I'm actually a year older than him, which he got some delight out of telling people. So we were two relatively young guys at the time.

During the meeting in London he challenged Whitelaw [William Whitelaw, the then British secretary of state for Northern Ireland] and I suppose that made an impression on me. I challenged Whitelaw as well, who was very nervous during the meeting. Towards the end of the meeting he made some remark in relation to the IRA or British troops, and there were a number of issues that they were to come back to us on. Martin challenged him, telling him he wasn't a referee, that the British Army had done what it did on Bloody Sunday [when fourteen civilians were shot dead by the army in Derry in January 1972], which would have been just four or five months before. You couldn't blame Whitelaw for being nervous. There was a certain political risk in it for him [if it became known he was negotiating with the IRA], although we were there in our own right and weren't that concerned about his sensitivities. We didn't rate a lot what Whitelaw was doing, meeting with us. Maybe it was the arrogance of youth?

I only got to know Martin well three or four years later. I'd come out of jail and we had a half-notion of reforming Sinn Féin, which at the time was a protest movement orientated very much as a support for the republican prisoners. This was the case in the north anyway – in the south they were a bit more politically involved, with councillors. I had the view that we needed to get back to our republican roots and build a genuine political party based on republican core values. With that in mind I naturally orientated towards Martin and people like Mitchel McLaughlin.

So Martin and I sort of came into each other's lives in 1972, then left, and then got back together after I left prison. After that we'd have had regular meetings. You fall naturally into a comfortable kind of comradeship when working for a common cause, particularly on realising that you have a similar outlook on many issues. But our relationship deepened a wee bit over time because I got to know Martin's kids and his mother, Peggy – if I was going to meet Martin I would meet him at his mother's house.

Peggy was a great woman – I think Martin got a lot of his sociability and affability from his mother. She was from Donegal and no one ever left her house hungry. She was always glad to see people and she was always genuinely interested. If my wife, Colette, and myself were going to Donegal for a break, we would naturally call into Peggy's, and we'd also meet with Bernie. An odd time I'd have our son, Gearóid, with me. If Martin was coming to Belfast he might have his two boys with him in the summer holidays.

At different times when we'd be away, we'd end up in the

same bed together. I used to joke that I spent many of my wedding anniversaries with Martin. If we were away doing meetings – we were quite poor – we'd end up in some republican house in Dublin or elsewhere, and you'd be shown the double bed upstairs. No, he didn't snore. But I did.

***

At times Martin could be very dogmatic and very assertive. You're talking about different periods in people's lives, so it's hard to speak in specifics. We all change and learn. I know that Martin, in terms of his public office, became much more thoughtful about how he might approach different issues.

His rise in the IRA was in the nature of things. I was up in Derry a couple of times before I met Martin. I always thought the set-up in Derry – while symbolically it was very important to have Free Derry and so on – it was something that didn't lend itself to anywhere else except there. You couldn't have had a sustainable Free Belfast, for example. Martin emerged from that situation. He was charismatic and able to articulate a position. The IRA was being presented as a terrorist organisation and being demonised; then someone from the world media comes in and here's this curly-haired Art Garfunkel lookalike articulating in a reasonable tone what he and the IRA at that time were at.

So you had his emergence within republicanism, which was something of a closed house, but also he developed this public persona. The equivalent in Belfast might have been Joe Cahill or Seamus Twomey, but they didn't have the same personality that Martin had.

We were part of that group which set about building a Sinn Féin movement. Speaking for myself, when we decided in 1982 to contest elections [for the Northern Ireland Assembly] on the back of the hunger strikes I didn't expect that I'd be a candidate. We went to a meeting to discuss who should be. I thought it might have been Tom Hartley or somebody else. I don't know whether Martin went through the same notional shock or surprise that we ended up in that position, contesting elections, but, more than me maybe, he was a natural. There were five of us contesting five seats and we won all five.

Martin and I were like people who'd come on the same journey – we were both very political, though we probably didn't see ourselves as MPs or MLAs. That almost came as a natural extension of the decisions we'd taken, where we were in a leadership position and were developing, talking internally, trying to get people on board.

I think Martin did enjoy the work of politics, even though there is a drudgery attached to it. We used to tell a story about Paddy McManus – who has since died. Paddy was a councillor and this office [Sinn Féin's office on the Falls Road] used to be a complete slum – parts of it you couldn't walk on. But there was a flat roof that let you out the back, which sometimes people would use if the Brits were raiding the place. One day some of the folks in the office noticed Paddy climbing over the flat roof and said to him, 'Are the Brits here?' And he said, 'No, but there's an oul' doll down there with a complaint – I don't want to see her!' Sometimes you have to get a balance in the whole thing. If you're able to help people, there's a satisfaction.

In those early days, nobody was dealing with us at all. We were censored; the party was banned; in the south, our voices were blocked out. The solution to that was to build the party. At some point around 1983 I ended up – at Martin's behest – as leas-uachtarán [vice-president] of Sinn Féin. There used to be two and one of them stepped down at very short notice. Martin grabbed hold of me and said, 'I think you should put your name forward.' He prevailed and I put my name forward.

It was only after I ended up having a responsibility for issues that we began to look at things such as abstentionism. We had to build the party, so how do you build the party? There's a natural ceiling to your growth if you're not in the market place, where most people expect their politicians to be. I would presume he went through a similar development.

***

Our entry to politics in Stormont created a reaction. The gasp that was heard on that bit of film where I nominated Martin as minister for education in 1998: that catches the unionist attitude to Martin. There are still unionists up there in Stormont who don't talk to me. There are still unionists up there who didn't talk to Martin ever. They used to tell a joke about one time he was in a lift with three unionists and he said, 'I've got you surrounded!'

I don't think the unionists took the attitude that it was better having Martin inside the tent rather than outside – I don't think it was as thoughtful as that. The Good Friday Agreement was negotiated without the Ulster Unionists negotiating directly with us, after all. The DUP weren't even at the talks – they were outside.

In the first talks I remember Ken Magennis calling us bastards, which became a matter of contention. Despite this response from some unionist politicians, Martin got on very well with the loyalists. I always thought that was interesting – I wasn't sure if it was a class thing or not. From day one, David Ervine and Billy Hutchinson and Gary McMichael – it was hand out and shake hands – there was no problem. There was also a bit of banter. I remember them slagging because Martin used to tell the story about not being able to get work after he told them the name of his school. The loyalists used to say, 'Don't be ever telling us that story again!' Or, 'If that man who didn't give you a job, if he knew what he was going to create!'

He did win over some unionists who'd have started out hostile. It's persistence, to a large extent. Unionism has really no place to go. The problem is that it can be content where it is and then the rest of us have to wait until some brave person emerges from within those ranks, just by virtue of getting to know people a bit better, having a bit of craic. I remember one time we had a meeting. David Trimble and John Taylor were at it, and I think Ken Magennis, although I can't be sure – and myself and Martin were also present. And whatever paper was being discussed, towards the end of the meeting they took the paper and slammed it down on the table and said, 'That's it!' Dismissing it completely. I stood up and said, 'I think we should all have a group hug', and made a hugging gesture. And Martin said, 'Count me out!' So he got on well enough with those folks.

Then fast-forward and consider all the different difficulties David Trimble had in persuading unionists to accept power-sharing. I would have been working quite closely with Trimble at the time to try to deal with difficulties both our constituencies would have had. In the course of all of that, you get to know people a wee bit better. If you're dealing with people every day, it's a natural, human response.

I would say the vast majority of unionists – and certainly the vast majority that Martin was working with – would have changed their attitude to him. I saw that especially after he died. We were up doing negotiations, and this was after the RHI scandal and Arlene Foster's remarks [comparing Sinn Féin to a hungry crocodile]. The first few meetings after Martin's death and the Assembly elections, we had made a conscious decision to take it very easy. It would have been quite simple to go in and have a row. But once the unionists there realised we weren't looking for a row, then the first couple of discussions were quite relaxed – and were mostly about Martin.

He had worked with some of these people for the last ten years. He had worked particularly with some of the senior support staff. They were genuinely shocked that he was gone. They were asking – because he'd been so stern in his resignation and his letter of resignation – 'Did he really not see there were some good days and good things that'd happened?' One of them asked me, 'Did he not enjoy his work at all?' I said, 'Yes he did enjoy his work; but what annoyed him immensely was that there was no reciprocation from any of you guys.' It was taken almost for granted. He had reached out and his mantra was: 'We're sharing power with you because we want to; you're sharing power with us because you have to.'

I remember away back, we were driving past Stormont, coming from the castle or Stormont House, and I said to Martin, 'You know, we're going to have to go in there some day, if we're going to make a success of this.' It was just a random thought at the time as we drove past. Then eventually he was nominated, had to go into the Department of Education. He brought all the officials – civil servants – together, he talked to them, he treated them very much as equals. And when he left that department some of them were in tears.

He also set about a process of genuine reform. As a progressive person he brought that into his work. His policy of reconciliation over the ten years wasn't tested to destruction because the unionists – civic unionism, the broad breadth of unionism, people who might be small 'u' unionists – I think they appreciated very much what he did and what he was doing. But he told me on more than one occasion, as we'd be going into a meeting with unionist politicians or the civil servants, some of whom were very conservative, 'These folk hate us.'

The difficulty lay at the political level. I often wonder did Peter Robinson regret some things – and remember the 'Twelve Apostles' [twelve DUP politicians regarded as particularly hardline] have been a constant in the DUP. We decided very consciously to go for power-sharing with the DUP because we couldn't get any sustainability out of David Trimble. I think Trimble absorbed intellectually what needed to be done, but emotionally he wasn't capable. So you got him on a good day and he was grand, but the next day it was totally different. In fairness, he was under constant pressure from the DUP.

So we decided to go after Paisley to try to get him on board for the idea of power-sharing with Sinn Féin. The very day that we had the deal done with the DUP [24 November 2006], and there was an agreed statement to be read by Ian Paisley, we got word just before he was to make that statement that he was going to renege on parts of it and make a different statement. He got up to make the statement. At which point enter Michael Stone. [On 24 November, Stone was arrested as he tried to enter Stormont carrying weapons. In 2008 he was charged with the attempted murder of Adams and McGuinness.]

It was just a mad coincidence. The bells went off in Stormont.

Martin and I actually escorted Ian Paisley out of the building because we didn't know what was happening. There were rumours that somebody was shooting, so we went out with Ian Óg and his father, straight down to Stormont Castle, and we said to the secretary of state, 'Don't let him out until we get this statement back again.'

Martin and Ian Paisley – that was a very genuine relationship. I found Paisley very easy to get on with as well. I think he hadn't been challenged on a lot of his theatrics and showmanship and all of that. I noticed a few times in the chamber he'd be listening to what Martin was saying. You could tell by the body language he was interested in whatever it was Martin was talking about. And to a lesser degree myself. I was only involved with Paisley in the early part of it, trying to keep it between the ditches.

I recall one occasion when some of his people had said something that our people were annoyed about. Paisley said, 'I agree with you entirely. You can't do business with a man if you're out there calling him names. What we need to do is come into a room like this, close the doors and do the business.' And that's what he did with Martin.

Martin was genuinely respectful of him as an older person. It was just good manners the way Martin related to him – you could see it in the body language. The issue of Martin being referred to as 'the deputy' – I resented that more than Martin. Then I went to Leinster House where they call everybody 'deputy' – it took me about a month to realise this wasn't offensive.

Martin got to know Paisley well. The two of them had a real relationship. Martin was in Paisley's house – I was never in Paisley's house. He was there quite a few times and he was there for the wake. He didn't have the same relationship with Peter

Robinson, but he had a good relationship with him – although Peter mightn't acknowledge that.

***

Martin didn't want to run as a candidate in the 2011 Irish presidential election. Who would? He was doing enough – he didn't want to put himself in that position. The idea came from Mary Lou McDonald and some of our comrades in the south. What persuaded him to run was the thought that he couldn't win, and the party wanted him to do it to help stretch out, reach into other areas.

There are places in the south where we don't have any structure whatsoever, but we have votes. Up until that point, the way you tested your support was during European elections. You could stand a person and you'd be dealing with eight or nine counties, depending on the size of the constituency. But in the presidential election it was the entire state. So it was to show there were no no-go areas for Sinn Féin; secondly it was a chance to argue the republican position on the issues of the day; and thirdly it was to break out of the position of isolation and do some party-building.

I thought Martin was a wee bit shocked by the southern media. Remember, by that point he had crossed the Rubicon in the north, so he was being treated quite decently by the media and by our political opponents. He was working with the unionists, was in partnership with them. He was taking initiatives, a lot of the big issues had been dealt with and he'd been very central to all of that. Then he opened himself up to attacks from the political establishment, including the media and our political opponents in the south.

I used to tease him. His campaign was only for six weeks and I pointed out to him that I'd been at it for four years.

I think he enjoyed the campaign. He got all over the place – in and out of *sraid bhailes* and boreens, meeting people and having a bit of craic. And, politically, it helped him to appreciate the antagonism there was within the political establishment towards Sinn Féin. It was OK when he was up in the north and going about business with the taoiseach or tánaiste of the day, but once he came into the presidential race he was seen as a threat and an interloper. Yes, Mary McAleese was also a northerner and got elected president. But she was from a different background and she'd spent a lot of time in Dublin. [From 1975 to 1987, she was Professor of Criminal Law, Criminology and Penology at Trinity College, Dublin.]

Martin got on famously well with the winner, Michael D. [Higgins], and that stayed with him. I've a lot of time for Michael D. as well.

Martin was annoyed when Miriam O'Callaghan asked him, 'When were you last at Confession?' And why wouldn't he be? We were well used to being treated as hostile witnesses by the media, but to take the moral high ground? He did have words with Miriam O'Callaghan afterwards. But that wouldn't be un-usual – that would happen quite a lot. I've done it myself a few times.

I'm convinced the David Kelly incident was a stitch-up. The guy wasn't living in the state – he was brought in from London. His father was a soldier. Martin saw it clearly as a set-up – but what could he do? Presumably if our people had been more alert it wouldn't have happened. But by then you're in the swing of a campaign and all of that.

I once did an interview with Miriam O'Callaghan along with Martin. It's quite funny because I was telling the story about how we were dancing together at a wedding, and Martin of course was affronted that I'd be saying such a thing on the public airwaves. It's actually a very funny interview because he's being very serious and earnest and I'm being a bit mad. I said in the course of the interview, 'We were dancing together. And I said to him "You're drunk" and then immediately he became sober.'

He did take a drink. He used to drink before 1968–69 – he used to drink whiskey. And then he stopped. And then, in more recent times, he would have had a wee glass of port or a wee glass of wine. But he stopped it entirely. In fact, some of us used to be scundered. You'd pick up a bottle of port and then Martin would tell of how he put the port into a casserole or something – and everybody was aghast at the waste of good alcohol.

So he didn't drink socially, but he was very sociable – I used to say to him it was like trying to get a drunk out of a pub. I could get out of a room in ten seconds flat just by not establishing eye contact. Martin would shake hands with every single person in the room, and would enjoy the fun and the craic of it.

He also did a lot of walking. Derry is blessed – and it's safer than Belfast. You're only across from the border. He and I, back in the 1970s, to avoid roadblocks, used to walk across the border – up towards Muff and Grianan Fort. That was one of his favourite places to walk. His love of sport was a matter of public record. He broke his leg one time playing soccer – was in plaster from the hip down to his ankle – and then a few days later he discovered he'd a broken arm as well.

***

Martin was really looking forward to coming out of the position of deputy first minister. He was frustrated at a personal level by the ten years in that job. He and I discussed his leaving, and he was to step down on 8 May, the tenth anniversary of the day he went into it.

He was very good in his illness. He told me of it in the early days – that the doctors had told him that he could be dead within three months if they didn't get it cured. They did some big operations with him – they put in a pacemaker and another yokey-bob into his heart. The illness meant he was creating too much protein and it was going to the heart, and they were trying to break that link. He knew how serious it was. I don't know if he knew he was going to die, although obviously that was a possibility. He embraced the treatment. He spoke really highly of all the medical people – from the nurses to the senior people.

I visited him a number of times in the hospital. One time I decided to bring him a present. Away back when Derry won the All-Ireland football championship [1993], a big guy called Brian McGilligan, who was in the football team at the time, got the jersey signed for me by all the players. It was lying in the wardrobe at home for several years and I said, 'I'm going to get that framed and give it to Martin.' Initially I'd decided I would give it to him on the day he stood down. In the end I went up to the hospital and I said, 'Look, I've got a present for you. I've had it for twenty years and I've kept meaning to give you it.' I brought it up to the hospital the next time I was up, as I just had this notion that he mightn't come out of it – and he didn't.

He died very quickly. I was in seeing him only days before that and then to see him in the coffin – he didn't look at all like himself. Even in comparison with his appearance on television.

He insisted on coming to Belfast to do the interviews. [On 9 January, the day he signed his resignation letter, he did interviews – an initial short press conference in his office and then several one-on-one interviews with a small group of media. When these were broadcast it was the first time most people saw how ill he was.] I said he'd no need to do those interviews. And do you know why he agreed to do them? So he could go in and talk to Arlene.

He said later on it was like climbing Everest. He'd just come out of the hospital. He'd decided he was going to resign on the back of Arlene's response [when she refused to step aside as first minister while investigations into the RHI scandal were conducted] and the fact that things were going from calamity to calamity on a daily basis – but he wanted to tell them face to face.

That was against my advice and my best wishes. I said to him, 'Stay in Derry. Don't be breaking your heart.' The capacity of his heart at the time, instead of being 100 per cent was something like 30 per cent. You can imagine the pressure that puts on you. And yet he came the whole way from Derry to Belfast because he wanted to go in and give people their face-to-face. That's probably the mark of the man. I wouldn't have bothered. My focus would have been on getting better.

He went to Dermot Gallagher's funeral down in Co. Meath. He was a senior civil servant. I was at the same funeral. This was during Martin's illness, but he insisted on going. And he insisted on coming up to Stormont for some reason. I remember getting very upset about it because he went in to do one meeting and ended up doing four or five. I said to him, 'Martin, you're mad.' This was during the period when he was very unwell. My concern was that he needed to mind himself. I remember saying to him, 'You've spent your whole life fighting for others; now you need to fight for yourself.'

I suppose in a grieving process, you have to come to a point of acceptance that the other person has gone. There's rarely a day, if I'm out in the public, where a complete stranger won't say to me, 'I'm sorry about your friend Martin McGuinness, I can't believe he's gone.' And I remember, during the South Down election, a woman in her forties saying to me, 'I can't believe Martin McGuinness is gone, because since I was a child, you two were always in my life. Always. Against the background of trouble or whatever – the two of you were always in my life. And now he's gone and I can't come to terms with it.'

Obviously Bernie is in a more concentrated form of that grief. There was also the unfairness of it – that she had hoped he was going to get better and he would have had the space to do the things he wasn't able to do.

He never gave up. There were times when he won an argument just by the force of his personality. That could be a good thing if you agreed with the argument but not so good if you disagreed with it. He had an emotional response to people, which sometimes could be wrong. If he thought you were sound on his first meeting you, then you were sound. That's the way he was. If he was glad to see you, he was glad to see you. It wasn't that he was pretending to be glad to see you.

I think he was sicker for longer than any of us guessed. I remember one time seeing him walking across Guildhall Square and I went to him the next day and said, 'Martin, you're not well.' He said to me, 'I'm tired.' He travelled a lot and had a very heavy schedule. He'd be up at 5 a.m., travelling every single day, then maybe not getting in until 11 p.m. He went home 99.99 per cent of the time.

He wasn't in the least way materialistic. He was genuinely happy about the house, cooking a bit, doing a bit of fly-fishing, taking a walk, being with Bernie, being with the kids, being with the grandkids. He was very ordinary in that way. Somebody said to me recently, 'Being retired means you can do what you want to do, when you want to do it.' He was a guy that that would have suited, because he did all the other things. But he had only been planning to retire from the position of deputy first minister – he wasn't coming off the Sinn Féin Ard Comhairle or any of that.

I tried to get him to write a book. When he was sick I said to him, 'You're now stuck here. You're not getting out of this bed for months. Even get a tape-recorder, talk about your childhood, talk about your mother, talk about your brothers and sisters, talk about meeting Bernie, your courtship, your kids – just do it.' And I think he was a good writer. So that's a long-winded answer to what would be his single best quality. I suppose if I summed all of that up, it would be his genuineness; regardless of the mission or event, he would give it his best. He was genuinely sociable, but he was also obviously a very good politician.

I miss him very much, every day. Every day. I miss him personally. I didn't work with Martin on a daily basis, particularly when I went south. But I would have been in touch with him very regularly, and particularly in times of decision-making or crisis. We were very close. I miss him – it's a personal thing, nothing to do with politics. I'm probably at the age now where quite a few friends of mine are gone – Cleeky Clarke was famously a very close friend of mine, a funny guy. I miss him as well. And you could pick other people. But I miss Martin every single day.

ALSO AVAILABLE FROM MERCIER PRESS

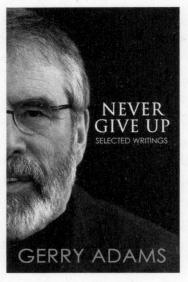

978 1 78117 537 8

Never Give Up gives an insight into the public and private life of Gerry Adams, and provides an in-depth look at the ardently held beliefs of Ireland's best-known politician. The book reveals Gerry's thoughts on the Irish peace process and Brexit, and recounts his experiences attending historic events, such as the inauguration of Barack Obama and the funeral of Nelson Mandela. We get a glimpse into Gerry's passions, including his love for the Antrim GAA teams and his dogs. Turbulent times are also explored, including his move from west Belfast to Co. Louth to run for a seat in the Dáil.

Renowned for his strong opinions and quirky sense of humour, this compilation of Adams' opinions ranges from the whimsical to the very serious indeed.

www.mercierpress.ie